THE CONDUCT

OF

ANTI-TERRORIST OPERATIONS

IN

MALAYA

(Third Edition—1958)

RESTRICTED

The information given in this document is not to be communicated, either directly or indirectly, to the Press or to any person not authorised to receive it.

The Naval & Military Press Ltd

Prepared under the direction of
the
DIRECTOR OF OPERATIONS, MALAYA
1958

Published by

The Naval & Military Press Ltd
Unit 5 Riverside, Brambleside
Bellbrook Industrial Estate
Uckfield, East Sussex
TN22 1QQ England

Tel: +44 (0)1825 749494

www.naval-military-press.com
www.nmarchive.com

In reprinting in facsimile from the original, any imperfections are inevitably reproduced and the quality may fall short of modern type and cartographic standards.

CONTENTS

	Page
Foreword	xi
Abbreviations	xv
Definitions	xvii

PART 1
GENERAL

CHAPTER I
MALAYA

Section

1.	The Country	1
2.	Climate	1
3.	Vegetation	2
4.	Aborigines	3
5.	Wild Life	3
6.	Communications	4
7.	Production	4
8.	Population	5
9.	Political Organisation	6
10.	State and Settlement Organisation	6
11.	Local Government	7
12.	Finance	7
13.	Commissioner-General	8

CHAPTER II
THE CT—ORIGIN AND DEVELOPMENT

1.	Origins of Communism in Malaya	1
2.	The Malayan Communist Party (MCP)	1
3.	The Malayan People's Anti-Japanese Army (MPAJA)	2
4.	Disbandment of the MPAJA and after	4
5.	Situation after the Liberation	5
6.	Organisation of the MCP	6
7.	Armed Forces of the MCP	8
8.	MCP Policy	8
9.	Notes on the CT Organisation	10

CHAPTER III
OWN FORCES

Section		Page
1. Introduction		1
2. System of Control of Emergency Operations		1
3. Main Tasks of the Security Forces		4
4. The Briggs Plan		5
5. Subsequent Developments		6
6. Pattern of Operations 1957		7
7. The Police		8
8. The Army		11
9. The Royal Air Force and Army Air Corps		12
10. The Royal Navy		14
11. The Home Guard		14
12. Psychological Warfare		16

CHAPTER IV
THE EMERGENCY REGULATIONS (ERs) AND METHODS OF SEARCHING

1. Introduction		1
2. Notes on ERs		1
3. The Emergency (Restriction and Prohibition of Foodstuffs and Other Supplies) Regulations, 1956		6
4. Food Denial Operations and Method of Searching		9

APPENDIX
A—Comparative Scale of Malayan Weights
B—Scale of Equipment at Gate Check Points

PART 2
OPERATIONS
CHAPTER V
PLATOON ORGANISATION, WEAPONS AND EQUIPMENT

1. Introduction		1
2. Organisation within the Platoon		2
3. Weapons		2
4. Equipment and Clothing		7
5. Weapon Handling		8

APPENDIX
A—Summary of Methods of Firing Weapons

CHAPTER VI
THE JUNGLE BASE

Section
1. Introduction
2. Deception
3. Siting a Base
4. Layout of a Base
5. Sequence of Establishing a Base
6. Security and Protection
7. Leaving a Base
8. Administration of a Base
9. Conclusion

APPENDICES
A—Suggested Layout of a Two-Section Base
B—Suggested Layout of a Three-Section Base

CHAPTER VII
PATROLLING

1. Introduction
2. Information
3. Planning and Control of Patrol Operations
4. Briefing by Battalion/Company Commanders
5. Planning and Preparation by the Patrol Commander
6. Debriefing and Rebriefing
7. Return to Company Base

APPENDIX
A—Patrol Orders—Aide Memoire

CHAPTER VIII
PATROL MOVEMENT AND FORMATION

1. Introduction
2. Movement—General
3. Movement of Patrols
4. Searching Ground
5. Formations
6. Position of Commanders
7. Position of Guides and Trackers
8. Maintaining Contact and Movement by Night
9. Maintaining Direction
10. Return to Base

APPENDICES

Section | Page

A—Silent Signals
B—Single File Formation
C—Open Formation

CHAPTER IX

JUNGLE NAVIGATION

1. Introduction 1
2. Aids 1
3. Planning 3
4. Checking 3
5. Obstacles 4
6. Conclusion 4

CHAPTER X

IMMEDIATE ACTION DRILLS

1. Introduction 1
2. The IA Drills 1
3. Action on Encounter 2

CHAPTER XI

THE AMBUSHING OF CT

1. Policy 1
2. The Principle of Ambushing . . . 2
3. The Layout of Ambushes . . . 2
4. The Sequence of Laying an Ambush . . 7
5. Prevention of Accidents - . . . 10
6. General 11
7. Ambush by Night 12
8. Wisdom in Retrospect - . . . 15

APPENDIX
A—Ambush Orders—Aide Memoire

CHAPTER XII

THE LOCATION AND ATTACKING OF CT IN CAMPS AND CULTIVATIONS

Section		Page
1. Introduction		1
2. Signs of CT		2
3. The Search		2
4. The Attack		4
5. General Points		5

CHAPTER XIII

MOVEMENT BY ROAD

1. Introduction		1
2. The Problem		1
3. Countering the Problem		4
4. Precautionary Measures		4
5. Action on Contact		11
6. Bailing Out Drill		13
7. Conclusion		14

CHAPTER XIV

INTELLIGENCE

1. Introduction		1
2. Own Organisation		1
3. Intelligence Sources		2
4. Air Reconnaissance and Photography		9
5. Military Security and Counter Intelligence		13
6. Conclusion		14

APPENDICES

A—Surrendered Enemy Personnel
B—Captured Enemy Personnel
C—Debriefing Aide Memoire for Patrols
D—Notes on CT Food Dumps
E—Report on Radio Interference
F—Requests for Air Photographs
G—Urgent Request for Air Photographs
H—Routine Intelligence Publications

CHAPTER XV

TRAINING FOR OPERATIONS

Section		Page
1.	Introduction	1
2.	Initial Jungle Training	1
3.	Training During Operations	2
4.	Junior Leader Training	6
5.	Jungle Warfare Technique	7
6.	Time for Training	8
7.	Courses and Cadres	9
8.	Conclusion	10

APPENDICES

A—Malayan Range Practices (Rifle and M1/M2 Carbine)
B—Malayan Range Practices (Owen and L2A1 Carbine)

CHAPTER XVI

WIRELESS COMMUNICATIONS IN MALAYA

1.	Introduction	1
2.	Wireless Sets in Use in Malaya	1
3.	Aerials	3
4.	Frequency Allocation	4
5.	Conclusion	4

APPENDICES

A—Methods of Tuning Simple Sky Wave Aerial for WS 68T
B—Aerial Lengths

CHAPTER XVII

AIR SUPPORT IN MALAYA

1.	Introduction				1
2.	Command, Control and Liaison				2
3.	Offensive Air Support				3
4.	Air Transport Support—General				7
5.	,,	,,	,,	—Air Supply	10
6.	,,	,,	,,	—Paratroop Operations	15
7.	,,	,,	,,	—Trooplifting	18
8.	,,	,,	,,	—Communication Flights	20
9.	,,	,,	,,	—Casualty Evacuation by Air	23

Section						Page
10. Psychological Warfare	-	-	-	-	-	25
11. Army Air Crops	-	-	-	-	-	27
12. Communications and Visual Signals		-	-	-	31

APPENDICES

A—Guide to Preparation of Request for Offensive Air Support
B—Specimen Request for Air Supply
C—Guide to Preparation of Request for Paratroop Operation
D—Guide to Preparation, and Specimen of, Request for Troop/Freight Air Lift
E—Guide to Preparation of Request for Communication Flight
F—Guide to Preparation of Request for Voice Aircraft
G—Light Signal Code—Ground/Air and Air/Ground
H—Ground/Air Panel Code for Use in Malaya
J—Air-Dropped Supply—Selection and Marking of DZs
K—Single-Engined Pioneer—Details of Performance and Emplaning/Deplaning Drill
L—Minimum Specifications for Helicopter Landing Zones
M—Marshalling and Reception of Helicopters, and Hand Signals for Helicopters
N—Whirlwind (Medium) Helicopter—Planning Data, Emplaning Drills, and Safety Precautions
O—Sycamore (Light) Helicopter—Planning Data, Emplaning Drills, and Safety Precautions
P—Ground Forces Follow-Up Report on Airstrike

CHAPTER XVIII

EMPLOYMENT OF THE ROYAL ARTILLERY IN ANTI-CT OPERATIONS

1. Artillery Resources	-	-	-	-	-	1
2. Allotment	-	-	-	-	-	1
3. The Advantages	-	-	-	-	-	1
4. Limitations in Malaya	-	-	-	-	-	2
5. Types of Support	-	-	-	-	-	3
6. Organisation and Administration	-	-	-	4
7. Ammunition	-	-	-	-	-	5
8. Aircraft Safety	-	-	-	-	-	5
9. Intelligence Reports	-	-	-	-	-	5

viii

CHAPTER XIX

HANDLING OF ABORIGINES BY SECURITY FORCES

Section	Page
1. Background	1
2. Government Counter-measures	1
3. Handling of Aborigines	2

CHAPTER XX

THE EMPLOYMENT OF DOGS ON OPERATIONS AND THE ADMINISTRATION OF WAR DOGS

1. General	1
2. Continuation Training	1
3. The Infantry Patrol Dog	1
4. Dog Handlers	4
5. Kennel Management in the Tropics	5
6. Feeding on Patrol	6
7. Veterinary Notes for Dog Handlers	7

APPENDIX

A—Advice to Dog Handlers

CHAPTER XXI

TRACKING

1. Introduction	1
2. The Sarawak Ranger (Iban)	1
3. The Visual Tracker	2
4. Tracker Dog	2
5. Tracking Teams	4
6. Tracking Techniques	5
7. Employment of Tracker Teams	8

APPENDICES

A—Cross Grain Search
B—Tracker Team Formation

PART 3

ADMINISTRATION

CHAPTER XXII

OPERATIONAL RATIONS

Section	Page
1. Introduction	1
2. Types of Packs Available in Malaya	1
3. Air Supply	2

APPENDICES

A—General Data on Special Ration Packs
B—Detailed Composition of BT 10 Men Compo Ration Pack
C—British 24 Hour Ration (GS)—Types A, B, C, and D
D—British Troops 24 Hour Pack Ration Mk III (Local)
E—British Troops 24 Hour Pack Ration Mk III (Local) SAS only
F—2 Men x 7 Day Light Weight Patrol Ration
G—Gurkha 10 Men Compo Rations
H—Gurkha 24 Hour Pack Rations
J—MT 2 Men Pack Rations

CHAPTER XXIII

FIRST AID AND PREVENTIVE MEDICINE

	Page
1. First Aid	1
2. First Aid to Health	4
3. Summary	6

FOREWORD TO FIRST EDITION

Since assuming my appointment as High Commissioner and Director of Operations in the Federation of Malaya, I have been impressed by the wealth of jungle fighting experience available on different levels in Malaya and among different categories of persons. At the same time, I have been disturbed by the fact that this great mass of detailed knowledge has not been properly collated or presented to those whose knowledge and experience is not so great. This vast store of knowledge must be pooled. Hence this book.

I wish to impress the following four points: —

Firstly, the absolute necessity for the adoption of the immediate action drills laid down in this book. All battle experience shows the very great value to be obtained from such drills and the saving of casualties which they bring about.

Secondly, the vital importance of accurate and quick shooting, particularly with single shot weapons. If only we can double the ratio of kills per contact, we will soon put an end to the shooting in Malaya.

Thirdly, the need for offensive action, both in planning on whatever level it may be, and also in minor tactical engagements. It is the automatic offensive action taught and practised by many units in Malaya that has brought such outstanding results.

And fourthly, the necessity in operations of this nature of discipline and all that it stands for. It is the vehicle load of men belonging to a unit which does not demand a sufficiently high standard of vehicle discipline which eventually gets caught out; it is the same thing with the foot patrol of the same unit.

The job of the British Army out here is to kill or capture Communist terrorists in Malaya. This book shows in a clear and easily readable form the proven principles by which this can be done. The book is by no means perfect. Criticisms and improvements are invited by GOC Malaya, who will produce a revised edition in six months' time.

In the meantime, the methods described are to be adopted not only by the Army, but also by the Federal Jungle Companies, the Jungle Squads and the Area Security Squads of the Federal Police. Many of the methods laid down for the movement of vehicles and convoys are also applicable to the Police.

Foreword

In the compilation of this book, the accumulated knowledge of the FARELF Training Centre organised and run by Commander-in-Chief, Far East Land Forces, has been drawn upon in full. We in the Federation are very grateful for what that school has achieved.

*High Commissioner and Director of Operations,
Federation of Malaya.*

FOREWORD TO SECOND EDITION

Since this book was produced by General Templer in 1952 much progress has been made in the fight against the Malayan Communist Party. But although the terrorists have mostly been forced back into the jungle the Emergency, after 6 years, is still with us. Many units of the Army and of the Federal Police have followed the principles and jungle drills laid down in the First Edition and have gained much thereby. But Army units are constantly changing and Police personnel being changed over. Hence the need to keep our ideas right up-to-date and hence this Second Edition. Recent experience underlines the supreme importance of quick, accurate shooting. As General Templer said 'if only we can double the ratio of kills per contact we will soon put an end to the shooting in Malaya.' Therefore all individuals and units while training and fighting in Malaya must keep in view a double aim:—

First—Stick to the tactics and drills in this book.
Second—Practise constantly to improve their shooting.

*Director of Operations,
Federation of Malaya.*

FOREWORD TO THIRD EDITION

THE PROGRESS to which General Bourne referred, in his foreword to the Second Edition of this book, has been maintained: the situation now is that a reduced Communist Terrorist Organisation has largely abandoned its aggressive attitude and is avoiding contact with the Security Forces. If therefore we are to find and root out these terrorists, it is vital that the Security Forces' battle-craft should be of the highest standard. In particular, General Templer's statement 'if only we can double the ratio of kills per contact, we will soon put an end to the shooting in Malaya' applies even more today than when he first made it.

The task of the Security Forces in Malaya is always arduous and often unexciting; they frequently spend long hours on patrol in trying climatic conditions without a sign of the enemy to reward them. It is quite essential that when a contact is made all that is humanly possible is done to turn it into a kill; that means first class discipline, and a very high standard of training in minor tactics and jungle shooting.

In particular, nothing must be left to chance when patrols or ambushes are sent out to make contacts on information. Only the best-trained men must be considered fit for selection for these operations. We cannot expect people to give us information unless we follow it up successfully.

This book contains the distilled knowledge and experience obtained during nine years of hard operations. That knowledge and experience will be wasted unless those members of the Security Forces who are new to this kind of operation read this book thoroughly. Do so!

Director of Operations,
Federation of Malaya.

ABBREVIATIONS

The following abbreviations are used in this pamphlet which are NOT contained in Appendix C to Staff Duties in the Field:—

ADO	=	Assistant District Officer.
AO	=	Administrative Officer.
AOP	=	Air Observation Post.
ASU	=	Area Security Units (Police Special Constabulary).
AWF	=	Armed Work Force.
BCM	=	Branch Committee Member (MCP).
CCP	=	Chinese Communist Party.
CEP	=	Captured Enemy Personnel.
CECM	=	Central Executive Committee Member (MCP).
CIS	=	Combined Intelligence Staff.
CPO	=	Chief Police Officer (State).
CT	=	Communist Terrorist(s).
CW	=	Continuous Wave (Wireless).
DCM	=	District Committee Member (MCP).
DIS	=	Director of Information Services.
DO	=	District Officer.
D of O	=	Director of Operations.
DSBO	=	District Special Branch Officer.
DWEC	=	District War Executive Committee.
ER	=	Emergency Regulation(s).
HPWS	=	Head Psychological Warfare Services.
HSB	=	Head Special Branch.
IA	=	Immediate Action.
JCLO	=	Junior Civil Liaison Officer.
JOC	=	Joint Operations Centre (Army/RAF).
MB	=	Mentri Besar.
MCP	=	Malayan Communist Party.
MIO	=	Military Intelligence Officer.
MPAJA	=	Malayan Peoples Anti Japanese Army.
MRLA	=	Malayan Races Liberation Army.
NMB	=	North Malayan Bureau (MCP).
OCPD	=	Officer(s) Commanding Police District(s).
OSPC	=	Officers(s) Superintending Police Circle(s).
PFF	=	Police Field Force.
PSS	=	Police Special Squad(s).
PW	=	Psychological Warfare (NOT Prisoner of War).
SB	=	Special Branch.
SCM	=	State Committee Member (MCP).
SEP	=	Surrendered Enemy Personnel.
SF	=	Security Forces.
SMB	=	South Malayan Bureau (MCP).
SMIS	=	Special Military Intelligence Staff.
SOVF	=	Special Operational Volunteer Force.
SWEC	=	State War Executive Committee.

DEFINITIONS

1. **Introduction.**—Frequent reference is made in this pamphlet to the following expressions which are defined below:—

2. **A Contact.**—A "contact" is made when the SF meet the CT and the SF open fire first. It should be noted that when the SF meet the CT and the CT open fire first, the encounter is referred to as an "incident."

3. **An Incident.**—There are two types of incidents which are classified as:—

   (a) *Major Incident.*—A major incident is one, caused by CT, which results in loss of life, serious injury or considerable damage to property.

   (b) *Minor Incident.*—All other CT caused incidents.

   (c) Major and Minor incidents are further subdivided as Type A or B:—

   (i) *Type A.*—Those which are the result of careful CT planning, showing aggressiveness by the CT, and which involve a degree of risk to CT.

   (ii) *Type B.*—All other incidents.

4. **Clearance.**—Police clearance, when given, means that the Police believe to the best of their knowledge that no loss or injury to innocent civilians will result from SF action in the particular area for which Police clearance has been given.

(This definition should be read in conjunction with Chapter III, Section 7).

5. **CT.**—Those who in any way actively further the subversive Communist campaign for the purpose of overthrowing the Government of the Federation by resorting to or instigating violence and who:—

   (a) By the use of any firearms, explosive or ammunition act in a manner prejudicial to the public safety or to the maintenance of public order.

   (b) Incite to violence or counsel disobedience to the law or to any lawful order by the use of any firearm, explosive or ammunition.

   (c) Carry or have in their possession or under their control any firearm without lawful authority therefor.

(d) Carry or have in their possession or under their control any ammunition or explosive without authority therefor.

(e) Adhere to the CT gangs as couriers or camp followers.

6. **SEP.**—(Surrendered Enemy Personnel). These are CT who willingly surrender to the Forces of Law and Order at a time when they could otherwise without difficulty have made good their escape. Two conditions must be fulfilled for such persons to come within this category:—

(a) They must leave or desert the CT organisation and,

(b) Must give themselves up at the earliest opportunity.

7. **CEP.**—(Captured Enemy Personnel). These are CT who come into our hands otherwise than as SEPs.

8. **Min Yuen.**—The term "Min Yuen" is short for "MIN CHONG YUEN TONG" meaning "The Peoples Movement." It covers all activities by the Masses, and the Masses leaders, in aid of the Party. It follows therefore that a Min Yuen worker can be a Party sympathiser living in the jungle but engaged in controlling the Min Yuen Organisation. The term Min Yuen is adjectival and is not a noun.

PART ONE
GENERAL

CHAPTER I

MALAYA

Section 1.—THE COUNTRY

1. Malaya is a peninsula stretching for 400 miles from the border of Thailand south-east to the Indonesian Archipelago. Its greatest width is 200 miles. In area—53,240 square miles—it is a little larger than England without Wales.

2. The peninsula has a backbone of jungle-covered mountains, rising to a height of 7,000 feet. From the mountains fast rivers run west to the Straits of Malacca and east to the South China Sea. Four-fifths of the land is trackless evergreen forest and undergrowth. A hundred feet above the ground the trees make a solid roof of green, shutting out the sky. From their branches curtains of vine and creeper join the undergrowth to make a jungle so dense that a standing man is invisible at twenty-five yards. The remaining one-fifth of the country is rubber plantations, rice fields, tin mines, villages and towns.

3. At the south-eastern tip of the peninsula is the island of Singapore, separated from the mainland by the Straits of Johore. Across the Straits there runs a road and rail causeway three-quarters of a mile long.

Section 2.—CLIMATE

1. The average noon temperature is 90°F, but there is little temperature variation throughout the year; winds are generally light, and rainfall is often heavy. The diurnal variation of weather is the predominant feature; it produces strong contrasts of rain and cloud between day and night although the weather of one day does not necessarily repeat that of the day before.

2. Four seasons can be distinguished:—
   (a) *North-East Monsoon*—Late October to the end of March. North-easterly winds blow strongly over the sea and the East coast, but lightly elsewhere. Much heavy rain and low cloud occur on the East side of the mountains—less elsewhere.

(b) *South-West Monsoon*—End of May or beginning of June to September. Intermittent rain in the south-west.

(c) *Two Transitional Seasons*—in April/ May and in October. Winds are generally light and variable. Thunder storms are frequent and rainfall is very heavy.

3. The nights are usually clear and quiet and reasonably cool. Towards morning mists may form in valleys and sheets of cloud mantle the slopes of the mountains, although the summits are usually cloudless. Soon after sunrise, however, the contours of distant mountains become less distinct and after an hour or two shimmer blurs their outline, the sun's heat increases, the sheets of cloud dissolve, and for a short time the sky becomes cloudless. By noon cumulus cloud frequently begins to form and the heat grows intense. During the later afternoon the cumulus clouds often increase to large drifting thunder-clouds, and thunder-storms occur. These may last only 15 or 30 minutes, but they are very heavy. During the early part of the night the thunder-clouds tend to flatten out, and by morning the sheets of stratocumulus over the mountain slopes and the mists over the valleys have returned.

4. The effects of topography on the weather and climate of Malaya are well marked. The windward sides of the mountains are apt to get heavier showers than the lee sides, sometimes even continuous rain. During strong winds the rugged nature of the country produces very uncomfortable turbulence with down-currents on the lee sides of the hills. Even during quiet weather the broken country gives rise to local wind currents and cloud, and over the bare worked-out mining land the heat sets up vertical currents.

Section 3.—VEGETATION

1. For operational purposes the vegetation of Malaya can be classified under four headings:—
    (a) Rubber.
    (b) Primary Jungle.
    (c) Secondary Jungle.
    (d) Swamp.

2. Interspersed with these is found open ground covered in belukar (low scrub and bushes), lallang (long grass) or cultivated land and padi.

3. **Rubber.—**
    (a) Visibility is often good up to several hundred yards. Trees are planted on a fixed pattern and at a fixed density. Except where an estate has been neglected there is very little, if any, undergrowth.

(b) It is difficult, if not impossible, to track in rubber on account of the lack of undergrowth and the nature of the ground. Movement at night in rubber is possible and by day a rate of movement of up to two miles per hour can be attained.

4. Primary Jungle.—

(a) This is very thick and contains trees 150 feet or more in height with comparatively little undergrowth on the jungle floor.

(b) Tracking is easier in primary jungle as signs left by CT in parting a way through the undergrowth are visible.

5. Secondary Jungle.—

Where for any reason primary jungle has been removed a secondary growth of every kind of bush, creeper or bamboo takes command quickly and soon forms a dense mass that is difficult to move through. The density and height of growth varies in accordance with the time that has elapsed since the cutting of the original forest.

6. Swamp.—

On low lying ground in coastal regions swamps extend over considerable areas. The swamp consists of water and mud into which a man may sink knee deep and frequently deeper. The whole area is covered with trees and thick undergrowth which reduces visibility to a few yards.

Section 4.—ABORIGINES

There are about 100,000 Aborigines in the Federation. They are not a homogenous people but fall roughly into three major groups —the Negritos, the Senoi and the Aboriginal Malays. The book "An Introduction to the Malayan Aborigines" by P. D. R. Williams Hunt, which has been issued to all units in Malaya, gives full details of their characteristics and the methods of handling them. Further up-to-date details are contained in Chapter XIX.

Section 5.—WILD LIFE

There is plenty of wild life in Malaya but it is possible to live for years in the country without actually encountering anything more than lizards, monkeys and birds. Tigers, elephants, wild pig, deer, buffaloes, crocodiles and snakes are all to be found.

Section 6.—COMMUNICATIONS

Compared with European countries there is a lack of road communication. Not all roads and paths are marked on the current maps, particular exceptions being the roads in rubber estates and the large number of tracks in Government Forest Reserves.

Section 7.—PRODUCTION

1. **Agriculture.**— The main agricultural crops of Malaya are shown below.

2. **Rubber.**— This is produced both on large (over 100 acres) estates and small-holdings. These covered an acreage of 3,500,000 at the end of 1956 from which was produced a total of 625,601 tons or an estimated 33 per cent of total world production. Export duties yielded a total of 144 million dollars. 291,390 persons were directly employed in the industry. Comparative estate and small-holding production was as follows:—

	Production in tons
Estates	352,233
Small-holdings	273,368

Conditions throughout the industry vary widely but in general it may be said that large estates are to a great extent replanted or being replanted with high yielding material whilst the small-holdings are still covered with the original tree stand, much of it 40 years old or more. Again as a very general rule large estates will be found to be cleared of undergrowth and well maintained whilst small-holdings tend to be overgrown: even in some cases to secondary jungle.

3. **Rice.**— In the 1955-56 season, 875,880 acres were under dry and wet padi and it was estimated that this area produced some 420,070 tons of rice. Accurate statistics of home consumption in rice producing areas are not available but even when taking these into account the Federation does not produce more than 60 per cent of its normal annual consumption. The greatest proportion of the very considerable imports required come from Thailand.

In view of the general overall improvement in the world rice position Government rationing of this commodity ended on August 1, 1954. Rations can, however, still be imposed for operational purposes.

4. **Coconuts.**— Some 500,000 acres were under this crop at the end of 1956, and total production of copra, coconut oil and copra cake was 154,054, 108,373 and 67,808 tons respectively. Three-quarters of the total acreage is small-holdings. Generally speaking, coconut production is confined to the coastal plains of the West Coast. Net exports were of the value of some 56 million dollars.

5. **Pineapples.**— After total extinction during the war this industry has recovered to the extent that some 44,777 acres were planted as at the end of 1956. Total exports of canned fruit from the Federation of 22,953 tons were valued at 19 million dollars.

6. **Tea.**— Approximately 5 million pounds of tea were produced during 1956 of which half was exported. Generally speaking Malayan teas are not of high quality.

7. **Cocoa.**— Cocoa is being grown on an experimental scale. It is a crop of high promise in view of the favourable climate and overall world shortage.

8. **Timber.**— Approximately 12,500 square miles, or 24.6 of the total land area of the Federation is now Reserved Forest. Despite the closure of logging areas from time to time on operational grounds, a total of 186,847 tons of timber of a net value of 30 million dollars were exported during 1956. General revenue from timber royalties amounted to 10.6 million dollars. It is of interest that Malaya now ranks third as exporter of raw non-coniferous sawn timber to the United Kingdom.

9. **Mining.**—
   (a) Tin is the main mineral resource of the Federation. During 1956 a total of 62,295 tons of metal-tin were produced in the Federation. This represents approximately 32 per cent of the total world production with a total value of 340 million dollars. It produced a revenue of 60 million dollars in 1956. At the end of the year there were 78 dredges, 633 gravel pumps, 26 underground and 47 other types of mines being operated. 37,515 persons were directly employed in the industry.
   (b) Other minerals are of secondary importance although there is promise of extensive development of iron-ore mining on the East Coast and aluminium (Bauxite) has certain prospects. The one coal mine (at Batu Arang) produces very poor quality coal.

Section 8.—POPULATION

1. The estimated populations of the Colony of Singapore and of the Federation of Malaya at the 31st December, 1956, were:—

Colony of Singapore

Malaysians	Chinese	Indians and Pakistanis	Others	Total
157,610	989,011	101,102	42,214	1,292,937

Federation of Malaya

Malaysians	Chinese	Indians and Pakistanis	Others	Total
3,092,788	2,413,325	759,753	97,987	6,363,853

The term 'Malaysians' embraces all members of the Malay race with the exception of Philippinos.

2. It will be noted that Chinese in the Colony of Singapore comprise some 77 per cent of the total population, whilst in the Federation 49 per cent are of Malaysian stock, 36 per cent are of Chinese origin (almost without exception drawn from South China) and 12 per cent from India and Pakistan—the vast majority of the latter being from South India. Both the Colony of Singapore and the Federation of Malaya with net 1953 increases in population of 4.15 per cent and 3.65 per cent respectively have one of the highest percentage population increases in the world.

Section 9.—POLITICAL ORGANIZATION

The Federation of Malaya includes the nine Malay states of Perak, Johore, Selangor, Negri Sembilan, Pahang, Kedah, Kelantan, Perlis and Trengganu and the two former Straits Settlements of Penang and Malacca. On August 31st 1957 the Federation of Malaya with the two Settlements now designated as States, achieved Independence within the British Commonwealth. The Government at that time consisted of fifty-two elected members (of which fifty-one belonged to the political party in power, an Alliance of the United Malay National Organization, the Malayan Chinese Association and the Malayan Indian Congress), while the remaining forty-six members consisted of the Chief Ministers of the States, and representatives of industrial interests and minorities.

Section 10.—STATE AND SETTLEMENT ORGANIZATION

1. The Ruler is advised by an Executive Council which consists of:—

   (a) The Chief Minister (the Senior State Administrative Officer).

   (b) The State Legal Adviser and certain nominated officials and unofficials.

2. The State Councils meet under the chairmanship of the Chief Minister to deal with the State Legislation required. These councils all have an elected majority.

3. **The State Administrative Machine.**— This consists of:—

   (a) The State Secretariat.

   (b) The District Officers, who are responsible to the State or Settlement Government for the overall policy in their districts and in particular for the Land Office, Treasury and in almost all cases for the Town Board. Both the State Secretariat and District Officer are normally staffed by Officers from the Malayan or State Civil Services.

   (c) The Penghulu or Penggawa who is responsible for the Mukim or Sub-District.

   (d) In Perak there is a system of Territorial Chiefs who are directly responsible to the Ruler and in Johore and Trengganu officers of the Malayan Civil Service, entitled Administrative Officers, assist the District Officers who are drawn from the State Civil Service. The Administrative Officers are invariably in charge of the Land Office.

Section 11.—LOCAL GOVERNMENT

1. The two Municipalities of Malacca and Kuala Lumpur have a nominated President who is an officer of the Malayan Civil Service, and they have in all cases an elected majority. The City of Penang has its own Mayor.

2. The pattern of Local Government in the Districts is at present mainly the nominated Town Board (but this is rapidly being changed to a Town Council with an elected majority) and the fully elected Local Council.

3. These latter are a successful innovation and are the only form of Local Government based upon an adult franchise. Chairmen of the Local Councils are usually men of substance and considerable local influence.

Section 12.—FINANCE

As is common in all forms of Federal Government the major items of revenue, e.g. Customs and Income Tax are Federal. State Revenues are drawn from Land and Natural Resources. Annual allotments from the Federal Government enable the State Government Budgets to be balanced.

Section 13.—COMMISSIONER-GENERAL

1. Her Majesty's Government is represented in Singapore by His Excellency the Commissioner-General for the United Kingdom in South East Asia. His role is twofold:—

   (a) To co-ordinate policy for the Colonial Office amongst the Colonies of Singapore, Sarawak and North Borneo.

   (b) To co-ordinate policy for the Foreign Office in Burma, Thailand, Indonesia and Indo-China; and for the Commonwealth Relations Office in the Federation of Malaya.

2. He is also Chairman of the British Defence Co-ordination Committee whose principle members are the three Commanders-in-Chief resident in Singapore.

CHAPTER II

THE COMMUNIST TERRORISTS (CT)

Section 1.—ORIGINS OF COMMUNISM IN MALAYA

1. The Emergency began in June 1948 and the Communist insurrection still remains a menace to the security of Malaya.

2. Communism in Malaya was not an indigenous movement. It did not develop from the grievances of its peasantry or labouring classes, nor from any frustrated desire for national independence on the part of a local population governed by a foreign power. It was the result of the direct injection of Communist virus into a small section of the Chinese community in Malaya, through the agency of the Communist Party in China, which in turn was directed by the Far Eastern Bureau of the Communist International (the Comintern), the directing agency of Soviet Russia in its pursuit of 'world revolution.'

3. It was part of a plan, sponsored by the Comintern, which embraced the whole of South-East Asia and aimed to spread Communism in the Philippines, Indo-China, Siam, Burma, the Netherlands East Indies (now Indonesia) and Malaya, with the consequent discomfiture of the 'Imperialist Powers' (Britain, America, France and Holland) which controlled colonial territories within those areas. This was part of a wider scheme of the Third International aimed at establishing Communism throughout the world by armed insurrection.

Section 2.—THE MALAYAN COMMUNIST PARTY (MCP)

1. The first organised Communist Party in Malaya was created in 1927/1928 by the Comintern organisation in China through the agency of the Chinese Communist Party (CCP). It continued to be influenced, if not directed, by the CCP until 1930 when Soviet intervention severed this direction.

2. In 1933 the Malayan Communist Party (MCP) was firmly set up on its own feet. External direction laid down its future policy which required the MCP to concentrate its entire resources and main activities in penetrating and controlling the labour field and in achieving leadership of the strike movement. Expansion of Communism amongst youth was also listed as a priority.

3. The MCP was not slow in using genuine labour grievances for its own ends and wide-spread strikes took place in 1936/1937. This policy of fomenting labour unrest was continued until Soviet Russia became part of the allied front in June 1941. In view of British economic aid to Russia, the MCP then found it expedient to prevent any unnecessary labour friction which would indirectly harm the Soviet war effort.

Section 3.—THE MALAYAN PEOPLE'S ANTI JAPANESE ARMY (MPAJA)

1. When the war against Japan began, the MCP offered its services to the British authorities. These were accepted and the first seeds of the resistance movement were thus supplied by the MCP. Some 200 Chinese were recruited by the MCP and trained with them and it was not at any time then suggested that they were under British command—the emphasis was on co-operation. Arrangements were made, however, to enable this body to maintain contact with parties of British officers which had already been placed behind the Japanese lines independently of the Chinese supplied by the MCP. While British contact with Malaya was lost between February 1942, and May 1943, these trainees played a major part in organising the military side of the MCP resistance movement known as the Malayan People's Anti-Japanese Army. In the beginning, they carried out a considerable amount of offensive action against the Japanese, but as Japanese control tightened and the arms and food situation deteriorated, most of this came to an end and the MPAJA was fully occupied in maintaining its existence on the defensive in the jungle. British remnants were contacted and looked after by them, and though they were treated with deference throughout and invited to help over training, they were refused any voice in the organisation or control of the MPAJA. Such was the position when contact was re-established by a British party from India in August 1943.

2. In December 1943, a preliminary agreement was made between the British party representing the Allied Forces (later SEAC) and a Communist leader representing specifically the MCP, the MPAJA and the Anti-Japanese Union (as the political side of the MCP was then known). In accordance with this agreement the resistance organisation undertook to co-operate against the enemy and to accept orders and instructions from the Allied Forces. This co-operation was to continue throughout any period of military occupation. The British on their part undertook to arm, train and supply the MPAJA so far as was possible. By this time the

MPAJA had become a fairly extensive organisation and was divided into eight groups, each with its own group leader. Each group was split up into a number of small camps hidden in the jungle. Food supplies were received from outside, especially from the Anti-Japanese Union and augmented by the produce of their small gardens in the jungle. Before the foregoing agreement could be implemented, however, all contact with India was again lost and the British were unable to fulfil their part of the bargain until February 1945, when contact was regained with India, and Malaya came within the range of Allied aircraft.

3. A further conference was now held, at which the organisation of the MPAJA was clarified and British liaison with it was settled. For co-operation with the British the MPAJA was organised into seven regiments each consisting nominally of five patrols of not less than 100 men each. British liaison officers were to be attached to each patrol headquarters and to each regiment or group headquarters. Patrols were to be under the operational command of the British liaison officers, but internal command and discipline remained a matter for MPAJA's own officers and headquarters. Arms, equipment and money to buy food, and possibly food itself, were to be supplied by air, but arms or equipment would not be supplied to patrols which had no British liaison officers. The period before D-Day for the Allied invasion was to be one of preparation, training and equipping and no offensive action was to be undertaken until orders were received from SEAC. The object of this was to preserve surprise for D-Day.

4. The plans were carried out with remarkable smoothness and rapidity, and at the time of the Japanese surrender over 4,000 members of the MPAJA were under operational control of British liaison officers. The majority of these units were grouped at strategic points near the main North-South road and railway line.

5. After the Japanese surrender, the MPAJA remained mobilised and under the control of the liaison officers. Other liaison officers were brought in and control was extended to remoter areas and patrols. This force, now employed on watch-and-ward duties, was fully rationed by the British Army and each man, regardless of rank, was paid at the rate of $30 monthly from the date of surrender. At the same time, in order to obtain some control over the large number of armed and uncontrolled bands roving the country, it was ruled that any alleged guerilla who produced an effective firearm and applied for enrolment in a controlled patrol before the day of disbandment should be accepted.

Section 4.—DISBANDMENT OF THE MPAJA AND AFTER

1. On 1st December, 1945, the MPAJA was disbanded. The principal conditions of disbandment were that all arms, explosives and equipment were to be handed in, the MPAJA was to cease to exist and its insignia and badge (three red stars) were never again to be worn as uniform. In return each guerilla was paid a gratuity of $350 and received a promise that the Government would do all that was possible to rehabilitate him in suitable employment.

2. Some 6,000 members of the MPAJA were disbanded (this figure probably included guerillas who had joined the MPAJA shortly before disbandment purely for the sake of obtaining the monthly pay and gratuity), and over 5,000 arms including all those supplied through British liaison officers for which receipts had been obtained, were handed in. In addition, a number of rifles and shot-guns, most of which had probably been obtained during the British retreat in 1942 or immediately after the Japanese surrender, were also given up. Nevertheless, a large quantity of arms and ammunition, including sten guns, carbines and pistols, together with numbers of weapons which had been dropped from the air and picked up by the MPAJA unknown to the liaison officers, were never brought in or handed over on the disbandment of the organisation. These arms were hidden in secret dumps throughout the country for future use by the MCP.

3. At the same time, a secret branch of the MPAJA, which ran parallel to the open MPAJA, was retained and its members kept their weapons and did not come forward to be demobilised. At the end of 1945, this clandestine organisation numbered 4,000 men and included as many members as possible of long and tried service, units of the MPAJA which had not come into contact with and were therefore unknown to the British liaison officers, and most of the important MCP leaders who had remained incognito.

4. This secret force, and the secret caches of arms were formed for the express purpose of waging a guerilla war should the British Government not introduce into Malaya a People's Republic to the liking of the MCP.

5. Following the disbandment of the MPAJA, the MCP organised the MPAJA Ex-Comrades Association, ostensibly to look after interests of the ex-guerillas, but actually to preserve and perpetuate MCP influence over them. The record of this organisation after the war was one of continued abuse of the Government for alleged failure to look after guerilla interests coupled with refusal to

co-operate with Government officers who attempted to carry into effect the Government's promises of rehabilitation. At the same time the MCP used the clandestine military organisation as a nucleus for mobilisation and training of their armed forces.

6. Such is the background of these forces which were born of British-Communist co-operation during the Malayan Campaign of 1941-42. Though motivated throughout by a political creed fundamentally antagonistic to the British, they were openly loyal to their agreement to co-operate throughout the war. The MPAJA units had never been a real menace to the Japanese authorities, but they had a considerable nuisance value and necessitated troops being held in readiness lest an attack should take place. They also performed signal service in helping to keep alive the spirit of resistance to the Japanese throughout the occupation.

Section 5.—SITUATION AFTER THE LIBERATION

1. While the MPAJA was occupied with active resistance to the Japanese, the political side of the MCP was concentrated primarily on the dissemination of Communist propaganda, the boosting of a spirit of resistance, and the maintenance of supplies to the armed guerillas. Already during the Japanese occupation the MCP had planned to take over the government of Malaya when the war was over, but when the British came in with strong military forces after the capitulation and set up the British Military Administration, the MCP realised that their plans could not be carried out at that time.

2. The MCP then followed a policy of apparent co-operation while at the same time following the normal communist procedure of infiltrating its agents into government departments, public utilities etc. It was also trying to get a firm grip of labour by controlling trade unions. During this time only a few of the lesser leaders worked in the open. The remainder and the greater part of the organisation worked under cover.

3. Throughout 1947 there was a great deal of internal dissension in the MCP. This coupled with the remarkable economic and political recovery taking place in Malaya made it clear to the MCP that a radical change of policy was essential if it was to continue to be effective.

4. In December 1947, the MCP decided on a more violent policy which became apparent through labour unrest and strikes. It was probably in March 1948, that it was decided to start an armed fight against the Government.

5. Up to this time the MCP had been permitted to function free of all legal restrictions, and, since the liberation, the Societies Ordinance had been deliberately left partially in abeyance. In the face of growing lawlessness in labour disputes and of increasing evidence that Communist agitators were using trade unions for political purposes, the Federation Government revised the Trade Union Ordinance. This was done not with the object of suppressing the unions, but to ensure that they should in fact be trade unions with their members organised for trade union purposes. But strikes and labour unrest continued to increase, and the MCP began a campaign of violence throughout the country. Vast quantities of rubber were stolen, rubber estate offices were burned down, British planters and miners and their Chinese, Indian and Malay employees were murdered.

6. On 18th June, 1948, the Government of the Federation proclaimed a State of Emergency and adopted emergency powers to deal with the outbreak of violence. On 23rd July, 1948, the Governments of Singapore and the Federation specifically prescribed the MCP as an unlawful society.

Section 6.—ORGANISATION OF THE MCP

1. **Introduction.**— Before considering the structure of the MCP, a brief examination of its main elements is appropriate.

2. The MCP may be broadly divided into two, i.e.:—
   (a) The Jungle Organisation.
   (b) The Open Organisation.

3. It is not proposed to deal with the Open Organisation in detail, as the individuals concerned cannot be classified as terrorists and therefore do not come within the scope of this pamphlet. It must be remembered however, that the Open Organisation plays a very important part in the Communist campaign.

4. **The Jungle Organisation.**— This may be divided into two main categories:—

   (a) *Malayan Races Liberation Army (MRLA)* (See Section 7 below).
   (b) *The Min Yuen Movement.*—The Min Yuen Movement is controlled by District and Branch Committees which are the spearhead of the political side of the MCP Organisation, and are in direct touch with the masses. In addition to their duty of indoctrinating the masses and spreading the

gospel of Communism, it is the task of District and Branch Committees to organise the collection of intelligence, money, supplies and materials from the Masses. From the nature of their duties, District and Branch Committees operate almost entirely in their local areas near the jungle fringes, and cannot retire to the deep jungle without breaking contact with "masses" and thus losing their efficiency. All members are usually armed.

5. **Present Organisation.**— The MCP is organised on orthodox Communist Party lines:—

(a) *Central Committee.*—The Central Committee is composed of approximately 12 top ranking MCP executives under the direction of the Secretary General. This Committee rarely assembles and the actual Policy direction emanates from the Politbureau consisting of 3-4 members including the Secretary General.

(b) *Military High Command.*—This is believed to exist in name only and is probably the title assumed by the Central Committee when it issues directives to the Armed Forces.

(c) *Regional Bureaux.*—Directives and decisions by the Central Committee are passed to the North and South Malaya Bureaux for transmission to the various State and Regional Committees below them.

(d) *State and Regional Committees.*—Although operational control normally exists at the State Committee level there are cases where, for geographic expediency, control in large states has been split between two Regional Committees, e.g. North Johore Regional Committee and South Johore Regional Committee.

(e) *District Committees.*—Each State/Regional Committee has under its control a number of District Committees (MCP Districts). The number of MCP Districts varies from about 4 to 7 according to the size and geography of each State/Region. The MCP District is the main functional level of the MCP.

(f) *Branch Committees.*—The Branch Committees work under the direction of District Committees, each District Committee controlling an average of 4 Branch Committees. The units controlled by the Branch Committees are known as Armed Work Forces (AWFs) or Branches and the rank and file of these units are the main link between the Terrorist Organisation in the jungle and their supporters living in the open.

(g) *Masses Organisation.*—The Branch Committees contact the 'masses' (MCP terminology describing the general public) through 'masses executives.' Masses executives live in the open and may be members of the MCP. Their activities include the organisation of the MCP supporters, the procurement of food and miscellaneous supplies, the collection of subscriptions and intelligence, the dissemination of communist propaganda and generally speaking, the fostering of communist-inspired subversive activities among the civil population.

Section 7.—ARMED FORCES OF THE MCP

1. The part of the MCP which carries out military tasks is the Malayan Races Liberation Army (MRLA). It was originally organised in Regiments but due to logistic difficulties these were disbanded though their HQ still exists in name. The MRLA now consists entirely of Independent Platoons some of which are employed on bodyguard duties and most of which, from time to time, perform Min Yuen activities.

2. Policy directions issuing from the MCP Central Committee and affecting the MRLA are sometimes issued in the name of "The Military High Command."

3. State and Regional Committees are, in fact, combined political and military commands and issue directives on broad matters of policy in the name of the Regimental HQ.

4. **Independent Platoon.**— The standard MRLA unit is the Independent Platoon. The number of these Platoons was greatly decreased by the formation of Armed Work Forces (mentioned below). Platoons usually operate under the control of a State Committee Member (SCM) and therefore may operate in several MCP Districts according to the jurisdiction of the SCM. Strengths vary considerably from about 15 to 30. When carrying out operations they may be assisted by the local Armed Work Force.

Section 8.—MCP POLICY

1. MCP policy is guided by that of the Communist Parties in Russia and China. Its aim has always been to establish a Communist peoples republic in Malaya by overthrowing the lawful government. Though this aim has never changed since the

MCP was created in 1927, the plan to achieve it has altered frequently. Every aspect of the political and economic life of the country has been watched and, where expedient, has been exploited to further the aim of the MCP.

2. Prior to the Emergency, the MCP policy was to gain power through the trade unions. When this policy created industrial strife causing the MCP to be proscribed, it was decided that power must be seized by armed rebellion. This began as terrorism in 1948.

3. By 1951 the MCP realised that its policy of terrorism was not going to achieve its aim. In fact, due to the suffering the terrorists were causing the people of Malaya, the party was losing ground. Because of this, directives were issued to the CT organisation to reduce terrorist activities and to concentrate attacks on military targets.

4. At the same time, the aim was to be furthered by what is now known as the "United Front." This policy was based on the fact that all political parties, racial associations, trade unions, etc. have certain common points of policy e.g. land for the peasants, expansion of industry and foreign trade, independence. By using such points the MCP has produced a manifesto which, if not entirely acceptable to everyone, has a wide appeal to many. The MCP's final aim of a Communist people's republic is, of course, not disclosed by the manifesto.

5. The immediate aim of the manifesto is to win the support of the middle and upper classes in whose hands is the political power so that, with their help, a United Front can be formed to take over the government or to compel the government in power to come to terms with the MCP, to withdraw the Emergency Regulations, and to force the British out of Malaya.

6. In addition to the United Front, the MCP is making widespread efforts to infiltrate secretly into the public life of the country. The continuance of the Emergency seriously hampers this and the MCP may be expected to do its best to bring the Emergency to an end on the minimum terms of no surrender and unrestricted return to civil life of party members in the jungle.

7. At the Baling peace talks in December 1955, it was made clear to the MCP that its terms would never be accepted.

Section 9.—NOTES ON THE CT ORGANISATION

1. CT Characteristics:—

(a) Approximately 90 per cent of the CT are Chinese. The remainder are Malay and Indian with one or two Javanese, Siamese and Japanese.

(b) They are mostly young, thoroughly familiar with life in the jungle and well acquainted with the topography of the areas in which they operate. They are able to withstand hardships and privations and if necessary, can subsist on jungle produce for lengthy, but not interminable periods. Their tracking, fieldcraft and standard of discipline are normally of a very high order. Their handling and maintenance of personal weapons as well as their general standard of shooting is adequate for the type of warfare they are engaged in.

(c) CT morale is an extremely variable factor depending upon such factors as SF pressure, food and supply situation, leadership, successes, etc. Generally the CT prefer hit and run tactics to pitched battle. Only the most fanatical elements amongst the CT will put up determined resistance when cornered.

2. Uniform and Personal Equipment.

CTs wear various types of uniform and plain clothes. Sometimes it is khaki or jungle green complete, including equipment and packs. Headgear varies from red-starred caps, civilian hats or caps, to no hats at all.

3. Arms and Ammunition:—

(a) The majority of CT arms and a high percentage of their ammunition is old and partly unserviceable. It is therefore of vital importance to prevent them from replenishing their stocks at the expense of SF. The capture of arms and ammunition is one of the principal aims underlying any CT attack on SF patrols, bases and transport.

(b) An example of the arms held by a strong MRLA Independent Platoon is:—

Two Brens	Seven Shotguns
Six Stens or TSMG	Two Pistols
Six Carbines	Ten Grenades
Twelve Rifles	

(c) Armouries exist where repair of damaged weapons and ammunition is carried out, and where grenades and landmines can be made.

4. CT Camps:—

(a) *Siting and location.*—Most camps possess the same major characteristics:—

   (i) Adjacent to a stream, river or swamp.
   (ii) Sentry posts on the main tracks or routes leading to the area of the camp. Quite frequently the sentry post is protected by some form of warning device e.g. a trip wire sited along a likely line of approach connected to a tin, or a string running from a bush or tree, which if moved rattles a tin by the sentry.
   (iii) Consist of bashas or lean-to huts, standing or collapsible.
   (iv) Except in small or temporary camps they have a small parade ground or out-door lecture hall. In the larger ones they have both.
   (v) Sited on the slopes of a hill or behind or in front of a swamp.

The extent of camp defences and degree of resistance to be expected will depend on the size and importance of the camp.

Patrols should be able to recognise likely places where a CT camp might be located, remembering that often camps, for reasons of security, are built in unlikely places, i.e. in swamps, belukar and lallang. Men should make a habit of appreciating the ground and the area around them as they move so as to be prepared for immediate action.

(b) *Camp protection drill.*—The normal CT protection drill for their camps is as follows:—

   (i) The sentry either fires at the SF as they approach his post or else he moves back to the camp unseen, and gives the alarm.
   (ii) On hearing the firing or on receiving information from their sentries the CT, who are always prepared, immediately disperse into the jungle and reassemble at a prearranged RV.

(iii) Sometimes, particularly in the large and better organised camps, one or more counter attacks are put in after the SF have entered the camp. These counter attacks are seldom pressed home with determination.

5. **Communications.**—For the maintenance of communications the CT depend on:—

  (a) *Jungle couriers.*—These usually move in groups of two or three on jungle routes between courier posts. Generally the rear member of the group carries the most important documents. Jungle couriers are also used for carrying bulky items such as packages of propaganda material.

  (b) *Open couriers.*—These provide the quickest means of communications. They are normally open members of the MCP and use public transport, taxis and bicycles. Messages are usually carried in the form of small rolled slips concealed about the person.

  (c) *Wireless.*—The MCP is known to possess a very limited number of wireless transmitters. It is doubtful whether wireless communications have ever been successfully established. They make considerable use of commercial radio receivers, mainly to listen to Radio Malaya and to Communist broadcasts from China.

6. **CT Tactics.**— Basic CT tactics, such as immediate action drills, siting of ambushes and defensive positions, the use of Bren, Rifle and Reconnaissance groups, resemble our own because the more senior military instructors in the MCP are ex MPAJA personnel who were trained by Force 136 officers. Training manuals include translations of British and Russian publications and original Chinese Peoples' Army pamphlets.

CHAPTER III

OWN FORCES

Section 1.—INTRODUCTION

1. The responsibility for conducting the campaign in Malaya rests with the Civil Government. The Police Force is the Government's normal instrument for the maintenance of Civil Authority but, in the current Emergency, the Armed Forces have been called in to support the Civil Power in its task of seeking out and destroying armed Communist terrorism. In addition, a Home Guard has been formed.

2. Since every function of Government is affected by the Emergency, a special system of control of operations has been evolved to provide intimate co-operation at all levels between Departments of Government and the SF. This system has remained the same in outline since its introduction in 1950. Because of the advance to Independence of Malaya, which has taken place while the Emergency has continued, the system has, however, varied in detail. An outline of the current system is given below.

Section 2.—SYSTEM OF CONTROL OF EMERGENCY OPERATIONS

1. **The Emergency Operations Council.**— A Committee—the Emergency Operations Council—is responsible to the Government of the Federation of Malaya for the overall conduct of the campaign and for ensuring that there is full integration of Civil Government and SF measures. The Council consists of:—

Chairman: The Prime Minister.
Deputy Chairman: The Minister of Defence.
Members: The Minister of Finance.
The Minister of Health.
The Minister of Interior and Justice.
The Minister of Agriculture.
The Minister of Labour and Social Welfare.
The Minister of Commerce and Industry.
The Federal Director of Emergency Operations.
The General Officer Commanding Federation Army.
The Secretary of Defence.

The Commissioner of Police.
The Flag Officer Malayan Area.
The General Officer Commanding Overseas Commonwealth Land Forces.
The Air Officer Commanding No. 224 Group RAF.

Secretary: The Principal Staff Officer to the Director of Emergency Operations.

NOTE: 1. The Flag Officer Malayan Area will normally attend only when matters directly affecting the use of the Royal Navy are being discussed.

2. The Deputy Secretary (Security and Intelligence), Prime Minister's Department, is in attendance at all meetings of the Council.

2. **The Federal Director of Emergency Operations.**— The Federal Director of Emergency Operations (normally described as the Director of Operations) is a General Officer seconded from the British Army for service with the Government of the Federation of Malaya. He is responsible to the Minister of Defence for the day to day conduct of Emergency Operations, in all their aspects. He is not in command of any Security Forces, but exercises operational direction and control of the forces assigned for operations against Communist Terrorists through respective SF commanders. He will, as appropriate, issue instructions to State War Executive Committees.

3. **Commanders' Sub-Committee.**— The Director of Operations is the Chairman of the Commanders' Sub-Committee of the Emergency Operations Council. The members of this Sub-Committee are:—

General Officer Commanding Federation Army.
Commissioner of Police.
Flag Officer Malayan Area (normally present only for discussions affecting the use of the Royal Navy).
General Officer Commanding Overseas Commonwealth Land Forces.
Air Officer Commanding No. 224 Group RAF.

In Attendance: Principal Staff Officer.
Director Special Branch.

This Sub-Committee makes policy decisions in regard to the use of SF, within the overall policy approved by the Emergency Operations Council.

4. **Director of Operations' Staff.**—To assist the Director of Operations and to issue appropriate instructions to implement the decisions of the Emergency Operations Council and the Commanders' Sub-Committee, there is a small joint staff headed by the Principal Staff Officer.

5. **SWECs, DWECs and WECs.—**

(a) In each State there is a State War Executive Committee (SWEC) which is responsible for waging the "war" in the State. This Committee consists of:—

Chairman: *The Chief Minister.

Deputy Chairman: *The State Secretary or such other Government Officer, especially appointed to this post.

Members: *The Chief Police Officer.
*The Senior Military Commander.
*The State Home Guard Officer.
The State Financial Officer.
The State Information Officer.
*The Executive Secretary.
Up to six selected community leaders.

The persons marked * form the Operations Sub-Committee of the State War Executive Committee (Ops SWEC). Ops SWEC is responsible for the day to day direction of Emergency Operations in the State: it normally meets daily.

(b) In almost every civil administrative district there is a District War Executive Committee (DWEC) which is responsible for waging the "war" in that district. The composition of the DWEC is:—

Chairman: †The District Officer.

Members: †The Administrative Officer (Johore only).
†The Senior Police Officer of the District.
†The Senior Military Commander.
†Home Guard Officer nominated by the SHGO.
The District/Area Information Officer.
Three selected community leaders (more in special circumstances).

The persons marked † form the Operations Sub-Committee of the District War Executive Committee (Ops DWEC). Ops DWEC is the District equivalent of Ops SWEC.

(c) In certain parts of the country it is not practical to base a DWEC on the civil administrative district. In these cases special War Executive Committees have been formed.

For example in Kedah there are no DWECs; instead there are three Circle War Executive Committees (CWECs) each based on a police circle: on Penang is Penang Island Rural War Executive Committee (PIRWEC). These are, however, equivalent to DWECs.

(d) In a few cases DWECs have been based on civil administrative sub-districts. When this occurs, the Assistant District Officer is Chairman—they function as normal DWECs.

6. Emergency Operational Chain of Command.— The Emergency Operational Chain of Command is:—

Emergency Operations Council.
Commanders' Sub-Committee
State War Executive Committees.
District War Executive Committees.

The Services chain of command is used only to enable the respective commanders to give orders to their own forces. For Emergency Operations, however, SF are placed at the disposal of SWECs/DWECs.

Section 3.—MAIN TASKS OF THE SECURITY FORCES

1. The methods used by the SF, to defeat armed Communism and re-establish normal conditions in Malaya, include the following:—

   (a) The close control of populated areas such as towns, new villages, kampongs and estate lines. These areas are potential sources of CT food supplies and, in addition, must be afforded security in the interests of the economy of the country.

   (b) The conduct of offensive operations on the fringes of the populated areas, with the object of eliminating CT and depriving them of contact with sources of food supply.

   (c) The mounting of deep jungle and other special operations designed to eliminate CT, to isolate them from the aborigines and to locate and destroy their headquarters, long term food and arms dumps and cultivation areas.

2. The most important factor in destroying the CT is to complete his isolation from the rest of the community. He must get no

money, no food or clothing; no help of any sort. Bases must be secured in towns, new villages and kampongs. With these bases secure the armed forces, with their attendant resources of mobility, flexibility and fire power can then go after the CT and destroy him, his dumps, camps and cultivation.

Section 4.—THE BRIGGS PLAN

1. The Briggs Plan, which came into effect on 1st June, 1950, aimed at bringing proper administrative control to a population, which had never been controlled before. The main aspects of the Plan were:—

  (a) The rapid resettlement of squatters under the surveillance of Police and auxiliary Police.
  (b) The regrouping of local labour in mines and on estates.
  (c) The recruitment and training of CID and Special Branch Police personnel.
  (d) The Army to provide a minimum framework of troops throughout the country to support the Police, and at the same time to provide a concentration of forces for the clearing of priority areas.
  (e) The Police and Army to operate in complete accord. To assist in this, joint Police/Army operational control is established at all levels and there is a close integration of Police and Military Intelligence.

2. The Briggs Plan established the SWEC-DWEC chain of command which has functioned ever since. This has ensured that:—

  (a) There was always complete integration of Emergency effort.
  (b) SF have always been acting in support of the Civil Power.

3. The Plan also created the principle of the Ops SWEC/Ops DWEC by which all members make a joint decision, and then issue appropriate orders to their subordinates through their Services chain of command.

4. The Plan was essentially a thorough but long term proposition and it would be unrealistic to look for speedy and decisive results. It envisaged a logical clearing of the country from South to North, leaving behind a strong police force and civil administration once an area or State had been cleared. It also aimed to isolate the MRLA from the rest of the rural population, thus enabling the latter to feel

safe to come forward with information, whilst at the same time depriving the MRLA of their means of support and so forcing them into the open where they could better be dealt with by the SF.

Section 5.—SUBSEQUENT DEVELOPMENTS

1. **White Areas.**— It has not proved possible to carry out the logical clearing of the country from South to North as envisaged in the Briggs Plan.

2. However, progress has been such that the CT organisation has been decisively broken in about half the area of the Federation. Consequently it has been possible to declare almost the whole of Kelantan, Trengganu, Pahang, Province Wellesley and Malacca, together with a strip of the West Coast White Areas; in these areas the majority of Emergency Regulations are lifted.

3. It has been explained to the population in these areas that it is their responsibility to keep the area White by refusing to co-operate with the CT and by promptly reporting any CT activity to the authorities.

4. **The Aboriginal Areas of Malaya.**— In December 1952, the Director of Operations in Committee decided that a forward policy would be adopted for the control of the aboriginal tribes of Malaya. This would involve taking protection and administration to the aborigines in their own areas and the avoidance in future of the resettlement of aborigines who live in the deep jungle.

5. This policy has been implemented by the following measures:—
   - (a) The expansion of the Federal Government Department of Aborigines by the appointment of additional officers as Protectors of Aborigines in the States concerned and the recruitment of 'Field Teams' to work in the aboriginal areas.
   - (b) Establishing a series of 'Jungle Forts' in selected deep jungle aboriginal areas.
   - (c) The mounting of special operations to find parties of aborigines under CT domination in deep jungle, and to bring them into Government protection.

6. The aims of jungle forts can be defined as follows:—
   - (a) To establish bases from which the Federal Police can give local protection to the aborigines and from which offensive operations can be mounted when the occasion arises.

(b) To allow the aborigines in the selected areas to continue their normal way of life without risk of CT domination and so to build up an intelligence network on CT activity.

(c) To improve the morale of the aborigines by having permanent SF garrisons in their areas and eventually by the recruitment of selected men to assist in local defence.

(d) To provide centres from which medical and trading facilities can be made available to the aborigines.

Section 6.—PATTERN OF OPERATIONS (1957)

1. Operations can be categorised as follows:—
    (a) Mopping-up Operations.
    (b) Framework Operations.
    (c) State Priority Operations.
    (d) Federal Priority Operations.
    (e) Deep Jungle Operations.

The definition of each of these type of operations is given in the following paragraphs.

2. **Mopping-up Operations.**— Operations to complete the destruction and prevent revival of the CTO in White or Selected areas. The Masses Organisation in such areas is usually disrupted, and the CTs rely for supplies on casual begging and extortion. Relaxation of Emergency Regulations precludes food denial. Operations consist mainly of patrols to prevent contact between the CTs and the population, and jungle patrols by Police and Home Guard.

3. **Framework Operations.**—These are the normal offensive operations by which a DWEC reduces its CTO when no State or Federal priority is allotted. It may include any or all the elements of a major operation on a limited scale—i.e., gate checks, patrols to prevent contact between the CTs and the population, ambushes, cordon and search operations, jungle patrols, central cooking or the operational rice ration in certain villages, and mass arrests. The essentials for success are resource, economy of effort and variety of methods.

4. **State Priority Operations.**—Operations in which the SWEC decides to transfer SF to exploit opportunities in specific areas— usually for limited periods. Examples are large scale cordon operations, multiple ambushes, and intensive patrols in areas where

CT groups are known to be, or the imposition of strict food denial on certain areas for a short time. On occasions the SWEC may be provided with Federal reinforcements including air effort, for State Priority Operations.

5. **Federal Priority Operations.**—Major food denial operations planned on a Federal level, for which reinforcements of SF are provided between target dates laid down by Director of Operations. Priority is also given before and during the operation to the provision of civil and police officers, and for central cooking, accommodation, roads, wiring, etc.

6. **Deep Jungle Operations.**—Operations separate from the above which are mounted to gain intelligence of the CTO in the deep jungle, to deny them areas for rest and retraining, to protect and bring administration to aborigines, and isolate them from the CTs.

Section 7.—THE POLICE

1. The Police Force is a Federal Organisation commanded by the Commissioner of Police, and consists of ten contingents, each commanded by a Chief Police Officer, (CPO). With the exception of Kedah and Perlis, which share a contingent, each State is policed by one contingent. Contingents are further divided into Police Circles which are supervised by Officers Superintending Police Circles, (OSPC). These Circles are themselves divided into Police Districts, commanded by Officers Commanding Police Districts, (OCPD).

2. The tasks of the Police Force are:—
    (a) Maintenance of law and order.
    (b) Preserving the public peace.
    (c) Prevention and detection of crime and the apprehension of offenders.
    (d) Protection of life and property.
    (e) Collection of information relevant to these tasks and to internal security, and their dissemination to departments of Government.
    (f) Para-military duties necessitated by the Emergency.

3. **Composition.**—The Police are divided into:—
    (a) Regular Police.

(b) Temporary and volunteer police, the main groups of which are:—
  (i) Special Constables (SC).
  (ii) Temporary Female Searchers (TFS).
  (iii) Special Operational Volunteer Force (SOVF).
  (iv) The Police Volunteer Reserve (PVR).

4. **The Regular Police.**—The Regular Police are permanent career policemen. They consist of:—

(a) (i) *Uniform Branch.*
    (ii) *Detective Branch.*

These are trained and organised to carry out orthodox Police duties.

(b) *The Police Field Force (PFF).*

These are para-military formations equipped and trained to operate on a platoon basis in any area of the country in the same way as army units. Their principal tasks are the manning of Jungle Forts and the mounting of trans-frontier operations in South Thailand. They also provide trained riot units.

(c) *Special Branch.*—The Special Branch is the Intelligence Department of the Police Force and is the instrument of Government for the collection and collation of all internal intelligence affecting the security of the country. In co-operation with the appropriate departments of Her Majesty's Government it shares the responsibility for the collection and collation of certain external intelligence affecting the security of the country. The principal task of Special Branch is to collect intelligence concerning subversive organisations with a view to destroying them. The Special Branch may supply such intelligence to the Security Forces and other Government departments for exploitation, and may itself exploit such information.

(d) *Special Constabulary.*—The Special Constabulary is deployed in the form of Area Security Units, (ASU) and Police Special Squads, (PSS) in the developed areas of the Federation. Its role is the carrying out of offensive patrolling against CT, the enforcement of food denial measures, the safeguarding of planters and miners and the static defence of vital public or semi-public utility installations against sabotage.

III

5. Police Clearance.—

(a) *Introduction*: —

(i) One of the underlying principles in all operations against the CT in the present Emergency is that the Armed Forces are acting in support of the Civil Power.

(ii) It is important to remember this when examining the relationship between Police and Military, particularly on the question of clearance. While generally all operational activity will be co-ordinated through Combined Operations Rooms, there have been and will be occasions when the Army is acting on its own and requires offensive air or naval support at short notice. In all cases Police clearance must be obtained, unless the SF are actually in contact with the CT, when an immediate air strike can be initiated without formal Police clearance.

(b) *Necessity for Clearance*

(i) While the operational responsibility for any particular area may be given to the Army, it is still the responsibility of the Police to ensure that no innocent person is killed or injured and no lawful habitation or property is destroyed or damaged as the result of SF action.

(ii) It is a comparatively simple matter for a Military or Police Commander to state at any given time the location of his own units; it is not so simple, however, to be sure of the location of woodcutters, aborigines and their clearings, and other lawful habitations, and this, allied with other Emergency considerations, may at times result in some delay before the local Police Commander is able to give clearance for a proposed air strike or operation. It is essential, therefore, that the Police Commander in whose area of responsibility it is proposed to request an air strike or SF are to operate, be informed at the earliest possible moment of such intention, to allow him to make the necessary enquiries, which will enable him to grant clearance.

(c) *Operations Requiring Police Clearance.* Most operations are mounted at SWEC or DWEC level and mutual clearances are arranged simultaneously. Where this does not occur and a military formation is acting on its own initiative, it should obtain Police clearance in the following circumstances:—

    (i) Minor operations, e.g., ambushes, in or adjoining Police patrol areas, or in rubber or other areas likely to be occupied by innocent civilians.

    (ii) All requests for offensive air support and artillery fire unless actually in contact with CT.

    (iii) All requests for Naval bombardment.

(d) *Clearance Procedure.*—Police clearance will initially be given by the OCPD in whose district the operation, artillery shoot, naval bombardment or air strike is to take place. This clearance for air strikes and naval bombardment must be passed via OSPC and CPO to Police HQ, Kuala Lumpur, where Operations Information Branch are in close liaison with JOC at Air HQ, Malaya. No Naval bombardment or air strike, other than the immediate air strikes referred to in paragraph 5 (a) (ii) above, will take place without such clearance.

(e) *Limitations of Clearance*

    (i) The object of Police clearance has been explained in paragraph 5 (b) (i) above. When given, it means that the Police believe, to the best of their knowledge, that no loss or injury to innocent civilians will result from SF action.

    (ii) This does not mean that SF can shoot on sight any person found in an area which has been so cleared. If in any reasonable doubt, the unidentified person or persons should be challenged and any subsequent action by SF should be based on the reaction of such persons to that challenge.

Section 8.—THE ARMY

1. Role.— The primary role of the Army is to seek out and destroy CT in the jungle and on its fringes. By the constant harassing of the CT, their lines of communication with sympathisers amongst the civil population are disrupted. Thus in an effort to maintain their food supply system they are forced into the open and so brought to battle.

2. The secondary role of the Army is that of supporting the Federal Police in the populated areas by helping to enforce food denial measures, curfews, etc.

3. **Deployment.**—The deployment of military formations and units is based on the principle of Army/Police/Civil co-operation at all levels as embodied in the Briggs Plan. The principle is to have, in each State:—
   (a) A senior military headquarters alongside Police Contingent headquarters in the State capital and responsible through the SWEC for military operations in the complete State.
   (b) A brigade or battalion headquarters near Police Circle headquarters at the administrative centre of the Civil District and responsible through the DWEC for operations in the District.
   (c) Infantry companies deployed in each Police District with the Company Commander in his turn working in close co-operation with the OCPD.

4. Superimposed on the above is the organisation of units into the normal military formations. This provides the normal Service and administrative chain of command, and ensures that the Army remains organised so that it can operate, if necessary, against a first class military enemy.

5. Under this system the Black area of the Federation is covered by a framework of military commanders each working in close co-operation with the Police and Civil authorities at his own level in his own area. Although this basic layout is adhered to wherever possible there are bound to be variations owing to such factors as the availability of units and the operational importance of different areas of the country. Thus in some cases there may be only one battalion in a State where there is little CT activity and the Battalion Commander will be the Military representative on the SWEC with his Company Commanders acting at DWEC level. Alternatively for a particularly important operation a complete brigade may be concentrated in one district for a limited period. As progress is made in establishing White areas in various parts of the country there will be an increasing number of Districts under Police control where no military unit is deployed.

6. Units of the supporting arms are either retained as HQ OCLF troops or as HQ Federation Army troops and deployed in support of operations as necessary, or are permanently allocated to Brigades.

Section 9.—THE ROYAL AIR FORCE AND ARMY AIR CORPS

1. The Royal Air Force in Malaya is available to support Emergency operations. The RAF may operate independently or in direct co-operation with ground forces. The main roles of the RAF and Army Air Corps are shown in the following paragraphs.

2. **Air Reconnaissance.**— Air reconnaissance in Malaya plays a major part in the planning and conduct of anti-CT operations. The most populated areas have been covered by recent air survey and tactical photographic cover can be supplied with little delay. Methods of demanding photo cover are explained elsewhere in this pamphlet.

3. Light aircraft of the Army Air Corps are responsible for visual air reconnaissance in Malaya. These aircraft are under the operational control of the Army; in current operations their use is subject to the overall direction of the Air Officer Commanding, No. 224 Group RAF, exercised through the Joint Operations Centre. These light aircraft are used in a number of other roles including Target Marking for the Offensive Air-Strike Force.

4. **Offensive Air Support.**— The jungle provides unlimited cover from the air and targets are rarely visible to the Offensive Strike Force. Because of this the RAF work in close co-operation with the ground forces, upon whom the RAF must rely to provide worthwhile targets.

5. The offensive air effort is limited, but the bomber force can lay down a lethal pattern big enough to cover targets which are reported accurately. Purely harassing attacks can be provided for larger areas.

6. An RAF representative can always be made available to advise and assist in preparation and execution of ground operations when air participation is included.

7. **Air Supply.**— In order that ground forces may mount sustained operations in deep jungle it is necessary to keep them sustained with food, clothing and equipment. This commitment is met by an element of the air transport support force.

8. **Troop Lifts.**— Medium helicopters and light air transport aircraft are widely used for lifting troops into remote and hitherto inaccessible parts of the jungle. In this way the effectiveness of the available forces has been increased considerably.

9. **Casualty Evacuation.**— Light helicopters are used mainly for communication flying and for casualty evacuation. Apart from the urgent need to evacuate casualties to hospital as quickly as possible, the ability to remove them by helicopter frequently enables patrols to continue operating when they would otherwise have had to return to base.

10. **Psychological Warfare:—**

   (a) *Voice Aircraft.*—Aircraft fitted with special broadcasting apparatus are used for making voice broadcasts over parts of the jungle known to be occupied by CT. The object of such broadcasts is to induce CT surrenders by the application of Psychological Warfare methods.

   (b) *Leaflet Dropping.*—Leaflets are dropped over selected areas of the jungle with the object of inducing CT surrenders.

Section 10.—THE ROYAL NAVY

1. The Royal Navy assists by carrying out:—

   (a) Anti-smuggling and anti-piracy around the coast of Malaya.

   (b) Amphibious landings.

   (c) Bombardment of CT areas. Full details and method of calling for support are contained in Director of Operations Instruction No. 33.

Section 11. THE HOME GUARD

1. The aim of the Home Guard is, by the provision of a part-time force composed of all races, to form a yet closer link between the people and the Government in the fight against the Communist Terrorists. This involves:—

   (a) Creating security by protecting their own homes and the immediate area in which they live and by denying the enemy access thereto.

   (b) Full co-operation with the Security Forces in passing information of the movements of Communist Terrorists and of their agents and in assuring that no food reaches Communist Terrorists from their area.

   (c) With the operational sections, active assistance to the Security Forces in offensive operations.

2. To achieve this aim, the Home Guard, other than the permanent staff, consists of:—

   (a) *Village Home Guards.*—These are mainly in the Malay Kampongs, and are entirely responsible for the defence of their villages.

   (b) *Operational Sections.*

3. **Home Guard Operational Sections.—**
   (a) These are of two kinds:—
      (i) Operational Sections (General Duties).
      (ii) Operational Sections (New Village).
      The basic organisation of both types is the section. Both types of section are armed, uniformed and equipped similarly.
   (b) Members of operational sections are volunteers and are paid allowances for duties performed.
   (c) It is essential that areas allotted to operational sections, when not working directly with other Security Forces, are accurately recorded in DWEC operations rooms. Owing to lack of communications it is very seldom possible for section commanders to notify operations rooms of the movement of their patrols.

4. **Operational Sections (General Duties).—** Members of these sections volunteer to take part in Security Force operations away from the area of their homes. These sections are organised in platoons of 3 sections. They should not normally, however, be grouped into sub-units larger than platoons, as they have no operational administrative organisation or signal system. They are best used as platoons attached to infantry battalions.

5. **Operational Sections (New Village).—** These are the village Home Guards of Chinese new villages who are totally responsible for the defence of their village. They operate from the village in which they are raised. They have full responsibility for the defence of their village, by means of a mobile defence, which includes an area immediately adjacent to and surrounding their village.

6. **Overall Control of the Home Guard—**
   (a) The Inspector-General Home Guard is responsible to the Minister of Defence for administration and organisation and to the Director of Operations for training. He is not directly concerned with the day-to-day operational use of Home Guards.
   (b) The State War Executive Committees are responsible for the operations carried out by Home Guards. Their responsibilities are exercised through State Home Guard Officers (SHGO) who command the Home Guards in their areas.

(c) At District level, the District Officer commands the Home Guard, but, in view of his wide responsibilities, is relieved of command duties, other than those concerning policy, by a Deputy District Home Guard Commander (known as a DHGO) appointed to him by the SHGO. This officer has a number of permanent staff appointed to assist him.

7. **Kinta Valley Home Guard.**—To provide protection for the predominantly Chinese owned mining area of the Kinta Valley of Perak, a full-time force known as the Kinta Valley Home Guard has been formed. Its members are Chinese, and part of the cost of maintaining the force is met by the mine owners concerned, through the Perak Chinese Mining Association. The tasks of the Kinta Valley Home Guard are to provide protective cover by patrolling over areas containing open-cast mines and by contact with mine owners and workers, to gain information of CT movements and plans. The Force Commander is responsible to the State Home Guard Officer, Perak.

Section 12.—PSYCHOLOGICAL WARFARE

1. **Introduction.**— Psychological warfare (PW) is directed at the Communist Terrorist Organisation with the object of bringing home to the terrorists the sense of military and political defeat and isolation from the people; undermining their confidence in the leadership and policy of the Malayan Communist Party (MCP); creating dissension and distrust within the CT organisation; turning individual terrorists into easier military targets; and securing surrenders. It should be noted that the object is to cause general demoralisation and is much broader than just increasing the rate of surrender and disintegration of the CT organisation.

2. It is important to note that PW must always operate within the policy directives laid down by the appropriate Government authorities. PW cannot be divorced from military operations and must be looked upon by military formations as a supporting arm in all operations.

3. **Organisation.**— On the Federal level PW activities are carried out by the Psychological Warfare Section (PWS), the Head of which (HPWS) is a member of the Director of Operations' Staff and is responsible to the Director of Operations through the Principal Staff Officer for co-ordinating the PW element in operations, controlling all propaganda material aimed directly at the CT organisation, whether on a Federal or a local level, conducting necessary research in connection with PW and advising the Director of Information Services (DIS) on the operational and PW aspects of publicity directed towards the civil population.

4. At State level PW is planned, co-ordinated and executed by the State Information Officer who is responsible to the SWEC. Local campaigns are planned within the framework of existing PW policy and calls are made on the Federal Department for support as required.

5. In some of the larger States it has been necessary to appoint Area Information Officers who are responsible to the State Information Officer and plan, co-ordinate and execute PW at District level.

6. **Tasks.**—The following are likely tasks:—
   (a) The immediate exploitation of a CT elimination, i.e. a kill or surrender;
   (b) The immediate exploitation of a situation arising in the course of operations;
   (c) The planned exploitations of a tactical situation as part of a planned operation.

7. **Methods.**—PW attacks the CT organisation by direct and indirect means. Direct means employ mainly leaflets and Voice Aircraft broadcasts. Direct PW is supported by the Information Services who attack the CT organisation indirectly through the public by means of Public Address through their Field Units, Press, Radio, Films and Dramatic Shows.
   (a) *Leaflets.*—Leaflets are divided broadly into two categories. First, strategic leaflets, dealing with themes of general application to any CT unit throughout the Federation; secondly, tactical leaflets, devised to exploit specific events or grievances. Leaflets are distributed by Medium and Short range Aircraft of the Far Eastern Air Force (Transport Command) or Light Aircraft Flights, at the rate of 5,000 leaflets per 1000 yard map square or flying line. Small quantities are also distributed by ground forces and by the Field Units of Information Services.
   (b) *Voice.*—Medium and Short Range Aircraft fitted with broadcasting equipment are available to carry out the tasks listed in paragraph 6 above. (These aircraft also undertake Search and Rescue operations).
   (c) *Public address.*—State Information Officers have at their disposal mobile Field Units which can be used to support operations. These vans are fitted with a Public address system and cinema projectors. The personnel manning the vans are fluent in the language of their audiences.

SEPs often accompany these vans to give special addresses. Dramatic troupes can be organised to accompany these vans for specific purposes.

(d) *Press.*—A daily communique covering the Emergency is issued by the Information Services at Kuala Lumpur. The news is obtained from the Daily Sitreps. It is normal to issue the facts concerning all incidents over the past 24 hours. If for operational reasons an item of news should be withheld from the Press the item must be marked on the Sitrep 'NOT FOR PUBLICATION.'

(e) *Radio.*—In co-ordination with Information Services, Radio Malaya operates a Community Listening Service in addition to its regular broadcasts. Wireless receivers fitted with loud-speakers are placed in the majority of new villages and a large number of Malay kampongs and are tuned to this Service which produces programmes in Malay, Tamil and several Chinese dialects. This network plays an important part in the PW campaign.

(f) *Tours by Surrendered Enemy Personnel.*—Special propaganda shock teams of SEPs are sent on tour to support special operations. They put over their points simply.

8. Requests.—

(a) *Leaflets.*—Requests for leaflets to be dropped will generally be made by or through State Information Officers. In cases where supplies of leaflets have been sent in bulk to State or Area Information Officers drops may be carried out by arrangement with local Lt AC Flights without further reference to HPWS. (For further details see Chapter XVII Section 10).

(b) *Voice.*—Requests for Voice Aircraft will normally be initiated by State or District War Executive Committees after clearance with local Special Branch Officers. Requests should be submitted through Police (NOT Army) signal channels addressed to Federal Police HQ, Kuala Lumpur (telegraphic address: COMPOL OPS) for HPWS. A guide to the preparation of requests is given in Chapter XVII, Section 10 and Appendix F.

CHAPTER IV

THE EMERGENCY REGULATIONS (ERs) AND METHODS OF SEARCHING

Section 1.—INTRODUCTION

1. This chapter has been written in order to give members of the SF a brief outline of the ERs and to assist them in their day to day duties in connection with the Emergency in Malaya. The important part of the Regulations is to be found on pages 1-54 of the latest volume published in 1953 by the Government Printers, as amended by subsequent legal notifications.

Section 2.—NOTES ON ERs

1. This section contains various notes of importance and interest on the Regulations except for those Regulations dealing with Food Restriction which are dealt with separately in Section 3.

2. **Definitions.**— It should be noted that the term "supplies" includes money.

3. **Confessions.**— It should be noted that confessions made at any time during investigations into offences against the Regulations are admissible in court. This is in distinction from the Criminal Procedure Code wherein no confession made to a Police Officer is accepted. Confessions must not, however, be obtained by any inducement, threat or promise; and no confession will be admissible in evidence unless the person making it has first been given a warning to the effect that he is not obliged to say anything and that anything he does say may be used in evidence.

4. **Detention and Deportation.**
    (a) *ER 17.*—The Secretary for Defence may order any person to be detained for a period of up to two years. Minors (under 17 years of age) are usually detained in an advanced approved school.

    ER 24 (1).—Gives the Police powers to detain for up to 28 days any person against whom detention orders are pending.

    (b) All cases of Detention are scrutinised by a Committee of Review who have authority either to confirm or to revoke the order of detention or to suspend it on suitable conditions.

5. (a) *ER 17C.*—The Yang di-Pertuan Agong in Council may order any person who has had an order of detention issued against him to leave and to remain out of the Federation. Such deportation order shall not take effect until the detainee has had an opportunity of presenting his case to the Committee of Review.

   (b) Neither Federal Citizens nor British Subjects may be deported, but use can be made of the Banishment Enactments.

   (c) When a deportation order has been issued all the dependents are also deported. For definition of dependents see Page 1 of ERs. In the event of a deportee returning he may be sentenced to three years' imprisonment. The Yang di-Pertuan Agong in Council may permit a deportee to return.

6. **Restricted Residence. ER 17 F.**—The Chief Minister of any State may order any individual and his dependents to leave any area and to reside in a specific locality. The family may not leave without permission from the OCPD. It should be noted that upon expiry of the time limit the individual against whom the order has been made is entirely free to move where he wishes. Note should also be taken of the powers of the OCPD to exclude people from his district under ER 21. An order must be in writing.

7. **Controlled Areas. ER 17 FA.**—The Chief Minister may declare any area to be controlled in which case no person shall reside in this area unless it be in a specifically declared residential part of such an area.

8. The Chief Minister in a State may also order that no person shall be in other than the residential part of the controlled area during certain specified hours.

9. **Miscellaneous Protective Measures. ER 18.—Protected Places.**— The CPO may declare any area where it is desirable to restrict the entry of unauthorised persons to be a "Protected Place." Any person found in a protected place without authority may be arrested. He may be fired on if it is reasonably necessary to do so in order to effect his arrest, to overcome forcible resistance or to prevent his escape.

10. **ER 19A.—Danger Areas.**—The Chief Minister in any State may declare any area to be a Danger Area, and any member of the SF may take any measures, including shooting, to prevent any unauthorised person entering, or remaining in a Danger Area.

11. **ER 19B.—Perimeter Fence.**— The Chief Minister in any State may declare the fence surrounding any specified area to be a 'Perimeter Fence.' Where there are two or more fences round the area, all of them and the land between them are legally regarded as being a single fence. It is an offence to cross, or to take articles through, a perimeter fence other than by a recognised gate, and any person doing, or attempting to do either, may be arrested. He may be fired on in the circumstances described above in paragraph 10.

12. **Curfews. ER 20.**—Curfews are imposed at the discretion of the OCPD. Written permits of exemption from curfew may be issued by any Police Officer holding the rank of Sub-Inspector or upwards.

13. **Arrest. ER 25 (2).**—Suspects may only be detained for 48 hours by the OCPD. If enquiries cannot be completed in that time further detention may be authorised for an additional 14 days. The circumstances must be reported to the CPO.

14. **ER 28 (1). Use of Lethal Weapons.**—Lethal weapons may be used legally under the following circumstances:—

   (a) as a last resort in self-defence;

   (b) against armed CTs who are resisting the SF;

   (c) as a last resort to overcome resistance to arrest for the following offences or as a last resort to prevent the escape of any person reasonably suspected of committing any of the following offences:

      (i) carrying firearms, ammunition or explosives without authority (ER 4);

      (ii) consorting with a person carrying firearms, ammunition or explosives without authority (ER 5);

      (iii) consorting with or harbouring persons acting in a manner prejudicial to public safety (ER 6A);

      (iv) failing to stop on being challenged in a Protected Place or a Special Area (ERs 18 (5) and 19 (2));

      (v) being in a Danger Area, not being a member of the SF (ER 19A (3));

      (vi) Perimeter fences 19B (6).

15. **Search. ER 29.**—This ER provides that any Police Officer or any member of H.M. Forces or of a Local Force may stop and

search any vehicle or individual in any place, if he suspects that any evidence of the commission of an offence may be found. The same ER provides that any Police Officer of or above the rank of Sergeant and any member of H.M. Forces or of a Local Force of or above the rank of NCO or Leading Rate may enter and search any premises if he suspects that any evidence of the commission of an offence is likely to be found. Home Guards may only conduct searches of premises, vehicles and individuals if authorised by the OCPD and a woman may only be searched by a woman.

16. **Seizure of Foodstuffs. ER 31.**—Any Police Officer or member of H.M. Forces or of a Local Force may stop and search any vehicle, vessel or individual in any place if he suspects that food is being carried which is intended for, or may become available to CT. Further, any Police Officer of or above the rank of Sergeant and any member of H.M. Forces or a Local Force of or above the rank of NCO or Leading Rate may enter and search any premises if he suspects that they contain food which is intended for, or may become available to CT. Home Guards may only conduct searches if specially authorised by the OCPD.

17. **Seizure of Property. ER 32.**—Any Police Officer of or above the rank of Sergeant and any member of H.M. Forces or a Local Force of or above the rank of NCO or Leading Rate can take possession of any building and any land belonging thereto, which belongs to or has been used by CT or CT supporters, or which is owned or occupied by a person or persons who are harbouring or have harboured CT. The seizure must be reported to the Chief Minister of the State who may make an order of forfeiture. Home Guards may exercise these powers if authorised in writing by the OCPD.

18. **Requisitioning. ER 35.**—The Chief Minister of a State may requisition property for use of the SF only. Rent is payable. An appeal against the order goes to an Advisory Committee.

19. **Destruction of Property. ER 37.**—The OCPD may order the destruction of any building which is liable to seizure under ER 32 if it is not practicable to seize or occupy it; of any building left unoccupied as a result of an order under ER 17F to any person to leave a given area; and of any building outside the residential portion of a "Controlled Area" declared under ER 17 FA. Compensation is payable in respect of such destruction.

20. **Control. ER 39.**—An OCPD may restrict the use of any road, waterway, etc.

21. **Clearance Orders. ER 40.**—This Regulation provides for clearance orders (signed by the Chief Minister of a State) upon owners of lands abutting on the roadside—50 yards have to be cleared—and upon owners of all lands cultivated with rubber, oil palms or coconuts. It should be noted that orders may be served upon individual proprietors or they may be made in respect of general areas. If proprietors disobey the order, officers authorised by the Chief Minister may clear the land and present the bill to the proprietor. In addition the proprietor is liable to a fine of $1,000 and $100 a day for the continuance of the default. Paragraph (6) of the Regulation states that the DO may require that the inhabitants of any Food Restricted Area clear undergrowth for 35 yards outside the perimeter fence. Where two fences exist the outer fence shall be the deciding factor.

22. **Miscellaneous. ER 41A.**—An Emergency Regulation which has just been gazetted gives power to the Chief Minister of a State to instruct Telecoms to withdraw any equipment. (This legalises the disconnection of telephones).

23. **ER 43A.**—The DO or the ADO may order any person or classes of persons to attend at such place in his District as he may think fit.

24. **ER 44.**—Where an area has been declared 'controlled' under Emergency Regulations 17 FA the competent authority may order any buildings to be erected or any work to be carried out within the controlled area. Orders may also be made concerning health and medical supervision.

25. **ER 44A.**—Provides that the Chief Minister of any State may for reasons of security (without enquiry) order the inhabitants of any area to:—

(a) take steps to protect themselves or others (e.g. clearance of undergrowth or construction of defence works);

(b) to repair damage caused by CT.

No payment is made for this work.

26. **General Note.**—In white areas all orders made under LN 169/56 or ERs 20, 39 or 40 are cancelled. No orders may be made under ERs 19, 19A, 35, 36 and 37 and 28 without unusually strong reasons and action must be reported to the Director of Operations.

Section 3.—THE EMERGENCY (RESTRICTION AND PROHIBITION OF FOODSTUFFS AND OTHER SUPPLIES) REGULATIONS, 1956

1. Regulations covering restrictions on foodstuffs and supplies are contained in the Emergency (Restriction and Prohibition of Foodstuffs and other Supplies) Regulations, 1956, and not in the main Emergency Regulations. Notes on these Food and Supplies Regulations are contained in this Section.

2. **Foodstuffs** comprise:—
    (a) any species of animal, whether alive or dead which is ordinarily used for human food;
    (b) any substance or commodity which is ordinarily used for human food, or in the preparation of human food;
    (c) any substance or commodity other than vegetable matter, which is ordinarily used for feeding animals including rice bran.

3. **Restricted articles** are:—
    (a) padi, rice products, flour, flour products, oil, sugar, salt concentrated foods, tinned foods, cooked food, dried fish;
    (b) paper suitable for use in printing, typewriting or duplicating words or figures or pictorial representations, wax stencils and printing ink;
    (c) drugs, medicines and other medical supplies;
    (d) electric torches other than one loaded electric torch for bona fide personal use, the onus of proving which shall be upon the accused, and any type of dry cell electric battery;
    (e) canvas or any article made wholly or partly from canvas;
    (f) green or khaki cloth, pliable plastic, or rubberised material; and
    (g) clothing and any articles made wholly or partly from the materials listed in sub-paragraph (f).

4. A Chief Minister in any State may declare a *Food Restricted Area*. This may be defined in any convenient manner. After declaration it is an offence to carry any restricted article or foodstuff into or out of a Food Restricted Area. This does not apply to:—
    (a) fresh meat, fresh fish, fresh shell fish, fresh prawns, fresh crabs, fresh fruits, live poultry, fresh eggs or fresh vegetables including sweet potatoes or tapioca in root form;

(b) liquids as approved by the DO;

(c) ice cream, cordial or beverages containing less than 15% sugar;

(d) any restricted articles or foodstuffs, the movement of which has been approved by the DO;

(e) clothing when worn on the person or conveyed as personal baggage;

(f) any restricted articles or foodstuffs loaded on a vehicle used exclusively for the purpose of trade, provided that it is consigned by a wholesaler to a retailer and that it is accompanied by a written record or manifest;

(g) drugs, medicines, medical supplies and essential articles of diet in reasonable quantities when carried with a medical certificate;

(h) reasonable quantities of food suitable for a child under the age of two when conveyed with the child.

5. Shopkeepers in gazetted Food Restricted Areas shall:—

(a) keep no restricted articles in excess of normal requirements;

(b) keep such records of his stocks and sales as the DO may require and produce them on demand of any Police Officer;

(c) not sell any restricted articles without production of an Identity Card.

6. The Chief Minister in any State may prohibit shopkeepers in a Food Restricted Area from carrying on business in any restricted article unless in possession of a licence issued by the DO.

7. The DO may order any shop in a Food Restricted Area to be closed or restrict business in a shop or make special orders relative to the sale of restricted articles.

8. When on duty any Police Officer, Home Guard, Food Denial Officer, member of a military force or Temporary Female Searcher authorised by the OCPD may search any person leaving or entering a Food Restricted Area.

9. No woman may be searched except by another woman.

10. Where an area has been declared a Controlled Area under these Regulations the Chief Minister in a State may declare that area (except the residential part of it) to be Food Prohibited. Any person found with any restricted article or foodstuff within such an area, shall be guilty of an offence against the Regulations.

11. The Chief Minister of any State may declare a rice ration or a ration of any specified foodstuff. He may also order the maximum quantity of any specified foodstuff which may be held by any person other than traders; and he may declare the maximum quantity of which any dealer may hold.

12. (a) No restricted articles or food may be moved outside a Food Restricted Area or Town Board or Municipality between 1900 hrs. and 0600 hrs. Certain fresh foodstuffs of a perishable nature as well as clothing worn on the person or carried as personal luggage are exempt from this Regulation.

    (b) When any restricted articles are being transported by road in an open goods vehicle they must be covered by a tarpaulin, securely fastened down.

    (c) The DO, Assistant Controller of Supplies or Chief Food Denial Officer may make such orders regarding the movement of any restricted articles as he sees fit. This is the legal backing for convoys.

13. Any Police Officer, Food Denial Officer, or any member of H.M. Forces or a Local Force excluding Home Guard may:—

    (a) stop any vehicle, make enquiry as to its contents, and, if not satisfied, search it;

    (b) give the driver any orders considered necessary to ensure that any restricted article or foodstuff in the vehicle is not used for an unlawful purpose and reaches the place for which it is intended;

    (c) detain any restricted article or foodstuff if it is likely that it will be used for an unlawful purpose;

    (d) detain any restricted article or foodstuff if it is suspected that an offence has been or will be committed in respect of it;

    (e) search any premises if it is suspected that an offence against these regulations has been committed.

The above powers may also be exercised by any Home Guard or any woman who has been authorised by the OCPD.

If within four weeks of seizure no charge is made the goods shall be returned to the owner or if the latter cannot be found disposed of by a Magistrate.

14. Upon conviction of any person who gives false information relative to a consignment on a vehicle or who does not carry a manifest when instructed to do so, the vehicle itself may be confiscated.

15. No vehicle may:—
   (a) stop outside the limits of a Municipality, a Town Board, a local council area or a gazetted village other than at a place to which any goods in the vehicle are consigned;
   (b) deviate from the normal route;
   (c) offload in any place except where the goods are consigned.

16. Goods carried on trains may be searched by Railway Officers or Police Officers.

17. The DO may prohibit or limit selling by itinerant vendors outside Municipalities, Town Boards, Local Councils areas or gazetted villages.

18. The Chief Minister of a State may prohibit the raising of any foodstuffs except upon such terms as may be specified in any food prohibited area and if the owner or occupier refuses or neglects to comply with such an order he may authorise a person to enter upon the land and destroy any crop and recover expenses from the owner or occupier.

19. Any Police Officer, or any member of H.M. Forces or a Local Force, or any Home Guard authorised to do so by the OCPD may arrest any person suspected of committing an offence against these Regulations.

Section 4.—FOOD DENIAL OPERATIONS AND METHOD OF SEARCHING

1. **Introduction.**— The CT jungle organisation cannot carry on its fight without constant re-supply of food, clothing, medicine and money. Although a small proportion of their food requirements are obtained from cultivations in the deep jungle, by far the highest percentage of their food, and all their other needs, must come from their supporters in towns, villages and other centres of population.

2. To deny these supplies reaching the CT in the jungle, SF action can be divided into two categories:—
   (a) *Food Denial.*—The imposition of gate checks, road blocks, curfews etc., to prevent illegal food and other essential

supplies from leaving towns, villages and estate labour lines.

(b) *Contact Denial.*—Operations on the jungle fringe (the frequent contact point between the CT in the jungle and the food supplying organisation) designed to eliminate the CT as he takes delivery of his supplies.

3. To facilitate the task of SF engaged on paragraph 2 (a) above, perimeter wire has been established around a large proportion of smaller towns, villages and estate labour lines. Two methods are, therefore, available to CT supporters to remove supplies from within the wire. Firstly, by its removal in small quantities at a time, concealed in the clothing of persons, or by concealment in vehicles as they leave the village etc., through the gates; and secondly, by passing the supplies, usually at night, over the wire to food carrying parties.

4. To prevent the removal of supplies concealed on the person or hidden in vehicles, gate checks are the most effective form of control. The following paragraphs show the method of setting up gate checks and the searching technique that should be followed.

5. **Implementation of Food Denial Measures.**— The manning of road blocks, gate check points, etc., is now normally the responsibility of Federation Army units and the Federation Police. On occasions, however, Overseas Commonwealth units may be called on to undertake these duties.

6. **Gate Checks.**—Ideally, and to ensure that no illegal goods leave villages etc., every person and vehicle should be searched. To carry this out would take considerable time and would, to a marked degree, dislocate the arrival of estate and other labour at their place of work. It is necessary, therefore, to carry out selective searching, ensuring that the element of uncertainty is ever present and that persons leaving the gate do not know who is going to be searched. This will depend on the number of searchers available and the numbers waiting to pass through the gate at one time. As a rough guide, a ratio of about 1 in 5 should be searched at peak periods (0600 hrs. to 0800 hrs.) and thereafter when relatively few persons are leaving at one time, it should be possible for practically everyone to be searched.

7. **Organisation of gate check points.**— The following principles should be followed when setting up gate check points:—

(a) wherever possible an officer should be in charge of each gate party.

(b) One man, either the officer in charge or a NCO specifically appointed, should take no part in the actual searching but should be responsible for the control of movement through the gate.

(c) If practicable, movable hurdles or barricades should be set up through which movement is channelled.

(d) Strict crowd control must be exercised, in order that men actually doing the searching are not crowded by persons waiting to move through the gate.

(e) It is important that adequate lighting is provided in order that searching can start before first light.

(f) No prior indication should be given as to who has been selected for search.

(g) A careful watch should be kept for any suspicious actions, e.g. attempts to evade search, movement back from the searching point, or uneasiness on the part of any person. (Think of your own reactions when carrying a bottle of whiskey through Customs!)

(h) Although anybody may be carrying illegal goods, it is more likely that the younger men and women will be carriers.

(j) The searching point must be secure and at least one armed sentry posted who takes no part in the searching procedure.

(k) Searchers must have both hands free. Their weapon should be slung.

(l) A recommended scale of equipment to be established at each check point is set out at Appx. B.

8. **Snap Control.**—Snap control is a defensive control having the following objects:—

(a) to ascertain a person's true identity;

(b) to ascertain a person's true character;

(c) to ensure that such person is not in possession of anything unlawful.

9. The methods adopted are entirely dependent upon the circumstances of each particular case but the best results are usually achieved by the operation of a road block or check point, where persons and vehicles are checked.

10. The road block or check point must be:—

(a) *Properly Manned and Sited.*—Ensure that precautionary measures are taken to give security to the persons manning the point, and sited so as not to cause danger or obstruction to through traffic.

(b) *Speedily Operated.*—Every person manning the road block or check point should know his job thoroughly, be methodical and move quickly to prevent delay to traffic using the road.

11. Each vehicle must be dealt with separately. Three persons are required to carry out the check:—

    (a) No. 1 will approach the vehicle from the offside, open the driver's door and request the driver to leave the vehicle.

    (b) No. 2 will approach the vehicle from the nearside and slightly to its rear; he will keep under careful observation any other occupants of the vehicle.

    (c) No. 3 will be armed with, if possible, an automatic weapon which he will hold in the ready position. He will stand on the offside of the vehicle always maintaining a clear view of the driver and not allowing No. 1 or No. 2 to cross his line of fire. No. 3's part in the operation is purely defensive. He takes no part in the examination of documents or search.

12. The driver of the vehicle will not be questioned as to his identity or requested to produce documents from his person until he has been frisked by No. 1.

13. **Summary or Routine Search of Persons.**— The word frisk, as used in this section, means the quick search of a person to ascertain whether or not any offensive weapons, i.e. pistol, hand grenade, knife, etc., are concealed within his clothing.

14. The person should be requested to stand facing his vehicle with his hands resting on the roof or side of the vehicle as the case may be, and No. 1 should then quickly, but thoroughly, run over the individual's person from head to foot.

15. The clothing of a person should not be patted, as any small flat object like a knife may be overlooked. The clothing should be rolled between the fingers.

16. Frisking must include searching under the arms, the stomach, inside the thighs and the crutch.

17. Women will only be searched by women. When searching a woman particular attention should be paid to her hair.

18. It is to be remembered that the greatest advantage there is in Snap Control is the element of surprise which in many cases prevents the person from disposing of an illegal article.

19. After the person has been frisked, he will be asked to produce his Identity Card and, if applicable, his driving licence (or in fact any other official document he might possess). These documents should be carefully checked against each other.

20. The following should be used as a guide for checking identity documents:—

(a) *Photograph.*—Compare the photograph on the card with the individual. When such a comparison is made one must endeavour to create the conditions under which the photograph was originally taken, i.e., a true likeness of a person photographed without a hat, as in Identity Cards, cannot be satisfactorily compared with the holder of the card who may be wearing a hat at the time of the check. Likewise a woman having had her photograph taken two or three years ago with straight hair looks very different after a permanent wave. A good tip in comparing the latter is to place a finger across the photograph thereby hiding the hair, and compare only the features of the person. A check of age will assist in checking the comparison.

(b) *Stamp (Chop).*—Careful examination of the chop across the corner of the photograph will assist the examiner when checking to see if the original photograph has been removed and another substituted. The authenticity of the chop itself should also be checked.

(c) *When questioning a person* in connection with particulars contained in their identity documents, such questions should be framed thus:—

    What is your name?
    Where do you live?
    How old are you?

Leading questions should be avoided.

(d) *Fingerprints.*—Because a positive means of fingerprint identification can only be dealt with by experts, a mark indicating a thumbprint must be accepted. Should, however, any queries arise as to the true identity of a suspect, he can be held for further questioning and his prints used for identification.

21. **Damaged Identity Cards.**—These should be the subject of very careful scrutiny, but provided the holder passes security scrutiny he will be allowed to proceed. The Police will take such action as necessary to ensure that he applies for a new card to the appropriate Registration Officer.

22. When No. 1 has satisfied himself as to the true identity of the driver, he will then frisk and check the identity of any passengers. He will then commence a casual search of the vehicle.

23. The No. 2 of the team having observed the passengers while the driver is being checked for any suspicious actions, will then assist in the search and checking of passengers and the search of the vehicle under the direction of No. 1.

24. **Casual Search of Cars.**—A car should be searched as follows:—

    (a) sun visors (examine behind and the item it is attached to);

    (b) dashboard pockets or cubby holes;

    (c) behind dashboard (wires, etc., leading from instruments. A letter or small weapon can easily be placed between the wires);

    (d) under the driver's seat;

    (e) between the driver's and passenger's seat;

    (f) at the back of driver's seat, i.e., between back of seat and bottom of back rest;

    (g) door pockets;

    (h) behind front seats;

    (j) any moveable mats in the car should be lifted;

    (k) back seats;

    (l) rear window panel shelf;

    (m) the luggage boot;

    (n) under bonnet and spare wheel compartment;

    (o) in addition, all loose baggage contained within the vehicle or boot should be carefully but quickly examined;

    (p) particular attention should be paid to umbrellas, newspapers, magazines, and any seemingly innocent parcels, etc., all of which may easily be used as simple methods of concealment.

25. The checking officer, when satisfied, will allow the car to go. Should, however, any doubts arise as to the true identity of any individuals in the car, or any suspicion remain that clandestine material(s) are concealed within the vehicle, then such vehicle must be removed under direct Police supervision to a suitable place for a thorough search.

26. **Search of Light and Heavy Goods Vehicles.**— The method of casual search of lorries and goods vehicles are similar to those adopted for cars. There are the following additional points to watch for:—

    (a) *Wooden Body Construction.*—Owing to the wooden body construction of lorries, it is very simple to make effective places of concealment by the addition of enclosed panels or false bottoms, or the boarding-up of spaces between the battens supporting the floor. The sides of lorries may be prepared in a similar manner, and the best method of search in such cases is a close examination from all angles and careful measurements.

    (b) *Twin Rear Wheels.*—The chances of concealment between the twin rear wheels are small, but should be examined carefully.

    (c) *Wooden Block (Chocks).*—Practically all goods vehicles, particularly those of the heavy class, carry a wheel chock which is used under the rear wheels of the vehicle to help the brakes should the vehicle have to stop on a steep gradient. These chocks are generally square or triangular probably about 9" x 9" x 6". Through regular use, they become dirty, worn and greasy, and are generally thrown in the rear of the vehicle or carried in the driver's cab when laden. Such blocks can be hollowed out and become good places of concealment. Examine all wooden blocks carefully.

    (d) *Gunny Sacks.*—All gunny sacks will be lifted and searched. A common subterfuge is the concealment of articles under a heap of gunny sacks in an apparently unladen goods vehicle.

    (e) *Driver's Cab.*—Particular attention should be given to search of the driver's cab, the driver's mate and the "jaga" usually found sitting on the top of the laden vehicle. Their actions should be very carefully observed.

27. **Search of Motor Cycles.**— Motor cycles are comparatively easy to search but attention should be paid to the following:—

    (a) *Petrol Tank.*—May be divided, one division being false.

(b) *Tool Box/Case.*—Open, remove all tools and examine.

(c) *Rubber Handle Grips-Controls.*—A few moments may be well spent on an examination of the handle grips.

(d) *Footrest-Supports.*—Examine footrests and machine support, which is hinged, and is used to support motor cycle in upright position during absence of rider.

(e) *General.*—Lamps, mudguards, and all hollow or tubular constructions should be examined. A search should also be made under the saddle. The piece of bent wire described in Appx. B. is very useful for this purpose.

28. **Search of Bicycles.**— Examine the following with care:—

   (a) Handle bars and rubber grips.
   (b) Bells.
   (c) Lamps, dynamos, etc., including behind reflector glasses.
   (d) The saddle.
   (e) All tubular frame-work, particularly open ends and joints.
   (f) Under mudguards.
   (g) In the case of very old bicycles some parts may appear to be damaged, i,e,. frame, pedals, etc., and have been repaired with wire or string. Remove and examine beneath.

29. **Search of Trishaws.**— Examine as for a bicycle, together with all tubular constructions attached to the actual passenger's hood.

   (a) Remove all tapestries, padding, etc., used for seat covering, and examine underneath.
   (b) Many trishaws have, underneath the seat. a shelf or tray containing sundries together with waterproof cover. Remove and examine these, particularly at the back and underneath the shelf.
   (c) Examine the roof and take considerable care when examining the edges.
   (d) For proper examination of the trishaw, it should be turned on its side.
   (e) Particular attention should be given to the 3rd wheel, i.e., the wheel on the passenger's side. The type and hub should be inspected.

30. **House Search.**— There is only one way to search a house, building, etc., and that is the thorough search after a carefully planned Police raid.

31. A procedure similar to the following should be adopted:

- (a) Arrests, whenever possible, should be made in the early hours of the morning to ensure the element of surprise.
- (b) The suspect will immediately be frisked as described earlier, and when the personal search is satisfactorily completed, he should be told to stand back against the wall with his back to the wall and his hands clasped behind his head. He will be covered by one member of the section.
- (c) No requests made by the prisoner at the time of arrest should be granted. He should be treated fairly but firmly. The initiative must be retained by the searching party.
- (d) All other members of the household should be collected together in one room. They also should be frisked.
- (e) One member of the section should visit at once kitchens, lavatories, etc., or any place where a person might well try to burn or destroy a clandestine communication.
- (f) All drawers should be quickly emptied and the contents examined.
- (g) Clothing belonging to the prisoner should be examined, also any pairs of shoes found in the premises.
- (h) Attention should be given to writing tables, desks, etc., and bedside furniture.
- (j) Kitchen utensils and partly consumed tinned goods should be examined.
- (k) Any dead birds or animals hanging up awaiting consumption should also be examined. (Ensure that a patrol or an arrest team consists of mixed religions otherwise such things as dead meat, etc., will not be examined or touched).
- (l) Rubbish heaps, fowl pens, pig styes, cow sheds, etc., should also be the subject of quick examination.

- (m) Private letters, documents, papers, diaries, address books, photographs, etc., should always be collected and taken back to Headquarters for careful and detailed examination. Any burnt papers should be carefully preserved by placing some large object over same (a bowl) and reported to Headquarters.
- (n) Any vehicle found on the premises should be searched as described earlier.

32. When carrying out a search it is often necessary to know the Malayan scale of weights. A comparative scale is shown at Appx A to this Chapter.

Appendix A

COMPARATIVE SCALE OF MALAYAN WEIGHTS

1. Scale of Weights: Pounds/Katty—

    | 1 oz. | = | $\frac{3}{4}$ tahil |
    | 1 lb. | = | 12 tahils |
    | 1 stone | = | 10 katties 8 tahils |
    | 1 qr. | = | 21 katties |
    | 1 cwt. | = | 84 katties |
    | 1 ton | = | 1,680 katties or 16 pikuls 80 katties |

2. Scale of Weights: Katty/Pounds—

    | 1 tahil | = | $1\frac{1}{3}$ oz. |
    | 1 katty | = | $1\frac{1}{3}$ lb. or 1 lb. $5\frac{1}{3}$ oz. |
    | 1 pikul | = | $133\frac{1}{3}$ lb. or 133 lb. $5\frac{1}{3}$ oz. or 1 cwt. 1 stone 7 lb. $5\frac{1}{3}$ oz. |

Note:

| 16 tahils | = | 1 katty |
| 100 katties | = | 1 pikul |

APPENDIX *B*

SCALE OF EQUIPMENT AT GATE CHECK POINTS

1. 3 foot length of flexible wire (one per man), for probing possible hiding places on bicycles, motor vehicles etc., not accessible by other means.

2. 2 x 4 gallon buckets or drums. One drum is used to empty night soil into, the other being used for wet refuse.

3. 4 foot prodder (broom handle with iron spike on tip).

4. Lamps electric hand (one per man).

5. 1 set hand scales.

PART TWO
OPERATIONS

CHAPTER V

PLATOON ORGANISATION, WEAPONS AND EQUIPMENT

Section 1.—INTRODUCTION

1. There is no standard platoon organisation in use by battalions on operations in Malaya. The organisation adopted depends on the tasks to be carried out and on the number of troops available. Other matters affecting the organisation are terrain, local CT characteristics and sometimes the duration of the operation.

2. The normal platoon organisation was designed for operations against a first class enemy in a normal theatre of war. This organisation has to be adapted to suit the characteristics of the terrain and of the jungle operations. The CT are lightly equipped and can move very quickly. Our organisation and equipment must therefore be such as to confer maximum mobility.

Section 2.—ORGANISATION WITHIN THE PLATOON

1. Where possible the platoon should be organised into a platoon HQ and three Sections each of three Groups.

2. The platoon HQ should consist of:—

    Pl Commander
    Pl Sergeant
    Batmen
    Signaller (Attached)

3. The section should consist of:—

  (a) *A reconnaissance group*, consisting of a group commander and two scouts.

  (b) *A support group*, consisting of a group commander, and Nos. 1 and 2 on the LMG.

  (c) *A rifle group*, consisting of a group commander and two or more riflemen.

4. In addition certain specialists may be attached to Platoon HQ, e.g. medical orderlies, police, guides, JCLO, Sarawak Rangers and SEPs.

5. When the strength of the platoon is low, the sections can be reduced to two, or the groups in each section reduced to two by discarding the Rifle Group.

6. The section should be organised into three groups because this organisation : —

- (a) Simplifies the section commander's job of control.
- (b) Provides the grouping needed for the effective minor tactics which have been evolved for use against the CT.
- (c) Helps to train potential junior leaders who can take over a section if necessary.
- (d) Provides small three men teams which experience has shown to be a good basic team.

Section 3.—WEAPONS

1. This section gives some notes on the best use of platoon weapons based on experience gained in operations in Malaya. Except when established in ambush positions, the terrain and vegetation in Malaya rarely allows for weapons to be fired from the lying position. Troops must, therefore, be practised in firing from the shoulder in the standing, sitting and kneeling positions. On fleeting encounters, experience has shown that aimed fire from the shoulder, in the standing position, is the most effective. A summary of the best methods of firing weapons is included in Appendix A to this Chapter; see also Appendix B to Chapter VIII for a possible distribution of section weapons.

2. Weapons in use include : —

No. 5 Rifle
7·62 mm Selfloading rifle (FN)
Bren LMG ·303 (Converted Bren (7·62 mm))
M1 and M2 Carbines
Owen gun
SMG 9 mm L2 A1
Shot gun

3. Experience on operations and detailed trials have shown that poor results are obtained when weapons are fired from the hip using ball ammunition, and that the chances of hitting a man when using this method at over 100 yards range are small. Even at closer

ranges hip firing, except with the Bren LMG, does not normally produce good results.

4. A rapid rate of fire will increase the chances of a kill. However it is important that a proper aim from the shoulder, using the sights, should always be taken.

5. In very close country, experience has shown that to be effective, fire should always be directed at a SEEN target. Firing at noise or sign of movement is seldom effective, unless it is possible to saturate the area with fire almost instantaneously.

6. Attention should be paid to the following points in order to ensure that weapons are reliable:—
   (a) They must be maintained correctly zeroed and in good mechanical condition.
   (b) Magazines must be kept clean.
   (c) Dirt and grit must be removed from ammunition.

7. **No. 5 Rifle:—**
   (a) The No. 5 Rifle is a single shot weapon with a magazine capacity of 10 rounds of ·303. This rifle is a precision weapon and must be fired from the shoulder in steady well aimed shots.
   (b) The number of rounds that can be fired in a short exposure depends on the skill of the firer. The rifle is reliable and hard hitting in skilful hands, and is light and handy to carry and can knock down a CT with one shot. Experienced shots have confidence in its capabilities and reliability.
   (c) This weapon is being largely replaced by the 7·62 mm Self Loading Rifle (FN).

8. **7.62mm Self Loading Rifle (FN):—**
   (a) The FN Rifle is a self loading weapon with a magazine capacity of 20 rounds of 7·62 mm ammunition.
   (b) The weapon, as issued in Malaya, is semi-automatic and separate trigger pressures have to be taken for each shot. Consecutive aimed shots may be fired without changing the grip, thus improving speed and accuracy.
   (c) Best results are achieved when the rifle is fired from the shoulder using the sights.
   (d) Pending the issue of UK production weapons, all FN rifles in Malaya are of Belgian manufacture and have certain inherent limitations.

9. **Bren LMG:—**
   (a) This weapon is still the unit of fire power of the infantry section and is most feared by CT.
   (b) Although the weapon can be fired from the shoulder by men of powerful physique it is more effectively used when fired from the hip using the sling. A high proportion of tracer (1 tracer to 2 ball) should be used and the gun fired in bursts of 5 to 6 rounds. Fire should be observed along the line of fire of tracer.
   (c) The pistol grip attachment for fitting to the forward part of the gun helps to steady firing from the waist and assists firing from the shoulder (when used).

10. **M1 and M2 Carbines:—**
    (a) This weapon has now been replaced in Commonwealth Battalions by the FN Rifle, but still remains an issue to units of the Federation Forces.
    (b) The M2 muzzle lifts strongly when the weapon is fired automatic, causing loss of control, therefore when fired from the shoulder single shots should be fired. This will also be the method used with the M1.
    (c) Using one method of firing will produce the best results at all ranges because of the varied degrees of skill of men who fire the weapons. It will also produce the best standard in a limited training time.
    (d) The trigger should be operated quickly in order to get the most shots off in a given time, consistent with accurate aiming.
    (e) The weapon must be stripped so that it can be cleaned satisfactorily, but owing to the possibility of losing parts and of incorrect assembly, stripping must only be carried out by qualified individuals.
    (f) The M1/M2 carbines suffer the disadvantage of having low muzzle velocity and consequently poor stopping qualities.

11. **Owen Gun:—**
    (a) The Owen gun fires single rounds or automatic. The magazine holds 33 rounds of 9 mm. The gun is heavier than the rifle but is steady and reliable. The magazine is above the weapon and gravity assists feeding.

(b) It should always be fired from the shoulder at targets which are up to 100 yards away. Bursts should consist of 3-4 rounds at short ranges and of 2-3 rounds at targets over about 50 yards.

12. SMG 9mm L2 A1:—

(a) This carbine, (Patchett) fires single rounds or bursts. (Magazine capacity 34 rounds of 9 mm).

(b) This weapon is much lighter and has a shorter barrel than the Owen gun. It is reliable and suffers from few stoppages.

(c) The carbine should be fired from the shoulder in bursts at ranges of up to 100 yards. Bursts of 2-3 rounds at the shorter ranges, and bursts of 2 rounds at the longer ranges.

13. Shotgun.—Magazine shotguns (Pumpguns) of 5 cartridge capacity are issued on a scale of 50 to each Commonwealth Battalion. These weapons, which cover an area target and are lethal at short ranges, will be the primary weapon used for night ambushes. Light and easy to carry, they are very effective for the forward elements of a patrol.

14. GF Rifle:—

(a) The 2" Mortar is not used in Malaya to fire HE, owing to the danger of the bomb striking trees. In its place the EY Rifle, known as the GF Rifle in Malaya, although obsolete in other countries, is used to discharge the 36 grenade.

(b) The GF Rifle can be used to drop No. 36 grenades behind the CT to prevent their escape. Care must be taken when firing to ensure that grenades do not strike tree trunks and rebound on to our own troops.

(c) The GF Rifle should be carried in Platoon HQ whenever there is a chance that it can be used.

(d) When the weapon is likely to be required for use at short notice the Platoon Commander can order a grenade to be placed in the discharger cup with the pin out, and the whole discharger cup covered with a 3-in. mortar bomb tail fin coverbag. The gas port should be set for approximately 120 yards. All that is necessary to fire the grenade is to load a round of ballistite into the rifle and press the trigger, thus blowing the grenade out of the discharger cup through the waterproof bag.

(e) The following drill will be used to remove the grenade after a patrol. The GF rifleman will move to the side of a re-entrant or depression, away from other troops. If a grenade fuze becomes ignited, the grenade can be thrown into the re-entrant or depression. No grenade will be removed from a discharger cup in the presence of other troops.

15. **2 in Mortar:—**
   (a) This weapon is impracticable for use in jungle. It has a contact fuze on the bomb, and there is a great danger of accidents due to the bombs striking the trunks, branches or twigs of trees, during its upward flight.
   (b) The 2-in. mortar can be extremely useful if carried in MT as an anti-MT ambush weapon. In this role it can be used either from the vehicle or from the ground after dismounting, when fire can be brought down initially on the ambush positions, and, if necessary, lifted to fall behind CT to block their escape. An assault can then be made on CT positions by the ambushed troops.

16. **36 Grenade.**—This grenade is difficult to use in jungle. The limited distance it can be thrown may result in casualties to our own troops. The grenade should only be used when our troops have height on the enemy, and on orders from the Platoon or Section Commanders.

17. **80 Smoke Grenade:—**
   (a) 80 Smoke grenades are useful lethal weapons, as well as smoke grenades. A good distribution is one to every fourth man, but men should not carry and use these grenades until they have thrown a number in training.
   (b) These grenades should be carried evenly distributed throughout the patrol. They are useful should the patrol walk into an ambush. Men should throw them in such a way as to hide them from CT view. The patrol can then manoeuvre behind the smoke and take aggressive action against the CT.

18. **Verey Pistol.**— Verey light pistols are usually carried by patrol commanders for signalling to aircraft or to dislodge air drop containers from high trees by burning the parachute canopy. They may also be used as a means of night illumination. The cartridges deteriorate quickly in Malaya. They should be protected from dampness and a reserve carried to allow for failures.

Section 4.—EQUIPMENT AND CLOTHING

1. **CT Identification Equipment:—**
   (a) Each battalion holds 5 cameras and 16 fingerprint sets for identification purposes.
   (b) Details of the use of these items are shown in Chapter XIV, Section 3, paragraph 12 and 13.
   (c) Additional cameras and fingerprint sets can be obtained by air drop.

2. **Entrenching Tools.**—These are carried for digging latrines, refuse pits, and improving water points. It is normally unnecessary in the present operations to dig-in against CT.

3. **Web Equipment.**—The equipment in use is the 1944 pattern web equipment. This should always be sufficient to carry whatever is necessary, including 4 days' rations. More rations can be carried by modification of the ration scale within the unit. No satisfactory ammunition pouch exists for the various clips and magazines of ammunition which are carried. In practice most men manufacture their own pouches.

4. **Clothing:—**
   (a) Spare clothing is carried only in order that troops may sleep dry. It is the normal practice for wet, dirty clothes to be put on again before leaving base in the morning, unless an opportunity to wash and dry out clothes has arisen on the previous day.
   (b) Although it is a matter for personal choice, underclothing is not recommended for use on patrol as it forms an accumulation of perspiration against the skin, and can be the cause of severe skin infection. One pair of underpants is recommended in order that troops in jungle base who are not on sentry duty may expose their skins to the air.

5. **Hand Saws.**—Issued on a scale of 50 per battalion; this equipment provides a more silent alternative to the machete.

6. **Stretchers—improvised.**—Although not on issue to units, it has been found that a strip of canvas approximately 6 feet 6 inches long by 3 feet wide with seams down the edges through which poles can be passed, makes a very useful improvised stretcher. It can be used not only for sleeping in patrol bases but for evacuation of casualties.

7. **Rubber Water Bottle Tops.**—The standard aluminium water bottle top rattles when screwed and unscrewed. A rubber water bottle top has been developed which is noiseless. Supplies of this equipment are available to units through normal channels, on demand.

8. **Poncho Capes.**—The Poncho Cape is carried rolled underneath the small pack. Rolled within it will normally be a man's dry change of clothing. The poncho should never be worn as a cape on operations as it restricts the action of the wearer. The cape is normally used in the construction of one or two-men shelters in a jungle base.

9. **Hammock—British Nylon Pattern.**—These are particularly useful when it is necessary to form a base in swamp, but can be used practically anywhere.

10. **The Pocket Altimeter.**—Held in a pool for issue to units as required, this equipment is of particular use when operating in mountainous country and is a useful aid in checking heights against the map.

11. **Preservation of Maps.**—Maps disintegrate very quickly when carried on patrol and the detail rapidly becomes illegible unless some method of protecting them is used. The following improvised methods of protection have been found effective:—

   (a) Enclosing the folded map in a small envelope of transparent plastic material, such as polythene, through which the map can still be read.

   (b) Painting the surface of the map with a mixture of clear shellac and gum. This not only protects the map but enables chinagraph pencil to be used on it.

Section 5.—WEAPON HANDLING

1. Particular attention must always be paid to safety precautions. In particular, attention will be given to the following:—

   (a) Loading before going on an operation or entering a vehicle should be done by sub-units as a drill under an NCO. Similarly unloading should be supervised in the same manner.

   (b) Individuals should not be permitted to load or unload without an order.

   (c) Loading or unloading in vehicles should be forbidden.

Appx A

Appendix A
SUMMARY OF METHODS OF FIRING WEAPONS

The best results with all automatic weapons are likely to be obtained when fired from the shoulder as aimed fire, 9 mm carbine shots in short burst, and M1/M2 carbines in single shots.

Serial	Weapon	Do's	Don'ts
1	*Owen*	Fire from shoulder in aimed bursts— 3-4 rounds at close range, or 2-3 rounds at longer range.	Don't fire single rounds. Don't fire from hip. Don't fire from rough alignment of sights from shoulder.
2	*SMG 9 mm L2 A1* (Patchett)	Fire from shoulder in aimed bursts— 2-3 rounds at close range or 2 rounds at longer range.	—do—
3	*M1/M2*	Fire from shoulder in single rounds at the highest possible rate.	Don't fire from hip.
4	*Bren LMG*	Fire bursts of 5-6 rounds using tracer/ball on ratio 1:2.	Don't fire continuously without observing line of fire of tracer.
5	*No. 5 Rifle*	Aimed fire from shoulder in single rounds.	Don't fire from the hip.
6	*7·62 Self-loading rifle (FN)*	Aimed fire from shoulder in single rounds.	Don't fire from the hip.

CHAPTER VI

THE JUNGLE BASE

Section 1.—INTRODUCTION

1. Owing to the difficulties of administering small or large forces operating in the jungle and of the limited time for which they can operate independently, it is necessary to establish bases forward of the company or platoon operational base camp.

2. These bases can be divided into two types:—
   (a) *Tactical bases.*—These may be company or platoon bases and are frequently occupied for some time. They form the firm base forward of which patrols or ambush parties operate. They are capable of being resupplied by either air drop or, in some instances, by ground troops or porters.
   (b) *Patrol bases.*—These are temporary bases occupied by either a company, platoon or section; are completely secret, should never be occupied for more than 48 hours, and ideally for not more than 24 hours.

3. The general principles governing the setting up of the two types of jungle base are the same, but it must be remembered that whereas the patrol base is virtually an overnight resting place, the tactical base may have to be occupied for protracted periods and requires far more elaborate facilities than does the patrol base.

Section 2.—DECEPTION

A jungle base depends largely on secrecy for its security, and it is always necessary to have a cover plan which will draw away CT attention from your base. Deception should always be planned. Some suggestions are as follows:—
   (a) If the terrain is suitable for night movement, the approach march should be made at night.
   (b) In the approach march, centres of population should be avoided.
   (c) It may sometimes be necessary to detain local inhabitants who have blundered into patrols during the approach march.
   (d) The further bases are away from obvious base sites the more secure they will be.

(e) Fires by day should be smokeless.
(f) Not more than one track should lead into a base. This track should be well camouflaged and guarded.
(g) The base must be established silently.
(h) Make a cover plan to conceal obvious preparations for operations and allow as few men as possible to be in the know.
(j) Hockey boots of local pattern are available for use to avoid certain patrols being given away by the well known pattern of the jungle boot.

Section 3.—SITING A BASE

1. Well-trained and hardened troops can make a base practically anywhere but obviously some places are better than others. The following are some of the factors involved in the siting of a base:—

(a) It must be sited so that the patrol can carry out its task.
(b) It must be secret and secure. If it is not secret the CT will quickly find out where it is and all chance of a contact will be lost, and therefore the use of a jungle base for more than 48 hours should be the exception rather than the rule. If the base is not secure, troops will be unable to rest as they will be uneasy about their safety. The type of place required is one remote from tracks and villages and with a good thick jungle canopy.
(c) It must have good facilities for the erection of wireless aerials. Communications are improved when the set is mounted on high ground.
(d) If it is anticipated that an air drop is required, the base should have a convenient DZ. DZ's are generally better if sited on high ground as supply dropping aircraft find it hard to manoeuvre in valleys. The base should not be too close to the DZ or its security will be prejudiced.
(e) It must allow men to sleep in comfort. Areas which are wet underfoot should be avoided. Men will not sleep comfortably on steep slopes. Flat and dry ground that drains quickly is the best.
(f) It should be close to water.
(g) Care should be taken to avoid siting base camps near dead trees or under trees with rotting branches, as these are liable to fall during sudden tropical storms causing casualties.

2. It is important that the area chosen for the jungle base should be suitable, or patrolling from it will suffer accordingly. Planning, forethought and study of the map and air photographs will give a good idea of where to go, but experience is the surest guide.

Section 4.—LAYOUT OF A BASE

1. Appendix A to this Chapter shows a suggested layout for a two-section base. Appendix B shows the layout for a three-section base.

2. It has been found from experience that once the set drill is clearly understood basing up procedure becomes a simple routine matter. All that is necessary is for the patrol commander to indicate the centre of the base and 12 o'clock. The men then adopt stand-to positions in pre-allotted areas which are checked and the necessary alterations made. Such a cut and dried procedure is far quicker than any impromptu arrangements which inevitably lead to numerous readjustments, general confusion and an unnecessary strain on the troops.

3. Once this drill is understood each man knows his own and his neighbours areas of responsibility.

Section 5.—SEQUENCE OF ESTABLISHING A BASE

A suggested sequence for establishing a base is as follows:—

(a) The patrol commander orders the patrol to halt, puts out whatever local protection is necessary and indicates 12 o'clock for the base.

(b) (i) As soon as the patrol arrives at the selected site for its base, a small security clearing patrol is immediately sent out to search around the site within hearing distance. The remainder of the patrol take up defensive positions and there should be no chopping, brewing up or similar activity until the security patrol returns.

(ii) The security patrol's task is to ensure that not only are there no CT, but that there are no wood cutters, cultivators, etc. present who could jeopardise the security of the base.

(iii) In the event of two clearing patrols being sent out, to avoid clashes they should both work in either a clockwise or an anti-clockwise direction.

(c) Sections under their commanders move into their positions according to a clock system and make contact with the sections on their right and left.

(d) The patrol commander goes round making adjustments among sections as necessary.

(e) Men start putting up shelters and settle in. (As a general rule, there should be NO chopping, although where a patrol is remaining out for a long period, and is changing its base nightly, this can occasion unnecessary hardship. The patrol commander should be guided in this regard by his appreciation of the degree of security of his base).

(f) A perimeter path can be cut around the front of the shelters. Another path may be required into the centre of the base from the section commanders to the patrol commander, but cutting should be avoided as much as possible. It is the clear trademark of a patrol's presence.

(g) If time permits the patrol commander holds an 'O' Group. The following are some of the points to be covered:—

- (i) sentries, passwords, stand-to, stand-down and alarm scheme.
- (ii) local patrolling.
- (iii) work for the next day.
- (iv) maintenance of weapons.
- (v) water and washing parties.
- (vi) cooking, fires and smoking.
- (vii) latrines.
- (viii) refuse pits.

Section 6.—SECURITY AND PROTECTION

1. **General:—**

(a) Although CT have attacked patrol bases on only a few occasions it would be unwise to underestimate their ability to do so. Every precaution must therefore be taken. The base must be well sited and well protected.

(b) When the majority of a patrol is out operating away from its base sufficient troops must remain in base in order to give it adequate protection. A base commander will be detailed to co-ordinate the defence. All duties such as sentries, local patrols and action in case of alarm must be clearly understood by every man. Base protection troops

will usually consist of troops due for a rest, and specialist personnel not on patrols such as wireless operators and dog handlers.
  (c) All movement to and from a water point must be controlled and have adequate protection.

2. **Stand-To.**— As in any other operation, morning and evening stand-to will be strictly observed. Special points to note are:—
  (a) Evening stand-to enables every man to check up that he knows the night dispositions of his neighbours to the flanks, front and rear. This is the safeguard against confusion amongst our own troops should shooting start at night.
  (b) Stand-to ensures that every man rises in the morning and retires for the night, properly dressed and with every item of his arms and ammunition to hand.
  (c) If an early move is planned for the following day, evening stand-to is the ideal time for a commander to check that every man is properly equipped so that there will be no delay on the following morning.
  (d) For the reasons given in (b) and (c) above, all men stand-to in their alarm positions, their arms and equipment close to hand.
  (e) Sub-unit commanders will detail day and night sentries and can check at stand-to that every man knows his tour of duty and his orders.
  (f) Commanders will check that each man:—
    (i) is in a sound tactically sited position.
    (ii) knows what to do in case of alarm.
    (iii) knows his fire task, and that each sub-unit commander knows his sub-unit task.
    (iv) knows what troops, if any, are outside the patrol base and their route and expected time of return.
  (g) Stand-to is an opportunity for commanders to ensure the strictest observance of all medical precautions.
  (h) Stand-to is an insurance against possible dawn or dusk attack and also enables men to accustom themselves to the growing and fading light.
  (j) Fires should not be allowed after the evening stand-down.

3. **Sentries:—**
  (a) *By Day*:—
    (i) Sentries must always be posted by day, particularly on tracks leading past or into the base.

(ii) They should be posted at the limit of noise. In a well conducted camp this should be 20-30 yards only.
   (iii) With troops new to the jungle it is advisable to post sentries in pairs.

(b) *By Night*:—
   (i) Sentries should be withdrawn to within the perimeter during the evening stand-to, before it gets dark. After this time nobody will be allowed out of the perimeter without permission of the base camp commander.
   (ii) In larger base camps, where numbers allow, double sentries will be posted.
   (iii) In the case of the small camp or resting place, where numbers are few, it may only be practicable to post a single sentry. In such a case the tour of duty of the sentry should be as short as possible to ensure maximum alertness.
   (iv) Sentries must have some means of waking their patrol commander silently.
   (v) Listening posts or ambushes may be laid on tracks into the position.

4. **Local Patrols.**— Local patrolling must be carefully controlled by the patrol commander so that tracks in the area of the base are kept to a minimum.

5. **Carrying of Weapons.**— Every man must be armed at all times and men must never move about singly. The reason is obvious but only strict discipline will ensure that this rule is observed.

6. **Alarm Scheme:**—

   (a) When firing starts, or when the signal for the alarm is given every man moves silently to his alarm position and remains there. From then on any movement seen or heard during the period of the alarm is regarded as being CT.
   (b) There should be no firing at night until the CT is a certain target. (Experience has shown that, by night, fire at ranges beyond 10 yards is ineffective). In no circumstances should there be any firing from the centre of the base.

Section 7.—LEAVING A BASE

1. When leaving a base every effort must be made to obliterate any signs of occupation, and in particular any tell-tale marks of the time of occupation. This will hinder the CTs, if they subsequently find the site of the base, from counting the exact number of men in the patrol.

2. Any basha type shelters should be destroyed before the base is vacated, because the location by Auster of a SF camp (which is then reported as a CT camp) might well cause a waste of valuable time by other SF sent out to locate and destroy the camp.

Section 8.—ADMINISTRATION OF A BASE

If base administration is bad, patrolling from that base will deteriorate because living in it will be unpleasant and tiring. Some of the points which require attention are:—

(a) *Siting and cleanliness of latrines and urinals.*—These are normally outside the base and will be protected by the sentry layout. Excreta must be covered or flies will cause dysentry.

(b) *Disposal of rubbish.*—Rubbish must be disposed of as it occurs. Empty tins must be buried. If this is not done flies will increase quickly. Before evacuating a base the commander must ensure that all rubbish and food is completely destroyed, or CT will use it. Food which is to be buried should be taken out of tins or packets so that it will deteriorate more quickly, and as an added safeguard against its use by CT should be buried in excreta pits.

(c) *Water purification.*—The patrol commander must ensure that water is sterilised. Water-borne diseases are common throughout Malaya and jungle water will not be drunk unless it has been properly sterilised.

(d) *Cooking.*—Where individual 24-hour ration packs are carried each man prepares his own food. However, if compo ration is issued cooking is usually done on a section basis.

Section 9.—CONCLUSION

1. A jungle base must be sited in a position from which its patrols can best carry out their tasks, but its exact location will be decided by the requirements of security and comfort. These two factors may conflict but they are interdependent, for without security there can be no comfort.

2. The extent to which a jungle base will be developed depends on the length of time it will be occupied. But every effort must be made to ensure that it is as secure and comfortable as possible so that patrols returning to it can rest.

3. This security and comfort can only be achieved first by good discipline and leadership, and secondly by paying careful attention to the following:—

(a) There must be a sound alarm scheme known to, and practised by, everyone.

(b) Adequate sentries must be on duty at all times.

(c) A careful duty roster must be kept, and rest must be organised.

(d) Strict hygiene rules, and water discipline must be laid down and observed.

(e) Well constructed shelters should be built.

(f) Cooking should be of as high a standard as possible according to the circumstances.

Appx A

APPENDIX A

Suggested Layout of a TWO-Section Base

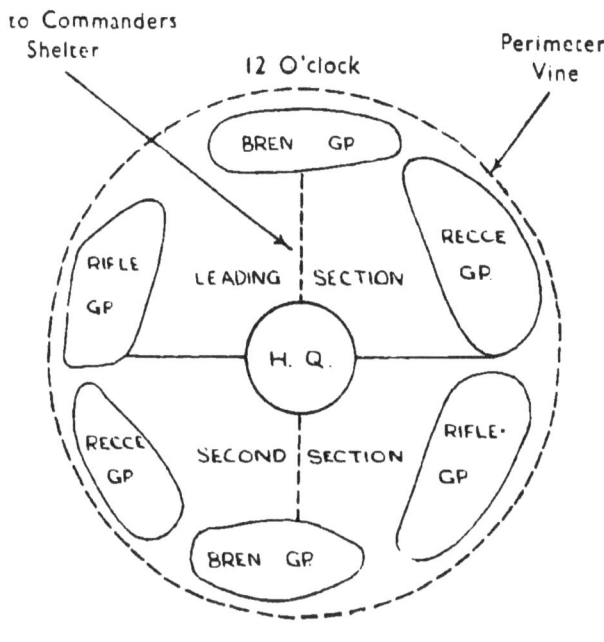

NOTES

1. The patrol commander having indicated 12 o'clock, the leading section of the patrol moves into position between 0300 hrs., 1200 hrs., and 0900 hrs. The second section moves into position between 0300 hrs., 0600 hrs., and 0900 hrs.

2. If the layout is kept standard within sub-units every man and group will know their approximate positions and who will be on their left and right.

VI
Appx B

APPENDIX B

Suggested Layout of a THREE-Section Base

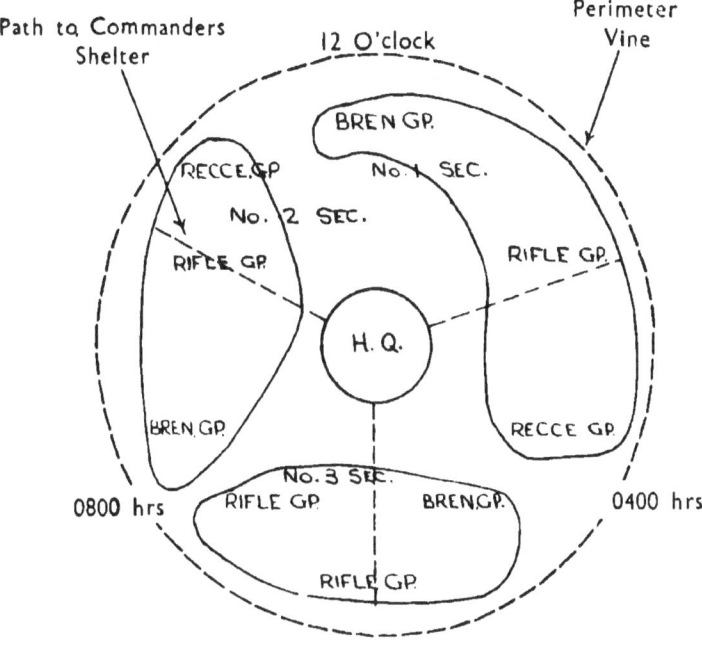

NOTES

1. The patrol commander having indicated 12 o'clock No. 1 section moves to take up position between 12 o'clock and 0400 hrs. No. 2 section between 12 o'clock and 0800 hrs. No. 3 section between 0400 hrs. and 0800 hrs.

2. The entrance to this base is at 12 o'clock.

CHAPTER VII

PATROLLING

Section 1.—INTRODUCTION

1. Although patrolling is important in every type of warfare, it has more than normal significance under jungle conditions against CT tactics. Patrolling in Malaya is no different basically from patrolling anywhere else, but because of the terrain, vegetation and characteristics of the CT, some modification to the normal technique is necessary.

2. In Malaya, as in other theatres, patrols can be classified as either Reconnaissance Patrols or Fighting Patrols.

   (a) *Reconnaissance Patrols.*—These are small patrols which seek information by stealth, avoiding contact. They consist normally of three to four men and are usually detached from a fighting patrol.

   (b) *Fighting Patrols.*—These vary in strength from a section to a company. They seek to contact and eliminate CT as and when encountered, and in particular to:—

   (i) attack CT camps and cultivations.
   (ii) pursue CT after a contact or incident.
   (iii) ambush CT.
   (iv) dominate an area to prevent CT contacting local inhabitants.
   (v) search remote areas.

3. All patrols of whatever type, are a source of intelligence and must be prepared to report all information, topographical or of CT, which they have discovered.

Section 2.—INFORMATION

1. Information on the following items must always be studied and passed on to a patrol commander before his patrol is sent out:—

   (a) *Topography.*—Full use should be made of maps, air photographs, air reconnaissance and local knowledge. A patrol 'going map' should be kept up to date. In addition to the maps kept at unit and sub-unit level it is essential that all new topographical and track data should

be recorded on going maps maintained at Combined Operations Rooms. This enables up to date information to be always available to new units moving into an area.
(b) *CT.*—Information may be available from Special Branch briefs, SEP, informers, air reconnaissance both visual and photographic, captured documents and diaries. The past history of CT activities in the area should be studied.
(c) *SF.*—Boundaries and movements of all SF in the area should be considered. These are recorded in the Combined Operations Room.
(d) *Civilians.*—Movements and habits of civilians must be studied if movement by troops is to remain secure.

2. All information from informers and SEP must be carefully considered and assessed.

Section 3.—PLANNING AND CONTROL OF PATROL OPERATIONS

1. All patrols require 'clearance' (full details are given in Chapter III Section 7). This requires that boundaries for the movement of the patrol must be given and agreed with other SF. It is often necessary to arrange this some days in advance in order to prevent loss of security by a sudden switch of task of a unit involved in routine work, such as an Area Security Unit.

2. The main problem when planning patrolling is the introduction of patrols into their operational areas without the loss of security. Every means of avoiding observation by civilians must be used e.g. deception; movement by night; the use of civilian vechicles (arranged through the Police) and the use of indirect routes. Security and deception are essential factors to consider when planning a patrol.

Section 4.—BRIEFING BY BATTALION/COMPANY COMMANDERS

1. All patrols must be sent out with a clearly defined mission. In a reconnaissance patrol this should take the form of a question or series of questions posed to the patrol commander. Fighting patrols will have tasks such as the attack and destruction of a party of CT, or the prevention of contact between CT and civilians in a fixed area, e.g. in food control operations. The mission must be clearly stated and understood by the patrol commander.

2. The officer despatching a patrol must make available to the patrol commander all possible information which may affect his mission.

3. It is essential that Battalion Commanders, and in the case of detached companies, company commanders, maintain patrol maps showing areas covered by patrols, and results and information gained. Consultation with the previous patrol commander, if an area is being re-visited, can often be of considerable assistance to the new patrol commander.

4. A sound communication drill must be arranged to avoid signallers giving away the presence of patrols by their efforts to open communications. This drill must be laid down by the officer despatching a patrol. It is suggested that fixed times are given for patrols to open listening watch. Control transmits the call sign for periods of 30 seconds at one minute intervals from five minutes before to five minutes after the fixed time. Sub-stations should net to control and reply during one of the 30 second intervals. Sub-stations should not, of course, reply unless the patrol commander has a message for control which MUST be passed. CW should be used for all transmissions from the jungle.

5. When arrangements are made for transport to bring in a patrol from a rendezvous and where empty transport has to return by the same route, more than normal alertness is required. Troops MUST be reminded of this and where possible escorts and armoured vehicles should accompany the transport. A similar danger arises when troops investigate incidents and where only one route to the site is available.

6. So that any member of a patrol can give comprehensive intelligence information on his return, he must have studied Section 3 and its Appendices of Chapter XIV before leaving base.

Section 5.—PLANNING AND PREPARATION BY THE PATROL COMMANDER

1. An '*Aide Memoire* for Patrol Orders' is attached as Appendix A to this chapter. This aide memoire gives a comprehensive list of headings for consideration by a patrol commander. The items which should be included in his orders will depend on the task and likely duration of his patrol.

2. Routes and timings are two of the more important considerations for the patrol commander:—

(a) Movement into the operational area must be secure if the patrol is to achieve success. This implies that any form of habitation must be avoided and that movement through rubber and other estates should take place before the arrival or after the departure of estate workers.

(b) Units and sub-units operating in or close to rubber estates should obtain a copy of the tapping task table from the estate manager. This normally shows the days on which certain divisions and lots of the estate are being tapped and is a guide to the likely presence of tappers in a particular area. Rain, however, affects the tapping cycle and there is no guarantee that the area concerned will be free of tappers. Weeders and other estate workers may be encountered at any time.

(c) The return should be by an alternative route. ONLY IN EXCEPTIONAL CIRCUMSTANCES SHOULD A PATROL RETURN BY ITS OUTWARD ROUTE.

3. 'Time in', as understood in normal military patrolling, must be very elastic. Speed of movement is very difficult to estimate and the possibility of a contact, and a resulting track or 'blood trail' make it necessary to allow extreme latitude in this matter. More important is the fixed listening time for the daily sitrep and location report.

4. When troops are to be committed to jungle, the problem of casualty evacuation must always receive prior consideration. Before leaving base a patrol commander should mark locations of possible LZs on his map or photograph. Then, if a casualty occurs, he is in a position to decide whether to move to an existing clearing or to search for and cut a new LZ. It is a good idea to have packs of cutting equipment (saws or explosives) held in unit store, ready for free drop by Auster.

Section 6.—DEBRIEFING AND REBRIEFING

1. **Debriefing:—**

   (a) The use of a debriefing aide memoire such as that in Chapter XIV, Appendix C greatly simplifies the task of the patrol commander in making his report. Remember, he will be tired.

   (b) Whatever the time of day or night, the company commander, or debriefing officer, must be up ready to interrogate the patrol commander. His information is required urgently so that commanders can plan the next operation and other patrols.

(c) The test of good interrogation followed by a good clear report is that few, if any, queries are raised later.

2. The value to other units and higher formation of information obtained from a debriefing must be borne in mind.

3. **Rebriefing for the next day.**— At the same time the patrol commander, must in addition to debriefing his patrol, start to think of action for the next day's operations. In this way full briefing of the patrol will be completed before the men are dispersed or go to bed.

Section 7.—RETURN TO COMPANY BASE

It is essential that a drill is arranged for the reception of patrols returning to base. This can have considerable morale value in a campaign where abortive patrolling is the rule rather than the exception. This drill, as well as catering for normal administrative matters, must include a post-mortem for every patrol which has had a contact or appears to have narrowly missed a contact.

Appendix A

PATROL ORDERS—AIDE MEMOIRE

1. **Situation**
    - (a) Topography.—Use maps, air photos, visual recce and patrol going map.
    - (b) CT in Area:—
        - (1) Strength.
        - (2) Weapons and dress.
        - (3) Known or likely locations and activities including past history.
    - (c) Movements of Aborigines and civilians in area.
    - (d) Own troops:—
        - (1) Clearance.
        - (2) Patrol activities of SF. Include means of identification.
        - (3) Air and arty tasks.

2. **Mission**
    This must be clear to patrol commander:—
    - (a) Recce Patrol.—takes form of question or questions.
    - (b) Fighting Patrol.—definite object.

3. **Execution**
    - (a) Strength and composition of patrol.
    - (b) Time out and anticipated time of return.
    - (c) Method of movement to patrol area.
    - (d) Routes out and in. If helicopters are to be used location and state of LZs.
    - (e) Boundaries.
    - (f) Probable bounds and RVs.
    - (g) Formations.
    - (h) Deception and cover plan.
    - (j) Action to be taken on contact.
    - (k) Action if ambushed.
    - (l) Action if lost.
    - (m) DO NOT:—
        - (1) Move in file through rubber.
        - (2) Move through defiles.
        - (3) Cut unnecessarily.
        - (4) Return by the same route as that used for outward move.
        - (5) Allow weapons to become jammed through dirt.
        - (6) Relax because you are nearing base.

4. **Administration and Logistics**
    - (a) Rations:—
        - (1) Type and number of days.
        - (2) Resupply.

Appendix A—*Continued*

- (3) Cooking.
- (4) Dog rations.
- (5) Rum.
- (b) Equipment and Dress:—
    - (1) Change of clothing.
    - (2) Large or small pack.
    - (3) Poncho capes.
    - (4) Footwear.
    - (5) Maps, compasses, and air photos.
- (c) Avoidance of noise:—
    - (1) Does equipment rattle?
    - (2) Leave behind men with coughs.
- (d) Weapons:—
    - (1) Types and distribution.
    - (2) Special weapons—GF rifle, etc.
- (e) Ammunition:—
    - (1) Type and distribution.
    - (2) Grenades, Hand and Rifle, including gas checks and clips for 80 grenades.
    - (3) Check grenade fuses.
    - (4) Signal cartridges.
- (f) Medical:—
    - (1) First field dressing, J packs.
    - (2) Medical orderly and haversack.
    - (3) Water sterilising tablets.
    - (4) Salt tablets.
    - (5) Paludrine.
    - (6) DBP clothing.
    - (7) Foot powder.
    - (8) Copper sulphate ointment for burns.
- (g) Special Equipment:—
    - (1) Saws and parangs.
    - (2) Cameras.
    - (3) Finger print outfit.
    - (4) Surrender pamphlets.
    - (5) Night equipment.
    - (6) Explosives.
    - (7) Dogs.
    - (8) Marker Balloons.
- (h) Inspect all equipment for serviceability.

5. **Command and Signals**
    - (a) Frequencies:—
        - (1) Times of opening.
        - (2) Special instructions.
        - (3) Air.

Appx A

Appendix A—*Continued*

- (b) Codes: —
    - (1) Net identification signs.
    - (2) Codes.
    - (3) Passwords.
- (c) Check and test sets: —
    - (1) Aerials.
    - (2) CW keys.
    - (3) Spare batteries.
- (d) Ground/Air Communications: —
    - (1) DZ panels and DZ letters allotted.
    - (2) Ground/Air signal code.

NOTE:

Check thoroughly that all points have been understood by patrol members.

CHAPTER VIII

PATROL MOVEMENT AND FORMATION

Section 1.—INTRODUCTION

1. All movement on operations in Malaya is tactical movement. The CT is cunning and ever ready to take advantage of any carelessness or relaxation by the SF.

2. The formations given in this Chapter are similar to those used in normal warfare, though the placing of individuals and weapons within the formations may be peculiar to anti-CT operations under Malayan conditions. The factors which have affected the evolution of these formations are:—

 (a) The requirement to produce maximum fire power immediately on contact.
 (b) Battle is largely at close quarters.
 (c) Formations must be such that troops are capable of taking immediate counter ambush action.

Section 2.—MOVEMENT - GENERAL

1. Rate of movement in primary and secondary jungle is seldom more than one mile per hour, which is fast going. More often it is not more than half a mile per hour. Every now and then small clearings are found and there are places where the overhead branches of trees are not thick. It is possible to receive an air drop through this type of jungle provided adequate smoke signals are given.

2. On account of the shade given by trees, movement in jungle and rubber can be made over reasonable distances without great physical discomfort. On the other hand movement in lallang or belukar is most exhausting because of exposure to the sun and also the hot haze off the ground.

3. Owing to restricted visibility in the jungle the only sure means of maintaining direction is by compass. Every commander down to the most junior must be able to use a compass with confidence and accuracy.

4. Movement by night in jungle is not often practical and should only be undertaken by well-trained troops. Movement by night in rubber is easier.

5. Movement through swamp is the most tiring and slowest of the conditions likely to be encountered. Some assistance can be obtained by clambering from the roots of one tree to the next. The CT have been known to build submerged tracks across swamps which enable faster movement. Such tracks are available to our own forces only with the assistance of a SEP who knows the area.

6. The chief characteristics of the jungle must be explained to men new to Malaya as early as possible. They must be trained to feel at home in the jungle and made to realise that it provides good cover which enables them to close unobserved with the CT and so more easily to kill them.

Section 3.—MOVEMENT OF PATROLS

1. **Silence.**— Silence is essential at all times. This refers both to voice and movement. With practice it is possible to move at considerable speed in comparative silence. Move steadily and carefully and part the undergrowth rather than crash through. Do not blunder forward—this will produce bruises, scratches and loss of direction besides loss of silence. Avoid treading on dry leaves, sticks, rotten wood, etc., wherever possible. Use the silent signals shown at Appendix A.

2. **Cutting.**
    (a) Cut only as a last resort and only to avoid excessive detours. There is nearly always a way nearby where movement is easier. Cutting has the following disadvantages:—
        (i) It is not silent.
        (ii) It reduces speed of movement.
        (iii) Fatigue is increased in the leading elements.
        (iv) Quick handling of weapons is prejudiced.
    (b) If it is necessary to cut:—
        (i) Make sure the matchette is always kept sharp.
        (ii) Do not slash—a sawing action is just as quick and is more silent.
        (iii) Cut upwards—this stops pulling vines, etc., down on you.
    (c) In many battalions cutting on the move is forbidden.

3. **Tracks and Track Discipline.**— Movement on tracks should be avoided, though it may sometimes be necessary when speed in follow-up is required, or when moving in mountainous country.

Movement on tracks simplifies the problem of the CT who constantly seek SF targets on tracks as a potential source of weapons.

4. Not only should established tracks be avoided but efforts should be made to disguise or hide signs of movement to prevent the leaving of a trail even in virgin country. Some aids in this problem are:—

  (a) (i) Wear hockey boots.

       (ii) Have the last man brush the trail lightly with a small branch after the patrol has passed.

  (b) Remember track discipline. Do NOT signpost the route with litter and waste food. These should be kept and buried. Do NOT while away the time by plucking leaves, breaking twigs—this blazes a trail.

  (c) When crossing streams a patrol should spread out along the bank, and be ready to give supporting fire to the leading troops.

  (d) When crossing established tracks signs of crossing should be obliterated by the rear man.

  (e) When moving through close, hilly country avoid handling small saplings. The shaking of overhead branches can be seen and heard at a distance.

  (f) When moving through rubber estates, keep off the tracks if only by walking parallel to a track and a few feet from it.

5. **Speed of Movement.**—Speed of movement is dictated by the nature of the country and the task. Speed in moving from one point to another will be better obtained by intelligent route planning than by trying to push quickly and blindly forward.

6. Speed will always be limited by the necessity to avoid noise of movement and will often be painfully slow. A commander must remember that movement in jungle is fatiguing, both physically and mentally, and that he must balance his desire for progress against the necessity for keeping his troops fresh and alert for action.

7. Halts must be frequent for observation and listening and less frequent for rest. When halted, always take up positions for all round defence. In single file formation it may be necessary to delegate responsibility for protection and lookouts down to groups. As a guide, when working out times for rest halts, start with the usual ten minutes in the hour. Do not march for longer periods.

Usually the halts will be more frequent especially when traversing difficult country. After passing through swamp or climbing a steep slope it is a good plan to have a short rest. Make sure the whole party has passed through a defile before halting or only the leading elements will be rested.

8. **Observation.**— In jungle a man observes with all his senses. On the move he must notice every sign of movement, marks on tracks and broken vegetation. His nose must be keen, and free from cigarette smoke, sweets, the smell of hair oil, so that he immediately notices any strange smell such as tobacco, cooking and woodsmoke. Every few minutes, depending on how close the commander suspects the CT to be, and certainly not less often than every ten minutes, a patrol must stop and listen.

9. Eyes must be trained to disregard the general pattern of foliage immediately to the front and to look through rather than at it. A better view is often obtained by looking through jungle at ground level.

10. As soon as any unusual sign or sound is noted a patrol must 'freeze' silently. There should be no further movement until the commander, and his tracker, have investigated.

11. The direction of responsibility for observation by the various men in a patrol is shown diagrammatically in the Appendices to this Chapter. This method must be practised before a patrol moves out from base. Observation to the rear must NOT be forgotten.

Section 4.—SEARCHING GROUND

1. When searching ground, or patrolling for information, the most that a platoon can be expected to search in a day even in ideal conditions, is one 1,000 yard map square. Commanders, when briefing patrols, must bear this in mind otherwise ground will be only partially searched and incomplete information will result.

2. A most effective method of search in jungle is the 'five finger' or 'fan' method. A patrol base is established from which reconnaissance patrols of three or four men are sent out towards the area in which CT activity is suspected. These patrols are sent out on compass bearings, at intervals of 10 degrees, like the ribs of a fan. Their radius of action should be limited to two to three hours outwards from base, i.e. approximately 1,000 yards. It is essential to limit their radius of action in this way because their task is an exhausting one and they must remain alert and ready for action all

the time. For this reason they should be changed frequently. There are several variations of the 'fan' method. One is for each patrol to turn right or left at the far end of its patrol line, move 100 yards to the flank and then return to the patrol base on the back bearing plus or minus 5 degrees.

3. These patrols wear no equipment and carry no rations, except for say, a packet of biscuits. They carry only their arms and ammunition, maps and compasses. They move slowly, pausing frequently to listen, and as silently as possible to avoid detection. They return on the back bearing. In the early stages of training, men may be permitted to bend twigs along their route to assist their return, but it must be remembered that such signposting of a trail may leave a weak reconnaissance patrol open to CT action.

4. If CT are in the area they leave signs of their presence. It is for these signs that the patrols search; both visual signs and noise. Ideally every man should be able to recognise a fresh trail (i.e. marks showing the passage of CT—they seldom establish permanent tracks) even if made by only one or two men. Some men will obviously be better than others at this, but all can be trained to notice the more obvious signs, e.g. disturbed vegetation, footprints, and marks made on the banks of a stream.

5. Equally important is the need to listen carefully all the time. The biggest give away of the CT is the noise of cutting and, as they use wood fuel for cooking they must cut fairly often.

6. Reconnaissance patrols used in this type of search must realise that their function is to obtain information on which their commander can make a plan. If they find traces of CT movement they should try to establish:—

(a) How many CT made the track.

(b) When tracks were made.

(c) Where found.

(d) Direction of movement of CT.

At this stage an unwise move by the reconnaissance patrol may disclose the presence of SF. The correct procedure is for the patrol to return and report to its commander.

7. If no information is forthcoming the patrol base moves on and a fresh series of reconnaissance patrols is sent out.

Section 5.—FORMATIONS

1. **Section.**— Two types of section patrol formations are considered sufficient for use in the various types of terrain to be met in Malaya. They are:—
   (a) *Single File formation* - - Appendix B
   (b) *Open formation* - - Appendix C

2. **Platoon.**—The platoon normally consists of two or three sections. Each section moves in groups as illustrated in Appendices B and C. The sections may follow one another in single file formation or move in open formation, one or two up, on parallel axes.

3. When a platoon is moving in its selected formation it may be necessary for the 'O' group to move behind the leading section, but in close country it may often be more important for the section commanders to be with their sections.

4. The patrol commander must continuously appreciate the ground and vary the formation of his patrol to suit it. Similarly he must continuously appreciate the tactical position of the patrol in relation to the ground so as to be able immediately to take action in the event of a contact.

Section 6.—POSITION OF COMMANDERS

1. The position of the patrol commander will normally be that shown in the diagrams.

2. The position of platoon and company commanders will be dictated by ground, tactical circumstances and formation. It should be sufficiently far forward for him to:—
   (a) be in a position to influence the encounter from the outset, and although it is not desirable for him to be caught in the opening burst of fire, he should be placed where he can quickly exploit IA drills.
   (b) exercise control, control his guides, read his map and air photos, give orders with regard to navigation and order halts when necessary.

Section 7.—POSITION OF GUIDES AND TRACKERS

1. The word 'guide', as used here, means somebody with an intimate knowledge of an area or someone who can lead SF to a known CT location. These may be SEPs, CEPs, Aborigines,

Malay, Chinese or Indian estate workers. They may expect to lead the patrol and have on occasions been allowed to do so, but this is wrong because:—

  (a) They are not trained scouts and are not part of the military team. Their function is merely to show direction.
  (b) If CT are encountered en route, guides may react badly and prejudice the patrol's chance of killing.
  (c) Cases have occurred of troops being led into ambush.

2. The correct position for a guide is with the patrol commander. The patrol commander will make decisions as to direction and tactics, using the guide's advice as he wishes.

3. The tracker has a different function—that of following a trail. Once a trail has been picked up, the tracker, be he man or dog, must move in the lead, otherwise faint signs of CT movement will be obliterated and confused. The tracker must be protected by the scouts who must not be allowed to relax their alertness or be distracted by the signs of the trail. The patrol commander must appreciate that a tracker, born to the jungle and lightly equipped, may tend to outstrip the patrol. The patrol commander must ensure that contact is maintained by seeing that the tracker conforms to the speed of the patrol. (See also Chapter XXI).

Section 8.—MAINTAINING CONTACT AND MOVEMENT BY NIGHT

1. **Maintaining Contact.**—The patrol leader must always adapt his speed of movement to that of his rear elements, in other words, responsibility for keeping touch must be from front to rear. The flanks must maintain their position by the centre. The only exception to this rule will normally be the leading group whose whole attention must be focused forward.

2. Obstacles must be crossed tactically. It must be remembered that obstacles and defiles are the CT choice killing grounds. A simple drill should be evolved to cover troops crossing obstacles to ensure that all elements are over before the patrol moves on.

3. **Night Movement.**—Movement by night in jungle, without a guide or an intimate knowledge of the area, is difficult but it must never be regarded as impossible. Movement on established tracks and up streams has been carried out with success, but away from tracks it is extremely noisy and maintenance of contact is difficult.

It is, however, normal to move through rubber by night in order to reach an operational area before estate workers are in position.

4. The following aids will help to maintain contact when moving by night:—
   (a) Sets of luminous patches worn on the back. These are issued through Ordnance channels.
   (b) White towels fixed behind the pack straps.
   (c) Where CT are NOT expected, the use of screened weak torch light directed at the ground.

5. If contact within a patrol is broken both parts of the patrol must halt and:—
   (a) the rear part of the patrol will stay where they are.
   (b) the leading elements must retrace their steps to bridge the gap, moving back on the route which they have already been over. In this way contact will be regained more rapidly and there is less chance of a clash between two moving parties.

Section 9.—MAINTAINING DIRECTION

1. The compass is the only completely reliable and constant guide to direction and should be issued on as generous a scale as possible. Because of limited visibility in jungle it is important that commanders carry their compasses in their hands and constantly recheck their direction. If this is not done loss of time and direction will result. Other commanders in the column should consult their compasses and maps frequently so that at all times they know where they are, both on the map and on the ground. This is always necessary, even if there is a guide with the patrol. The leading group commander should indicate directions to his scouts. Orders for change can be given by some pre-arranged signal.

2. Chapter IX deals with Jungle Navigation.

Section 10.—RETURN TO BASE

A patrol is most vulnerable to CT action when it is tired. After several days' operations men may relax as familiar land-marks near their base appear. This is known by the CT and is the time when many successful CT ambushes have been sprung. Remember the first sentence of this Chapter—'All movement on operations in Malaya is tactical movement'—and keep men alert and ready for action until they are inside their camp. Do NOT use tracks close to camp as a normal route for returning patrols.

Appendix A

SILENT SIGNALS

These signals are additional to those normally taught, e.g. advance, halt, close, turn about, and double.

Meaning	Signal
1. Seen or suspected CT	Thumb pointed towards the ground from a clenched fist.
2. No CT in sight or All Clear or OK	Thumb pointed upwards from a closed fist.
3. Support group	The clenched fist.
4. Recce group	The clenched fist with forefinger upright.
5. Rifle group	The Victory Sign.
6. Section Commander	Two fingers held against arm to indicate Cpl's chevrons.
7. Platoon Commander	Two fingers held on the shoulder to indicate Lieut's stars.
8. You	Point at man concerned.
9. Me	Indicate the chest.
10. Give covering fire	Weapon brought into the aim, indicating direction.
11. Track Junction	Arms crossed.
12. House or hut	Thumb pointing down from an open hand with fingers extended and together so as to form an inverted V between thumb and forefinger.
13. Recce	Hand held up to eye as though using a monocle.
14. Attack	Clenched fist swung vigorously in direction attack is required.
15. Freeze	Halt Signal. (Arm raised above head with open palm to the front).

Appendix B

SINGLE FILE FORMATION

1. This formation will NOT normally be used in rubber or other plantations.

2. Single file formation is used in jungle where troops cannot move in a more open formation.

Recce Group.

3. Distances between individuals and groups will vary according to visibility.

4. Generally there should never be less than five yards between each man. Distance between groups should be governed by the nature of the ground and vegetation, and the necessity for maintaining control.

5. A tracker group, if accompanying the patrol, will be located in a suitable position for immediate employment.

Support Group.

Rifle Group.

NOTE: For key to symbols see overleaf.

Appendix B—*Continued*

SINGLE FILE FORMATION—*Continued*

Key to Symbols in Appendices B and C:—

- (a) S1 — Leading Scout.
  - S2 — No. 2 Scout.
  - SC — Recce Group Commander
- (b) PC — Section or Patrol Commander.
  - G — Guide.
- (c) B1 — Bren Gun No. 1.
  - B2 — Bren Gun No. 2.
  - BC — Support Group Commander and Section 2 IC.
- (d) RC — Rifle Group Commander.
  - R1 — No. 1 Rifleman.
  - R2 — No. 2 Rifleman.
- (e) Small arrows indicate the direction of responsibility for observation.

Appx C

Appendix C
OPEN FORMATION

1. **'One Up'**:—

   (a) *Advantages.*—
      (i) Ease of control.
      (ii) Good fire power to front and flanks.
      (iii) On contact the leading group only is committed and two are available to manoeuvre.

   (b) *Disadvantages.*—
      (i) With the fleeting targets which are offered in Malaya fewer men are likely to see the CT on first contact.

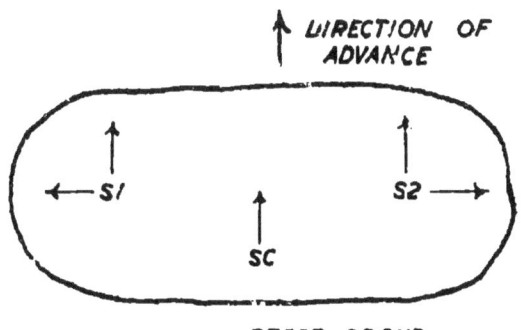

OPEN FORMATION—ONE UP

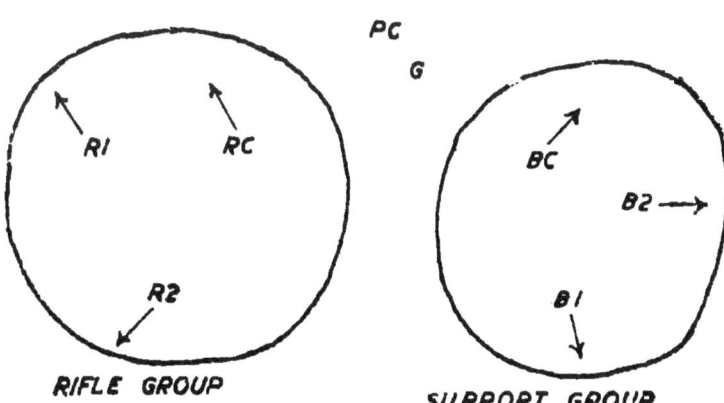

Appx C

Appendix C—*Continued*

OPEN FORMATION—*Continued*

2. **'Two Up'**:—

   (a) *Advantages.*—

   (i) A wider front is covered.
   (ii) The formation is less vulnerable to ambush.
   (iii) More weapons are available to fire forward in event of a sudden contact.

   (b) *Disadvantages.*—

   (i) On contact the two forward groups may be committed and there are less troops available for manoeuvre.

3. **'Three Up'**.—Although this formation will cover more frontage it is difficult to control and allows nothing for manoeuvre.

4. Distances between individuals and groups will vary according to the ground through which troops are passing.

OPEN FORMATION—TWO UP

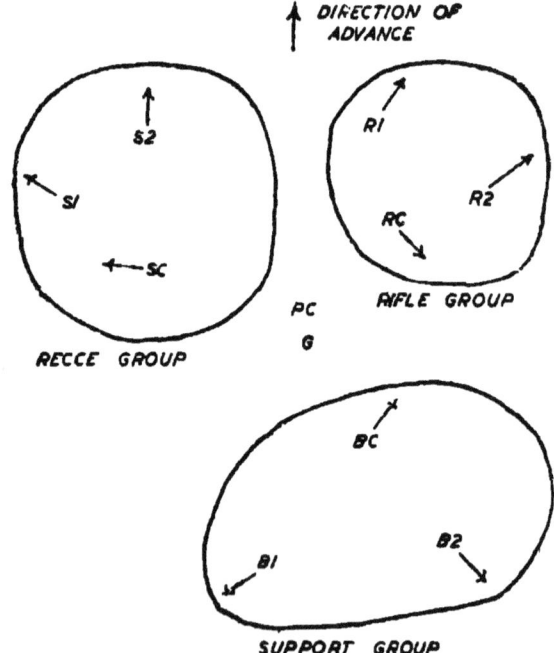

CHAPTER IX

JUNGLE NAVIGATION

Section 1.—INTRODUCTION

1. Map reading and navigation in Europe, where landmarks are easily seen and recognised, is fairly straightforward. In Malaya with its large areas of dense jungle it is more difficult.

2. In jungle it is possible to see for only very short distances—25 yards and upwards, sometimes even less, and therefore skill in the use of the compass is essential. There are few artificial features. Landmarks, therefore, consist largely of jungle covered hills (making it impossible to see one hill from another), streams and rivers. However, as in any other theatre, these natural landmarks are the surest guides in map reading.

3. The aim of this Chapter is to explain the elements of jungle navigation and to show how to make the best use of the available aids.

Section 2.—AIDS

1. **Maps:—**

   (a) *General.*—For obvious reasons map survey in Malaya is difficult and has been mainly carried out from the air. However, main hill features and streams are accurately shown, and maps can be relied on, although maps of some areas do not show enough detail.

   (b) *Map Study.*—Careful study of the map is an essential preliminary to jungle navigation. This study will provide the answer to many questions, e.g. the best route to be taken and areas to be avoided. It will reward the individual by helping him to visualise the lie of the land, to assist his sense of direction and to increase his confidence. If this careful map study is not carried out before going on patrol the chances of being lost are doubled.

   (c) *1 in. to 1 mile.*—This map is in general use. It is gridded in 1,000 yard squares. Some of its topographical detail is out of date and checks should be carried out with the unit operations room in order to ascertain the latest topographical information, e.g. rubber and jungle edges.

(d) *1:25,000.*—There is not a complete map coverage of Malaya on this scale. The map is not always clear, but local data can be added more easily than on the 1 in. to 1 mile.

(e) *Going Maps.*—Going maps lose their value if they are not kept up to date. Information contained on them must be checked and confirmed by at least two patrols. Going maps should include all data about types of cultivations.

(f) *Estate and Forest Department Maps.*—A library should be kept in unit operation rooms of local estate and forestry maps. They contain valuable and accurate information which is normally shown on a large scale.

2. **Air Photographs.**— A complete photographic coverage of Malaya is available. These air photos provide a valuable check, when used in conjunction with the stereoscope, to map reading. It is important when reading air photographs to check the date of printing because tracks and clearings can become overgrown in three or four months. When air photographs are available they must be used.

3. **The Compass.**— The value of the compass is equal to that of the map. It is used in jungle as for night movement, and must be continuously used as a check to direction keeping. Straight forward marches on a set bearing are seldom possible because of the terrain, but when used correctly in conjunction with the map the compass makes it virtually impossible to be lost. Account should be taken of tin mines and weapons which may upset a compass's accuracy.

4. **Compass Navigation.**— Despite the most accurate jungle navigation, patrols returning to their small patrol bases frequently have difficulty in striking their objective. A suggested method of navigation is to "aim off" so as to miss the base by say a hundred yards or so. When the patrol has reached a position that is thought to be approximately level with the base, a series of short sorties to the known flank will soon locate the base.

5. **The Protractor.**— This must be used in conjunction with the compass and is invaluable.

6. **The Sun.**— The jungle canopy frequently hides the sun from view but it is often a valuable aid to direction which should be taught to all other ranks.

Section 3.—PLANNING

1. Map study has been mentioned in Section 2 as the essential preliminary to planning. In deciding the best route from one point to another the following factors should be considered:—

(a) *The grain of the country.*—It is far easier to follow the grain of the country than to go against it, and therefore a direct route in the form of a straight line is practical only in flat jungle. It is useless in hilly jungle.

(b) *Watersheds.*—Tops of ridges and hills contain sparser jungle than the valleys. Animal tracks are often found on these ridges and therefore it is easier to march on the ridges. It is less tiring and much quicker. Once the effort of climbing the hill is over a relatively easy march follows.

(c) *River Lines.*—While rivers are useful aids to maintenance of direction, it is poor policy to follow them. They always wind about and are bordered by dense jungle. The further one keeps away from them the faster one can usually go.

Section 4.—CHECKING

1. Once the march starts checking must be continuous. The following means of checking should be used:—

(a) All features, hills and rivers should be checked as they are reached, and identified on the map. Note the direction of flow of all streams and rivers and check with the map.

(b) Tracks should be identified, but should always be regarded with suspicion. It is easy to place too much confidence in a track which may not be the one marked on the map.

(c) Forest boundaries may be useful checks.

(d) Pacing is a doubtful method of checking distance unless you are moving on flat ground. Time taken, the type of country and estimated speed and above all common sense will be a good guide to the distance travelled. The normal error is to overestimate the distance moved.

(e) Fatigue is the greatest enemy of good navigation. To blunder on, hoping for the best is a sure way of getting lost. Having stopped, obtain data—possibly by casting about with small patrols—and check with the map. If this rule is followed you will NOT get lost. If it is not followed the contents of the following paragraph should be remembered.

(f) *Action if lost*.—The feeling of being lost tends to create mental panic, and therefore the first essential is to **sit down and calm down.** Then:—
  (i) Work out where you are.
  (ii) Make a careful map study. Make a plan which aims to take you to a recognisable feature, preferably a river, and then if still in doubt move down-stream towards civilisation.
  (iii) Some use can be made of the sun and stars.
  (iv) Above all—do not panic.
  (v) It may be possible to obtain a Lt AC Contact Patrol. See Chapter XVII, Section 11 paragraph 2(a).

Section 5.—OBSTACLES

1. Preliminary map study will reduce the number of obstacles likely to be encountered, but some may be met, e.g. unmapped swamps and lallang.

2. The natural tendency is to follow round the edge of the obstacle, but this process is usually slow and tends to make direction keeping difficult. It is quicker to cast wide, checking the bearing carefully. When on the far side of the obstacle, resume the original course.

Section 6.—CONCLUSION

Jungle navigation is not easy, but the difficulties are easily overstated. Providing methodical map study and planning are undertaken, followed by careful use of the map, compass and protractor, all ranks can find their way about. With experience the individual will gain confidence in himself, his map and his compass. Once this confidence has developed a feel for the grain of the country and a sense of direction will become instinctive.

CHAPTER X

IMMEDIATE ACTION DRILLS

Section 1.—INTRODUCTION

1. Encounters with the CT are sudden, short, and often so unexpected that the opportunity to inflict casualties is lost if a leader has to give orders at the time of the encounter. What is required is immediate, positive and offensive action.

2. For this reason it is essential for simple Immediate Action (IA) Drills to be taught and thoroughly practised. It is impracticable to attempt to cover every contingency by committing to paper numerous IA Drills, because not only would they tend to cramp initiative but they would not be read or digested or remembered in the stress of action. It is however, important to teach one IA Drill to cope with each situation commonly met. The principles underlying each drill must be simplicity, aggression and speed.

3. Before a patrol leaves its base, the commander in his briefing, should include directions on IA Drills. This is necessary each time because patrols vary in strength and organisation according to the nature of their task. In addition the mere quotation of the standard drills applicable to the operation in question, will act as a reminder to the troops taking part and so help them to avoid being surprised.

4. IA Drills are of little value unless the standard of weapon handling and marksmanship is high and unless troops understand and remember instinctively the capabilities and limitations of the weapons with which they are armed. A guide on this subject is contained in Chapter V.

Section 2.— THE IA DRILLS

1. Four IA Drills are described in this Chapter. These are considered sufficient for use in the varied terrain of Malaya and they suit any standard patrol formation. It should be noted that the drills suggested are a sound framework on which units may build as their experience dictates.

2. The drills quoted are as follows:—

   (a) Freezing.
   (b) The immediate assault.

(c) The immediate assault on a CT camp.

(d) Counter ambush action which includes an immediate assault as above or the encircling attack.

3. Sub-para. 2(d) generally applies also in countering an MT ambush, but detailed IA Drills for MT ambush are contained in Chapter XIII, Sections 5 and 6.

4. It is important to note that although these drills are usually taught on a section basis, they can be adapted for use by a platoon.

5. These drills are applicable to close country. In open country normal infantry minor tactics will usually obtain.

6. Although the members of a patrol will know and have practised their IA Drills, a patrol may be accompanied by other people who have only a little knowledge of these drills. In general, guides, informers and SEP should be kept strictly under command and in view of the commander. They must be briefed as thoroughly as possible before the patrol starts (See Chapter VIII, Section 6).

Section 3.—ACTION ON ENCOUNTER

1. **Freezing.**— This drill is designed to deal with a situation where a patrol, without being seen itself, sights a CT party approaching, either on the same track, across a clearing or in jungle. It is obviously advantageous to allow the CT to approach as close as possible before opening fire on them. There may only be time for a silent signal to be passed for all members of the patrol to freeze in their tracks. It remains then for men of the patrol to remain absolutely motionless until the CT reach a position in which they are most vulnerable.

2. The technique to be followed should be:—

   (a) The leading scout, having sighted the approaching CT, gives the silent signal for halt and freezes in his tracks.

   (b) The remainder of the patrol freeze in their tracks in the aiming position.

   (c) Fire is opened, usually by the patrol commander, when the CT present a suitable point blank target.

   (d) If CT and SF are approaching each other on the same track the leading scout should give the silent signal to freeze, at the same time moving behind the nearest cover off the track, to right or left. The remainder of the patrol should follow his lead. It is essential that the whole patrol move to the same side of the track as the leading scout.

3. As many CT as possible should be allowed into the killing zone, but fire must be opened as soon as a kill is certain. In the event of the CT giving an indication that they have sighted the patrol, troops must be trained to fire at their own accord, and the freeze will then turn into an immediate assault.

4. It may sometimes happen that the CT are not approaching directly head on to the patrol but are moving to a flank, and by remaining at the freeze an opportunity to secure a kill may be lost. The patrol commander must then make an appreciation of the CT course, and if there is sufficient time available, move the patrol into ambush positions. In this event, to avoid confusion, the ambush should be sited on one side only of the CT line of advance. This subsequent action then becomes a minor tactical problem and not an IA Drill.

5. **The Immediate Assault.**—This drill is used when our troops and the CT become aware of each other at the same time.

6. The assault and follow up may well strike a CT camp or resting place. Alternatively if a patrol is fired on by a single CT and an immediate assault results, the single CT may well turn out to be a sentry placed outside a CT camp perimeter and once again the assault may lead into the camp. For these reasons the Immediate Assault should always be considered in relation to an Immediate Assault on a CT camp.

7. As contacts are often made at some distance from a CT camp, the Immediate Assault is considered as a separate drill, but the facts set out in para 6 must be kept in the forefront of the commander's mind.

8. As the name suggests, the drill is a controlled and immediate frontal attack led directly at the CT.

9. The assault will probably start with the first member of the patrol, who may or may not be the leading scout, sighting the CT, firing at the CT and shouting 'CT front (left or right) charge.'

10. The commander must control the distance to which the assault is allowed to go. The assault should continue until there is no CT in sight. In close country a very careful search should be made of the area where contact was lost as the CT may have gone to ground. After the search the patrol should follow up any tracks found. This is the time when the tracking team, can be employed to its best advantage.

11. It is essential that the assault should be pressed home by the whole patrol. If the ground allows, the GF rifle can be used to good advantage by immediately putting down grenades on or in the rear of the CT. Remember, however, that our reactions must never be stereotyped. For example, the immediate assault presents to the CT a chance of luring our patrols into an ambush. On contact, if the patrol has been in single file, it should shake out into line. The advantages of line are:—

    (a) More men can search for and engage CT.

    (b) There is less chance of ambush.

    (c) More ground is covered, should the CT go to ground.

12. The immediate assault must be applied in the event of a patrol being totally within an ambush in open country. On these occasions, when through lack of cover, manoeuvre is precluded, a determined and immediate assault by the survivors is usually the only solution to the problem.

13. **The Immediate Assault on a CT Camp.**— This drill is applied only when a patrol:—

    (a) Contacts a sentry on a CT camp, resulting in an Immediate Assault which reaches the edge of the camp

OR

    (b) Contacts several CT and the resulting assault leads the patrol on to a camp.

14. It is stressed that the drill will not be used when a patrol locates a CT camp and the patrol is unobserved by the CT. For action when the patrol is unobserved, see Chapter XII.

15. The normal CT protection drill for their camps is as follows:—

    (a) The sentry either fires at the SF as they approach his post or else he moves back unseen to the camp.

    (b) On hearing firing or on receiving information from their sentries the CT, who are always prepared, immediately disperse into the jungle and reassemble at a prearranged RV.

    (c) Sometimes, particularly in the larger and better organized camps, one or more counter attacks are put in after the SF have entered the camp. These counter attacks are seldom pressed home with determination although a great deal of ammunition is usually expended.

(d) In well defended camps, when held in strength, the CT may stand and fight in dug-in positions, or fight a delaying action to cover the withdrawal of a CT VIP.

(e) Recent experience has shown that (c) and (d) are seldom practised, and that almost invariably there is immediate withdrawal from the camp.

16. If a camp is located as the result of an unexpected contact as opposed to reconnaissance, the following drill is suggested: —

The leading scout, or whoever sees the camp, shouts 'CT camp' in a loud voice. The patrol commander shouts 'Charge' and the whole make a frontal attack into the camp.

17. In this way not only is there a better chance of catching CT in the camp before they evacuate, but in the event of fire being returned from the camp the patrol will be a more difficult target to hit.

18. Pursuit is continued until contact is lost after which the patrol re-organises. The camp and its vicinity is searched for: —

(a) CT casualties.

(b) arms, ammunition, stores and documents.

(c) food dumps.

(d) CT tracks and blood-trails.

The procedure thereafter for the follow up cannot be taught as a drill.

19. **Counter Ambush Drill.**— The IA drills to be practised when a SF patrol is caught in ambush are of two kinds: —

(a) Where only the foremost elements of a patrol are caught in the ambush—an immediate encircling attack carried out by the remainder of the patrol.

(b) Where the whole of the patrol is ambushed in open ground—an immediate assault (as in paragraph 12 above) mounted by the survivors.

20. It should be borne in mind that the CT normally site their ambushes on high ground dominating the axis of SF movement, and either IA Drill must take this into consideration.

21. **The Encircling Attack.**— The encircling attack is the correct reaction to a CT ambush and is based on the normal principles of fire and movement, taught in basic section leading.

The difference lies in the speed at which the manoeuvre is carried out.

22. The CT do not like having their line of withdrawal cut. By cutting it we undermine their confidence and prevent them escaping.

23. Our formations are designed so that part only of a patrol should be caught in the ambush. If these formations are practised and the distances correctly observed, the whole patrol should not be involved in the opening burst of fire.

24. It may be that speed of movement dictates the use of tracks and in consequence troops must be prepared for an ambush. This drill is designed to counter an ambush when a track or defile must be used.

25. As he advances the patrol commander should be constantly appreciating ground and thus when the recce group comes under fire the patrol commander's mind should already be made up. He must now take control of the battle by shouting 'Encircling Attack—(LEFT or RIGHT). This should be all that is necessary. The troops will have practised the drill and will know their positions in the assault—they will not have had time to go to ground or get out of control.

26. This drill is not suitable for action on encountering a CT patrol.

27. **The Immediate Assault.**— Experience has shown that some CT ambushes are laid on a considerable frontage and can occupy in excess of 100 yards by track. Under these conditions a small patrol, even when preserving its correct spacing, can all be caught within the ambush.

28. Scope for manoeuvre is often limited to an immediate assault being mounted directly at the CT position by the survivors. It will seldom be possible or desirable, to attempt to take up fire positions and exchange fire with the CT, so long as the patrol is in the killing ground. The patrol should therefore move as quickly as possible to a fire position outside the killing ground and thence assault the CT position.

CHAPTER XI

THE AMBUSHING OF CT

Section 1.—POLICY

1. A high proportion of total CT eliminations are achieved in ambushes, and better opportunities exist to obtain kills than in any other form of contact. With the dwindling targets offered by the CTs it is essential that full advantage is taken of every chance offered, and ambushes laid as the result of direct high grade information must be based on sound and detailed planning, executed by specially selected troops.

2. This Chapter sets out the basic doctrine for the planning of ambushes laid as the result of information or suspicion, or as part of a large scale operational plan. The aim of such an ambush is to contact the CT under circumstances of the attackers' choosing.

3. The majority of ambushes in Malaya are laid as a result of:—

   (a) Intelligence provided by SB through direct or indirect information from SEPs, agents or informers.

   (b) Chance information.

   (c) An appreciation of likely CT movement and activity based on familiarity with an area coupled with the history of CT movements in the area concerned.

4. In order to exploit fully the information received from SB agents it is essential that the best possible team is chosen to make the contact. This may frequently entail a company commander commanding an ambush group, even although it may consist of only a handful of men. Men specially selected for their marksmanship or other particular qualities should be drawn from any element of the unit, and in fact the ambush group may consist of men from different services. The over riding consideration in selecting the ambush party should be to choose the team most likely to succeed in that particular case.

5. A high proportion of ambushes laid as the result of information occur at food pick up points, either on the jungle/rubber fringe, or at the approaches to New Villages or estate labour lines. Even although the information concerning the time and place of such food lifts may be absolutely accurate, within the knowledge of the informant, the CT take extraordinary precautions

to attempt to preserve the security of the lift. It may not take place on the time and date arranged, the area being kept under observation for some days, and Masses Executives, tappers and small children are employed to search for sign of SF activity and ambush positions. Commanders must always take this into consideration and not become despondent if a carefully laid ambush fails to achieve its object. A clear distinction must, however, be drawn between such an occasion and an ambush that *is* at the right place at the right time but fails because of mismanagement.

6. As an illustration of the necessity of taking full advantage of opportunities, it is worthy of note that during a six-month period in 1956, out of 50 ambushes laid, 34 were unsuccessful of which only 6 were due to circumstances outside the control of the SF.

7. The observance of the detail contained in the remainder of this Chapter will do much to improve this kill to contact rate.

8. Action by SF when sighting approaching CT who are unaware of the SF presence is dealt with in Chapter X, IA Drills.

Section 2.—THE PRINCIPLES OF AMBUSHING

1. To achieve success, spontaneous co-ordinated action on surprised CT held within a well covered killing area is needed. This requires:—
    (a) Good shooting from all positions—kneeling, sitting, standing, lying, and firing behind cover.
    (b) A high standard of training in ambush technique.
    (c) Careful planning and briefing.
    (d) First class security in all stages of the ambush.
    (e) Intelligent layout and siting.
    (f) Concealment.
    (g) A high standard of battle discipline throughout the operation.
    (h) Determination by all members of the ambush party to wait and kill.
    (j) A simple clear cut plan for springing the ambush.

Section 3.—THE LAYOUT OF AMBUSHES

1. **Principles.**— There are two fundamental principles of general layout:—
    (a) All possible approaches should be covered.
    (b) The ambush must have depth.

2. **Approaches.**—Information may frequently give the destination of the CT but will rarely give the exact route they will take. However good information may be, CT have a flair for arriving from an unexpected direction. This has caused a high failure rate in our ambushes. It is therefore essential that all possible approaches be covered.

3. **Depth.**—At the first burst of fire CT scatter with remarkable rapidity and the chances of getting a second burst from the same position are small. It is important, therefore, that groups should be so sited that when the CT scatter after the first burst, subsequent groups take a progressive toll of any survivors.

4. **The Ambush Group.**—An ambush is made up of a series of small groups of men. The size of these groups will vary, but two to six men can be taken as a guide.

5. The group should be self contained. A leader must be nominated and arrangements made for rest. It is not possible for men to remain alert for six to eight hours. One or two men in a group will be listening and watching, while the others rest in the ambush position. By rest, is meant that a man relaxes in his position, resting his eyes and ears. This should eliminate fidgeting and dozing.

6. In siting the men of his group the commander must:—
   (a) Consider concealment as his first priority. Movement in the area must be kept to a minimum, even at the expense of indifferent fire positions. Each man should enter his position from the rear. The group commander must ensure that all traces of movement into the position are removed or concealed.
   (b) Ensure that the man detailed to spring the ambush has a good view of the killing ground.
   (c) Ensure that other men of the group will have good fire positions when they break through their concealment, i.e. to stand up to engage moving CT.
   (d) Site his men in a position of all round defence.
   (e) Choose his own position for maximum control of his group.
   (f) Organise a simple and clear system for alerting his group.

7. **Types of Ambush.**—Groups may be employed in two ways, bearing in mind the principles of layout:—
   (a) *Area Ambush.*—Where there is more than one approach, all must be covered. Approaches should be covered in

depth to catch CT scattering from the position of the ambush. Such an ambush is known as an area ambush (see Diagram 1). It consists of a series of small groups, each with its own commander, sited as part of an overall plan to encompass a particular CT party which is expected. The groups may be laid out as limited ambushes (see 7(b) below). Area ambushes have proved much more successful than limited ambushes.

(b) *Limited Ambush*.—When, because of the ground, there is only one likely approach, a group or groups may be sited in depth with all round defence at a place on that route which gives adequate concealment. This is a limited ambush (see Diagram 2). It is used when the area ambush is impossible or as part of an area ambush, along a very likely approach track.

DIAGRAM 1

AREA AMBUSH

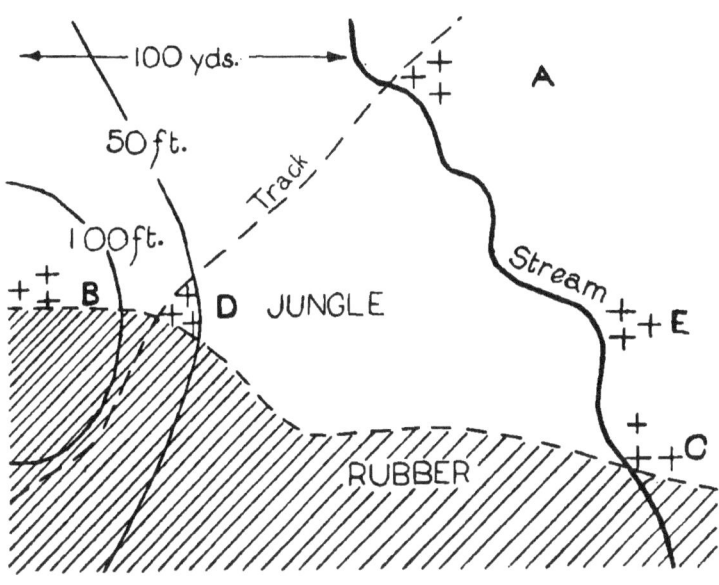

NOTES

1. Information received that CT will contact tappers at or near track junction 'D'.

2. It is decided that CT will probably approach through primary jungle along side of slope. Alternative approaches are 'A' to 'D', 'B' to 'D', 'C' to 'D' or through rubber.

3. Ambush groups are posted at 'A', 'B', 'C', 'D', 'E'.

4. If CT approach from 'A' to 'D', 'A' will allow them to pass through.

5. 'D' will probably spring ambush. CT will scatter and may run into 'A', 'C' (both downhill) or 'B'. If they hit 'A' or 'C' they may rebound along stream on to 'E'.

DIAGRAM 2

LIMITED AMBUSH

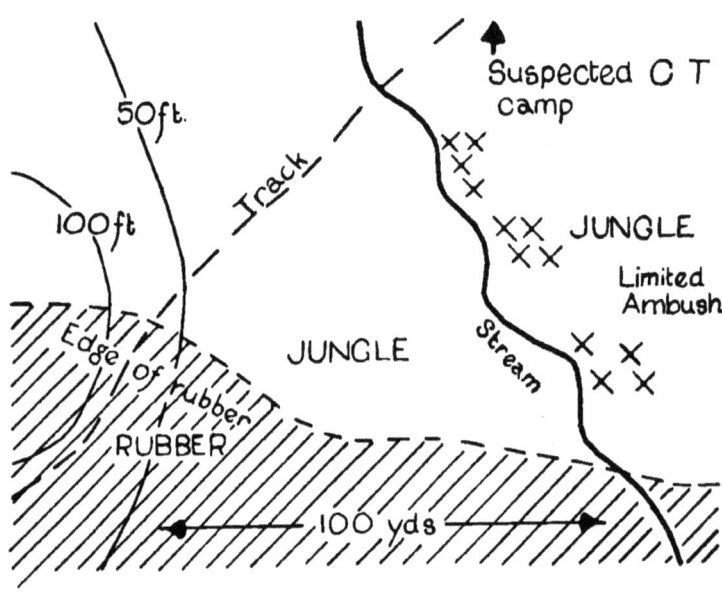

NOTES

1. A camp is known to be in an area approximately 1,000 yards square.

2. Information has been received that a party of three CT will collect subscriptions from tappers. The party will approach along the line of the stream. The ambush is therefore sited along this stream.

3. The ambush could be improved by siting the LIMITED AMBUSH as one element of an AREA AMBUSH thus covering all approaches.

Section 4.—THE SEQUENCE OF LAYING AN AMBUSH

1. **Planning.**—Many factors affect a plan for ambush. The following are common to all ambushes.
    (a) *Information.*—Information on the ambush area can be obtained from maps, previous patrol reports, Police, SEPs and air photos.
    (b) *Clearance.*—Movements of other SF in the area must be considered.
    (c) *Time Factor.*—The necessity of being unseen, coupled with knowledge of the habits of the local population will dictate the time at which it is safe to move into the ambush area.
    (d) *Security.*—The CT have a good intelligence system. Intentions of our own troops must be disguised from the start, e.g. by moving out to the ambush position by dark, and making false moves. The telephone should not be used when discussing plans for an ambush. A cover plan should always be made when time is available.
    (e) *Ground.*—All possible approaches should be considered. When considering likely ambush sites such as defiles and water crossings, the obvious should be avoided.

2. **Preparation for Ambush:—**
    (a) Success depends on adequate preparation. The time available for preparation is often limited. Certain items must therefore be kept in a state of constant readiness, e.g.:—
        (i) Weapons must be kept zeroed and tested.
        (ii) Ammunition, magazines and chargers must be kept clean and frequently emptied and refilled.
    (b) Preparation on receipt of information should include:—
        (i) Thorough briefing.
        (ii) Rehearsal, when time allows.
        (iii) Firing practice, if time allows.
        (iv) Final checking of weapons.

3. **Briefing.**—All members of the ambush party must be fully briefed. It is suggested that briefing be divided into two parts:—
    (a) Preliminary briefing at static location. This should include the items shown in Appendix A to this Chapter.

(b) Final briefing in the area of actual ambush by the commander of that ambush. This will be kept to the minimum but must include:—
  (i) General area of each group including direction of fire.
  (ii) Orders for springing the ambush.
  (iii) Orders on completion of ambush.

4. **Rehearsal.**— The more time that can be devoted to rehearsal the greater will be the chances of success. Rehearsals should not be carried out at the ambush site, as security will be prejudiced immediately. As the majority of ambushes are laid on either the jungle fringe or at food pick-up points at the approaches to labour lines/new villages it should usually be possible to select a site for rehearsal closely resembling the actual ambush position. All possible and likely CT action should be simulated and the ambush groups practised in springing the ambush under a variety of circumstances, including the unexpected eventuality.

5. Rehearsals for night ambushes should be done at night, and where it is proposed to make use of night illumination aids, these should also be employed.

6. **Siting:—**
  (a) *Area Ambush:—*
    (i) The ambush commander will first choose the killing ground and the general area of each group from his personal knowledge of the area, aided by maps and air photos. He will lay down the directions of fire for each group in order to obtain the maximum fire effect from the weapons at his disposal, and to ensure safety to his own troops. He will nominate the RV and give the administrative plan.
    (ii) The ambush party then moves to a dispersal point from which groups then move by carefully selected routes to their various group positions. The ambush commander may only be able to site one position in detail, leaving the remainder to be sited by group commanders.
    (iii) Each group commander will then carry out his reconnaissance, siting and issue of orders.
  (b) *Limited Ambush.*—On reaching the ambush area, the commander will:—
    (i) Make his reconnaissance to choose a killing ground and consider the extent of his position bearing in mind

that CT move with intervals varying from 10-50 yards. A killing ground of 60-100 yards is desirable. The ambush position should offer concealment but should not be too obviously a position suited to ambush.

(ii) Ensure that the man nominated to spring the ambush has a good view of the killing ground.

7. **Occupation.**— The occupation of an ambush position should be carried out with great care. All routes made by the ambush party must be carefully concealed. Remember that suspicious items such as paper scraps, foot prints, and bruised vegetation put CT on their guard. It is essential that all items with a distinctive smell which will betray the presence of the ambush party to the CT be left behind. Men's hair should be washed free of hair oils and hair creams, cigarettes should be withdrawn, sweets, chewing gum and other scented food, including curry powder, must not be carried. It is frequently necessary to wear PT shoes or have bare feet for the move into the positions. When allotting tasks and fields of fire for weapons it is seldom possible to site each weapon with a good field of fire. Each individual must be able to see his arc of responsibility and must be prepared to fire from any position, on the ambush being sprung.

8. **Lying in Ambush.**— Once a group is in position there must be no sound or movement. This is a test of training and battle discipline. Men must be trained to get into a comfortable position and remain still for long periods. During the wait weapons must be cocked and in a state of instant readiness to fire (i.e. safety catches forward).

9. **Springing the Ambush.**— The ambush should be sprung when all possible CT are in the killing ground and the range has been reduced to the minimum. There must be no half-heartedness or premature action. All men must clearly understand the orders and drill for opening fire:—

(a) The principle to be observed when springing an ambush is that fire should not be opened so long as CT are moving towards someone in a better position to kill. A limited ambush will normally be sprung by the commander.

(b) Should any CT act as though he has spotted the ambush, any man who sees this should spring the ambush.

(c) All shots must be aimed to kill. Once fire has been opened targets become more difficult and to cope with moving targets men may have to stand up.

(d) A signal must be arranged to stop firing, so that immediate follow up action and search can start as soon as CT become impossible to engage.

(e) When the ambush has been sprung men who have been previously detailed will search the immediate area under cover of ambush weapons and covering each other. They will:—

   (i) check CT in the killing area and secure any who are still living.
   (ii) search surrounding area for dead and wounded.
   (iii) collect arms, ammunition and equipment.

10. A definite signal for calling off the ambush must be arranged. This is particularly important in area ambushes and night ambushes in order to avoid groups running into other ambush parties. No movement to contact an ambush *in situ* should ever take place in darkness.

11. **Rendezvous.**— An easily found RV must be selected at which troops will rally at the end of an action on the receipt of the prearranged signal. This item cannot be stressed too strongly as several officers and men have been killed when returning to collect a man left in ambush.

Section 5.—PREVENTION OF ACCIDENTS

1. Cases have occurred where soldiers and police are shot by parties of SF which are waiting to ambush the CT on information.

2. The primary cause is that the ambush party is keyed up to expect the arrival of the CT in the area of the ambush and on seeing any movement fire is opened. The conditions are such that it is not possible for them to recognise the identity of the people fired at.

3. Once an ambush has been set there should be no movement of any kind by our own forces anywhere near the ambush position, unless it is essential.

4. Where it is essential for such movement to take place it must be very carefully planned and rehearsed. In all other cases once clearance has been given for the ambush to take place no movement of any kind is to be allowed.

5. It is important to ensure that fire discipline is observed in ambush operations in close country as in any other form of operations.

Section 6.—GENERAL

1. **Training.**— As ambushing is a most successful means of killing CT, time must be given to training for it. This is particularly important for group leaders. Training must be aimed at eliminating common faults and improving technique. Its objects are to:—

   (a) Achieve silence and stillness in ambush.

   (b) Train troops to occupy ambush positions without advertising their presence by smells (curry, chewing gum, cigarettes), by paper scraps, crushed vegetation, and foot prints.

   (c) Ensure good siting of weapons, and positioning of commanders.

   (d) Improve fire control and particularly the even distribution of fire.

   (e) Practise clear, well understood drills for springing ambushes, follow and search.

   (f) Ensure accurate shooting at difficult moving targets.

   (g) Improve care of weapons and eliminate stoppages.

2. **Tracker Groups and Patrol Dogs.**— A great many CT, wounded in ambush, get away. In many cases they probably escape by rushing into the undergrowth and laying low until the hue and cry has died down and they can crawl away. The employment of tracker groups, full details of which are given in Chapter XXI, will quite often lead to their capture or elimination.

3. Experience has shown that the blood trail left by wounded CT is not always an aid to a tracker dog, and is sometimes more useful as a visual aid to the human tracker.

4. The tracker group should not form part of the ambush party, but should stand by at some convenient RV ready to move when shooting announces that the ambush has been sprung.

5. Under certain circumstances patrol dogs may form part of the ambush group. They may be most profitably employed where several alternative routes lead into the ambush position and it is not known which route the CT will take. It must be borne in mind, however, that their presence may give the ambush position away to the CT as they pant, make other noises and are smelly. However when used they will invariably be alert before any human being.

6. **Administration—Long Term Ambushes.**— Eighty per cent. of ambushes are sprung within nine hours of setting and require no administration other than arrangements for rest within groups. These are called short term ambushes and are the normal ambush.

7. Where ambushes are set for periods of more than twelve hours they become long term ambushes and administrative arrangements for relief of groups for feeding and sleeping are necessary. Such an ambush may be placed on the approaches to a cultivation area which is ready for harvesting, or on the approaches to a known CT camp.

8. In long term ambushes an administrative area must be set up. It should be sited at least 500 yards from the ambush position, far enough to avoid noises and smells disclosing the presence of troops. Communication lines may have to be cleared and swept to enable silent reliefs to be carried out. Water should be available.

9. Careful consideration must be given to the problem of reliefs, particularly in the case of the area ambush. Normally the relief will come from the administrative area along the communication lines. Although the whole party in the ambush will eventually be relieved, only one fire position should be changed at a time in case CT come during this period. The reliefs should take place when no CT movement is expected.

10. The ideal is that ambushes should be divided into three parties, one in the ambush position, the reserve, and the party at rest. On relief the party at rest takes over the ambush position; the men in the position go to the reserve; and reserve goes to the rest area.

11. If the party is less than six and the duration of the ambush long, the whole party should be withdrawn during set periods to rest. Such a party would be responsible for its own security when resting.

12. When an ambush party is over six, but not large enough to carry out the three group method, sufficient men for all round observation should man the ambush. The others move away from the ambush position, post sentries and rest. The party at rest will act as reserve and will not, therefore, go far away. It will not be able to smoke and its food will be pre-cooked.

Section 7.—AMBUSH BY NIGHT

1. **General.**— The doctrine for day ambush also applies to night ambush. In darkness concealment is easy, but shooting is obviously less accurate. Much therefore depends on good siting of weapons so that the killing ground is interlaced with fire.

2. **Factors.**— The following factors apply to night ambushes:—
   (a) The shotgun will be the primary weapon used in night ambush.
   (b) The remaining ambush weapons should contain a high proportion of automatics. The M1/M2 carbine is not a good weapon for ambush parties since, owing to its poor stopping power they are unlikely to kill first shot.
   (c) In darkness all weapons, particularly LMGs firing down tracks, should have their left and right arcs of fire fixed by means of sticks to eliminate danger to own troops.
   (d) The ambush party must never move about. Any movement will be regarded as CT.
   (e) Clear orders, precise fire control instructions, clear RVs and signals are essential.
   (f) Men and groups will be sited closer together than by day. Control at night is all important.
   (g) It is difficult to take up an ambush position at night. where possible, therefore, it should be occupied before last light.

3. **Night Illumination Aids.**— More often than not a night ambush will depend on artificial illumination. Only in open country with a bright moon and no chance of cloud is it possible to rely on an unilluminated ambush. As a general rule all night ambushes should be provided with artificial illumination in some form. When ground marker flares are used, care should be taken to site them so that the ambush party suffers from a minimum of glare. A variety of night shooting aids are available, details of which are shown below.

   (a) *RAF Ground Marker Flare.*
       (Flares ground, illuminating No. 1 Mk 1 Yellow).
       (i) A light metal tube containing an illuminating chemical with a burning period of approximately 3 minutes. The tube is fitted with a metal spike and can be fixed to the trunk of a tree or spiked into the ground.
       (ii) In use the flare is generally initiated by means of a No. 33 electric detonator connected to a No. 68 WS battery. This entails a modification of the basic flare.
       (iii) The flare is used to illuminate the entire area of the killing ground and to canalize CT movement into SF killing grounds and away from likely escape routes.

(iv) In order to minimise glare and smoke the flare should be either suspended from or stuck into a tree some 6 feet from the ground, away from the direct line of sight of the ambush party.
(v) This flare, is the most satisfactory device yet produced for night illumination in support of ambushes.

(b) *Trip Flares.*
   (i) Used either in their normal role and designed to be sprung by the CT or mounted on a board and detonated electrically by a member of the ambush party.
   (ii) When used in the latter role they consist of three flares mounted on a board and detonated by a No. 33 electric detonator wired to a torch exploder.
   (iii) The tactical siting and use of this device is similar to the RAF ground marker flare.
   (iv) The period of illumination is up to approximately 50 seconds and the light provided is somewhat whiter and harsher than the RAF ground marker flare.

(c) *Torch Attachments.*
   (Bren, Owen and Patchett Rifle (FN))
   (i) Consist of torches with clip attachments for the weapons concerned.
   (ii) The beam of the torch is zeroed to coincide with the MPI of the shots at 20 yards.
   (iii) The switch for the torch is positioned so that the torch can be switched on and fire opened immediately.
   (iv) The maximum range up to which effective fire can be applied is approximately 50 yards.

(d) *2-in. Mortar Illuminating Flares.*
   (i) Can be fired from the flank of an ambush when terrain and vegetation permit.
   (ii) Are unsuitable for ambushes laid inside the jungle fringe.

(e) *Verey Pistol Flares (Cartridges Illuminating 1 inch).*
   Can be fired from within the ambush position when vegetation permits.

4. **Grenade Necklace.**—A useful ambush aid is a grenade "necklace." This consists basically of a series of No. 36 Grenades, with the striker mechanism and base plug removed, connected at approximately 12-foot intervals by a length of Cordtex. The whole is detonated electrically.

5. Possible uses in ambush of this device are:—
   (a) Laid as a stop along likely CT lines of retreat from an ambush killing ground.
   (b) Laid in dead ground difficult to cover by the weapons of the ambush group.
   (c) Laid in the likely halting place of the main body of a food collecting party, (usually a tactical bound in rear of the food dump).

6. When used, members of the ambush party should be protected from, or outside the lethal area of the grenades.

Section 8.—WISDOM IN RETROSPECT

1. The following are some reasons for failure which have been reported by ambush commanders. These may help in the training for and mounting of future ambushes:—
   (a) 'Disclosure of the ambush by the noise made by cooking weapons and moving safety catches or change levers.' Check your weapons, practise men in their silent handling and ensure that all weapons are ready to fire.
   (b) 'There was a tendency to shoot high at the light face of the terrorist.' This must be corrected on the jungle range.
   (c) 'Disclosure of the ambush position by foot prints made by the ambush party moving into position and by movement of individuals at the crucial time, when the CT were approaching.'
   (d) 'There was a lack of fire control and commanders were unable to stop the firing and start the immediate follow up.'
   (e) 'Commanders were badly sited with consequent lack of control.'
   (f) 'There was a lack of all round observation resulting in CT arriving in the area of an ambush unannounced.'
   (g) 'There were misfires and stoppages through failure to clean, inspect and test weapons and magazine.'
   (h) 'There was a lack of a clearly defined drill for opening fire and orders were contradictory.'
   (i) 'There was a tendency for all to select and fire at the same target.'
   (j) 'Fire was opened prematurely.'

Appendix A

AMBUSH ORDERS—AIDE MEMOIRE

REMEMBER SECURITY—DO NOT USE THE TELEPHONE. DO NOT ALLOW MEN OUT AFTER BRIEFING

Suggested Headings

1. **Situation**

    (a) *Topography.*—Use of air Photographs, maps and local knowledge consider use of a guide.

    (b) *CT.*—
    - (1) Expected strength.
    - (2) Names and anticipated order of march. Photographs.
    - (3) Dress and weapons of individuals.
    - (4) Which is the VIP.
    - (5) What are habits of party concerned.

    (c) *SF.*—
    - (1) Guides or SEP to accompany.
    - (2) What other SF are doing.

    (d) *Clearance.*—
    - (1) Challenge.
    - (2) Password.
    - (3) Identifications.

    (e) *Civilians.*—
    - (1) Locations.
    - (2) Habits.

2. **Mission**

    This must be clear in the mind of every man especially when a particular CT is to be killed.

3. **Execution**

    (a) Type of layout.
    (b) Position and direction of fire of groups.
    (c) Dispersal point.
    (d) Weapons to be carried.
    (e) Composition of groups.
    (f) Timings and routes.
    (g) Formations during move in.
    (h) Orders re springing.

Appendix A—*Continued*

    (j) Distribution of fire.
    (k) Use of grenades.
    (l) Action on ambush being discovered.
    (m) Order to cease firing.
    (n) Orders re immediate follow up.
    (o) Orders for search.
    (p) Deliberate follow up.
    (q) Signal to call off ambush.
    (r) Rendezvous.
    (s) Dogs—if any.
    (t) Deception plan.
    (u) Alerting.

4. **Administration and Logistics**
   (a) Use of transport to area.
   (b) Equipment and dress:—
          Footwear for move in
   (c) Rations—if any.
   (d) Special equipment:—
       (1) Night lighting equipment.
       (2) Cameras.
       (3) Finger print equipment.
   (e) Medical:—
       (1) First field dressing, first aid packs.
       (2) Medical Orderly.
       (3) Stretcher and ambulance.
   (f) Reliefs.
   (g) Administrative Area, if required orders re cooking, smoking
   (h) Transport for return journey.
   (j) Inspection of personnel and equipment:—
       (1) Men with colds not to be taken.
       (2) Is zeroing of weapons correct?
       (3) Is ammunition fresh?
       (4) Are magazines properly filled?

5. **Command and Signals**
   Success signal.

CHAPTER XII

THE LOCATION AND ATTACKING OF CT IN CAMPS AND CULTIVATIONS

Section 1.—INTRODUCTION

1. The action taken when a CT camp is unexpectedly encountered (the CT sentry firing) is described in Chapter X and it will be appreciated that the Immediate Assault is the only answer under those circumstances. However, it has been proved over a period of years that such an attack seldom succeeds in killing many CT in the camp because they make good their escape immediately after the CT sentry fires the first shot.

2. The deliberate method described in this Chapter will result, if carried out successfully, in the extermination or capture of every CT in a camp or cultivation. To ensure success it requires both training and rehearsal.

3. As already laid down (D of Ops. Instr. No. 14, paras 5 and 6), under conditions which are favourable to their use, priority will be given to the use of strike aircraft on located occupied CT camps. The decision whether the camp will be attacked by either air strike or by ground forces will normally be dependent on the following factors: —
 (a) Length of time that the camp is likely to be occupied.
 (b) The proximity of the camp to habitations.
 (c) The immediate and potential resources available to the ground force commander.
 (d) The accuracy with which the camp has been pin-pointed.

This decision will usually be taken at bn or coy level, when the camp is located by ground reconnaissance.

4. Attacks on CT camps located as the result of information will quite frequently be done by strike aircraft, particularly in cases where the information indicates that the camp is likely to remain occupied for some time. It is unlikely however that the information will be sufficiently precise for the camp to be pin-pointed exactly and reconnaissance patrols may still have to be sent out in order to determine its exact location. The patrol will quite often be accompanied by the SEP, CEP or other person providing the information. The procedure to be followed in these circumstances will be as set out in Chapter VII (Patrolling) and in Section 3 of this Chapter.

5. The succeeding paragraphs, however, deal with the deliberate attack by ground troops where neither bombing nor artillery fire are to be employed, and although for simplicity, it refers only to camps, the method of attacking a CT cultivation is the same.

Section 2.—SIGNS OF CT

1. CT disclose their presence by tracks, marks on the ground and noise. It is therefore essential that every man should be able to recognise the marks of the passage of CT, even when made by only one or two. CT seldom use permanent tracks. Some men will be better than others at tracking, but all can, with training spot the more obvious signs of CT passage, e.g. disturbed vegetation, footprints in soft ground and the marks of a water point on a stream bank.

2. Noise is an important factor in locating CT. Men patrolling must listen carefully all the time. CT do make a noise. They use wood for cooking and their biggest give away is the noise of chopping. They also cough, talk and rattle tins like any other human beings.

3. Full details of tracking technique and the employment of tracker teams are contained in Chapter XXI.

Section 3.—THE SEARCH

1. A great deal of tactical skill and patience are necessary to discover CT in their camp. This is done, as in other theatres, when exact locations are not known, by reconnaissance patrols.

2. Although the suspected area of a camp may be known, only by careful and often prolonged searching of the area will the camp be located on the ground. At the same time a force must be at hand to take immediate action on receipt of information from reconnaissance patrols.

3. A company is the ideal size of force for this type of operation, though the task can on occasions be undertaken by as few as thirty to forty men.

4. Once the force has moved into the suspected area, the commander sends out reconnaissance patrols in the direction in which he judges the camp to be. The paths of these patrols radiate from their base like the ribs of a fan, on compass bearings at intervals of 10 degrees. There may be as many as eight or nine patrols. There will seldom be less than five.

5. Each patrol consists of three or, at most, four men. The men wear no equipment and carry no rations. They carry only their

weapons, ammunition, maps and compasses. They search silently and must remain alert all the time. The lightness of their equipment tends to limit their radius of action but is basic to this method of working. The whole search may take days or even weeks, yet men patrolling must remain as fresh and alert as possible. Even lightly equipped, the task is an exhausting one. Each patrol must therefore be out for limited periods only and must be changed frequently.

6. The distance that reconnaissance patrols move away from base may vary but, as a rough guide, they can be told to move out for approximately two to three hours. They then return on the back bearing of their outward route.

7. The reconnaissance patrols move slowly and silently, pausing frequently to listen. On their skill depends the success of the operation. If and when they find traces of CT they must try to establish what the commander wants to know: —

    (a) How many CT were there.
    (b) How old are the signs.
    (c) Where are the signs.
    (d) In what direction were the CT moving.

8. Having found traces of CT and the answers to these questions, the patrol should return immediately to base. It is unwise to be dogmatic about this but, if CT are close at hand the company commander must be informed and must direct all future action. An unwise move by a junior leader may disclose the presence of the attacking force. Above all, a reconnaissance patrol must never move along the track it has discovered.

9. Now it is the job of the company commander to conduct further searches. He will often himself cast forward, accompanied by two or three men, in the direction taken by the CT, or towards the noise. Listening becomes vitally important, since noise may disclose the CT camp, if it is near.

10. The search does not always follow this pattern. It is possible that a reconnaissance patrol may return having actually located the camp. In any event, once the camp is located, the next step is for the company commander to make his plan.

11. Ideally, the Company Commander and his 'O' Group should view the camp, guided if possible by the patrol commander who found it.

12. The extent to which the Company Commander can show his 'O' Group the actual camp and his decision whether to do so or not must depend on a variety of factors, the most important of which are:—

(a) Risk of compromise to security due to the danger of the SF party being seen or heard by the camp sentry(ies) or by CT returning to the camp.
(b) Danger of making fresh tracks and thereby disclosing the presence of SF.
(c) Time that would be taken by further reconnaissance and likelihood of camp being evacuated before an attack can be mounted.
(d) Weather conditions prevailing (heavy rain would screen the movement of the SF party).
(e) Siting of the CT camp.

Section 4.—THE ATTACK

1. Meanwhile, the main body should have been moved up to a position of readiness for the attack. The movement of troops into position demands extreme stealth; all equipment and packs should be dumped and, in the final phase, men should carry only their weapons and ammunition.

2. The attacking force will be divided into:—

(a) An assault party.
(b) A cut-off party.

3. The task of the assault party is to flush the CT. This party can normally be small, as the usual reaction of CT is to flee in all directions when attacked. However, where a camp is equipped with prepared defences, a larger party, organized as for a set piece attack, may be necessary. The bulk of the force will form the cut-off party or cordon, which must be complete and as close to the camp as possible, in order to catch the CT as they scatter.

4. By virtue of previous training and rehearsal, the commander should be able to limit his orders to the:—

(a) composition of the assault party.
(b) arcs of responsibility of sub-units in the cut-off party.

He will, if possible, give these to the 'O' Group during reconnaissance. However, if it has not been possible to indicate arcs, it may be necessary to move the cut-off party in one line to their positions about 100 yards distant from the camp perimeter.

They will then crawl silently forward to their action stations. At least an hour must be allowed for this difficult final move.

5. Commanders must devise and practice their own drill for encircling camps. Most prefer to indicate arcs and move their cut-off party into position from opposite sides of the camp; others prefer to move in on a succession of compass bearings from a selected point. Where the camp is in a clearing, the light filtering through the trees may be used as an aid, men keeping it just visible on their flank as they move into position. Sometimes noise from the camp will help. The encircling of the camp is the crucial manoeuvre and must be carried out with the greatest patience and stealth.

6. Experience has shown that unless an occupied CT camp is completely surrounded the attack is often abortive and the majority of CTs escape. The assault must be timed to start when the cordon is complete. The assault party moves into the camp picking its targets and opening fire as it does so. As soon as fire is opened the men in the cut-off party assume the best possible fire positions and wait for targets to present themselves. There must be NO indiscriminate firing and NO movement out of their positions. If this order is observed, the cordon remains complete and the risk of accidental shooting of our own troops is negligible.

7. All men must be briefed that, if they are seen while moving into position or if it is obvious that CT are trying to escape, any group may open fire. In that event all men double to their allotted positions.

Section 5.—GENERAL POINTS

1. When a patrol returns with information of a track, the Company Commander should normally wait for the remaining patrols to come back. If one has information of a track, another may have discovered the camp.

2. The Commander must know the limitations of his troops. If their jungle craft is weak, he may have to limit his reconnaissance of the camp, not risking too close a move before his cordon is in position.

3. Reconnaissance patrols must be permitted to shoot if they are actually seen by CT or fire is opened on them.

4. This method demands high standards of jungle craft and self-reliance, which can only be achieved and maintained by training and rehearsal.

5. The detailed procedure to be followed for an attack by strike aircraft on to an occupied camp is contained in Chapter XVII.

CHAPTER XIII

MOVEMENT BY ROAD

Section 1.—INTRODUCTION

1. SF must constantly use the roads in Malaya and the danger of ambush by CT is ever present. The risk of such ambush varies in different parts of the country and for this reason a system of road classification has been evolved. This system is dealt with in detail elsewhere in this Chapter.

2. It is the duty of all commanders to keep the problem of counter ambush action constantly in mind and to keep themselves informed as to CT tactics and activity in any particular area.

3. It is also extremely important that troops appreciate the problem, take precautions against ambush, and are prepared for immediate offensive action should the need arise.

4. This Chapter deals with movement by road as it affects sub-units of the infantry battalion and sets out measures which can be taken to counter any attempt by the CT to ambush military vehicles. It should be noted that these principles apply to units of other arms. In considering these measures two main principles should be borne in mind:—

   (a) An ambush is a contact with CT and by offensive retaliatory action the opportunity must be taken to inflict the maximum casualties on them.
   (b) The primary object of the CT in staging an ambush is to gain arms and ammunition and every effort must be made to prevent this equipment falling into their hands.

Section 2.—THE PROBLEM

1. The following paragraphs deal with the 'why, where and how' of CT action in laying a road ambush.

2. The aim of the CT in ambushing vehicles can be summarized in the following order of priority:—

   (a) To obtain arms and ammunition, without which they cannot continue their campaign.
   (b) To inflict casualties on the SF with the minimum risk to themselves.

(c) As part of a deception plan to draw off SF from another area.

(d) To demonstrate to the local population the CT freedom of initiative and potential striking power.

(e) As a quick and easy method of 'blooding' new recruits to their organization.

3. It will be appreciated from the above that military and police vehicles are the most likely target for road ambushes and incidents have been reported in which CT have allowed civilian vehicles to pass an ambush position and then opened fire on the first military vehicle to appear. This is not to say that CT never fire at civilian vehicles, but these are obviously less attractive targets.

4. The CT has no difficulty in finding good ambush positions as most roads run through country offering covered lines of approach and withdrawal and affording covered positions from which to fire on road transport. The CT therefore tend to select that part of a road where it is easy to place a road block or where vehicles have to move slowly, such as a climb into a cutting, a sharp bend or a climbing turn.

5. The CT are willing to accept the risk of remaining concentrated for up to three days. However, they prefer to carry out an ambush on a road where a target can be expected to appear fairly quickly.

6. There is ample evidence to show that the CT plan and execute a road ambush with very great care. They gather information from all sources, choose the ground very carefully, make a detailed plan—and often rehearse it—and altogether organize their forces in a workmanlike manner. The points in the succeeding paragraphs should therefore be noted carefully.

7. An ambush position may be sited on one side of a road or on both and may be up to 400 yards or more in length. Cuttings and embankments on the side of the road are obviously first choices.

8. A CT unit carrying out an ambush will usually be organized into a number of groups each having a special function. Thus there may be:—

(a) *Firing Group*.—Their task is to bring concentrated fire to bear on the vehicle or vehicles selected as the target and to wipe out opposition quickly.

(b) *Assault Group*.—Their task is to advance, probably under cover of fire from the Firing Group, to finish off survivors.

(c) *Follow Up Group*.—They seize arms and ammunition and carry them away without waiting to see the final outcome of the engagement.

(d) *Protection Group*.—In addition there may well be protection and/or warning groups and there are always scouts and look-out men. Where CT plan to use a road block look-out men are posted from half to one mile up and down the road.

9. A great deal of care is usually apparent in the preparation of the actual ambush positions which will be dug in if there is no other means of protection from fire. Individual positions will be well concealed and fire lanes and escape tracks may be cut. The main body of the ambushing party will usually be deployed along the length of the ambush position in groups of various sizes according to the organization (as mentioned above), the nature of the ground and the kind of convoy being ambushed.

10. The CT use the bren, sten, carbine, rifle, shotgun and grenade. They may be dressed in uniform, in civilian clothes or in a mixture of both; or even as police or soldiers.

11. The CT will employ various methods to block the road. Thus he may mine the road with explosive to disable the first vehicle of a convoy, fell a tree or use a civilian vehicle. On an estate road he can also make a crater to hold up movement.

12. While CT normally carry out ambushes by day, they are prepared to lay them at night when they can deploy greater fire power because of less difficulty of concealment. These ambushes may take the form of:—

(a) Fairly heavy sniping at odd vehicles, on a particular section of road.

(b) The deliberate ambush of a convoy based on information.

(c) The deliberate ambush of any SF vehicle using a particular section of road on a certain day.

13. As stated in the introduction to this Chapter CT will often stage an ambush as part of a deception plan. Thus they will frequently create a minor incident in order to bring the SF out in transport through an area in which a deliberate ambush has been laid. They try many tricks to conceal their intentions and numbers. For example three CT stop a civilian vehicle, take identity cards and a few odds and ends from the occupants and send them on their way to report the incident to the police or military. A small patrol on its way to investigate in one or two vehicles may later be ambushed by 20 or 30 CT in the area of the first incident, or on the way to it.

Section 3.—COUNTERING THE PROBLEM

This is considered in two parts:—
(a) Precautionary measures to reduce the chances of being ambushed and to ensure instant readiness for action.
(b) Action on Contact. Immediate action drills designed to gain the initiative by offensive action.

Section 4.—PRECAUTIONARY MEASURES

1. **The Military Classification of Roads.**— Roads in Malaya are classified in three main categories for military purposes. This classification is based on the estimated risk of CT action in the area concerned. The road categories are:—
   (a) UNRESTRICTED.
   (b) WHITE.
   (c) BLACK.

2. UNRESTRICTED roads are those which lie within the Town Board limits of major towns and other roads as decided by the responsible headquarters. Subject to any particular restrictions which local commanders may wish to impose, military personnel are permitted to travel on these roads unarmed, in uniform or civilian clothes, and in any type of vehicle.

3. WHITE roads are those upon which there is considered to be only a very limited risk of CT ambush activity. Nearly all of the main trunk roads in Malaya come under this category. The following regulations apply to the movement of military personnel on WHITE roads:—
   (a) All ranks travelling in military or police vehicles will be armed.
   (b) Vehicles may move singly but every military vehicle will carry one armed man in addition to the driver.
   (c) Military personnel may travel alone in civilian cars whether in uniform or plain clothes but must be armed when travelling on duty.
   (d) Single and unaccompanied motor cyclists on WD machines are NOT permitted.

4. BLACK roads are those roads which are not classified as UNRESTRICTED or WHITE. The rules governing the movement of military personnel and vehicles on such roads are as follows:—
   (a) All ranks will be armed when travelling on duty irrespective of the type of vehicle being used.

(b) Travel at night (1900 to 0630 hours) will be restricted to cases of operational necessity.

(c) Movement of single military 'soft' vehicles is NOT permitted and the minimum combination of military vehicles will be—two soft—one armoured and one soft—or—one armoured.

(d) Every Military vehicle will carry one armed man in addition to the driver.

(e) All ranks when not on duty and travelling in civilian clothes in a civilian vehicle may travel unarmed.

5. If considered necessary BLACK roads may be divided into sub-categories by the Formation HQ responsible for the area concerned and additional precautions to be taken on certain sections of road may be laid down at the same time.

6. Detailed instructions on the road classification scheme and a list of UNRESTRICTED and WHITE roads in Malaya are given in appropriate Standing Operation Instructions.

7. **Movement of Military Convoys.**— For the purposes of these instructions a convoy is defined as a group of two or more vehicles.

8. There are no special regulations concerning the movement of military convoys on UNRESTRICTED roads.

9. **On WHITE roads:—**

(a) An armoured vehicle as escort is not considered essential.

(b) Convoys of up to 10 vehicles will move at normal density (i.e. 20 or 30 vtm.) and in blocks of not more than 5/6 vehicles.

(c) Non-operational convoys of more than 10 vehicles (i.e. from units not in the combatant arms) will NOT move without the authority of the Formation HQ concerned who will make special arrangements for escort if it is considered necessary. All convoys of more than 10 vehicles will also move in blocks as in (b) above.

10. **On BLACK roads:—**

(a) Troop convoys of operational units will be primarily responsible for their own protection but the fullest use will be made of armoured vehicles as escort according to availability.

(b) Groups of non-operational vehicles such as RASC supply convoys will be escorted by armoured vehicles whenever possible. The scale of escort for such convoys should be one armoured vehicle to every five soft vehicles.

(c) Soft vehicles will move a tactical bound behind each other, i.e. approximately 150 yards apart, depending on the type of country. Armoured escort vehicles will move within this overall density so as to position themselves where they are best able to give protection.

(d) Non-operational convoys will not be moved without the authority of the Formation responsible for the area concerned who will ensure that adequate arrangements are made for escorts.

11. Particular attention is directed to the convoy density on BLACK roads as given at para 10(c) above, which will also be applicable to groups of less than 5/6 vehicles. On this type of road it is important that vehicles move sufficiently close to each other to be able to render mutual assistance in case of emergency but not so close that an ambush is likely to catch several vehicles. Thus if two vehicles are moving very close CT fire will bear on them both and neutralize offensive action from either. If, however, the second vehicle is further back its occupants may be able to debus unmolested and take rapid organized offensive action.

12. **Unit Standing Orders for Convoys.**— Every unit should have comprehensive orders covering movement by road based on the classification system described above. These orders should state clearly who is authorised to put a convoy on the road and should cover in detail the following points:—

(a) The appointment and duties of convoy and vehicle commanders.
(b) The organisation of the convoy.
(c) The weapons and ammunition to be carried. Automatic weapons should be included.
(d) The state of vehicles, e.g. detailed instructions regarding canopies, tailboards and windscreens.
(e) IA Drills.
(f) Security measures.

13. **Security.**— The CT intelligence system is carefully and widely organised and is very effective. It is essential, therefore, that the movement of convoys should never become a routine matter and that the maximum precautions are taken to prevent the CT gaining advance information of vehicle movement. In this connection it should be remembered that:—

(a) The telephone system in Malaya is not secure.

(b) Wireless messages in clear can be picked up on an ordinary civilian type receiver.

(c) The loyalty of civilian employees cannot be guaranteed, although they are subjected to screening.

(d) Troops tend to be talkative both inside and outside their lines.

In short, the fewer people who know about the timing, route and composition of a convoy before it sets out the better. Generally speaking, therefore, drivers and escorts should be warned as late as is possible and the use of alternative routes and other deception measures should not be overlooked.

14. **The Convoy Commander.—** A commander must be detailed for every convoy of vehicles moving by road. This will not necessarily be the senior officer or NCO travelling. The convoy commander will position himself where, according to the circumstances, he can best control the convoy. This will not necessarily be in the first or last vehicle.

15. **Briefing.—** Briefing by the covoy commander before moving off must be detailed and explicit. All drivers, vehicle commanders and if possible all men travelling in the convoy should be present at the briefing. Briefing should include:—

(a) Details of timings, route, speed, order of march, maintenance of contact and action to be taken if contact is broken.

(b) The distribution of men to vehicles.

(c) The distribution of all weapons.

(d) The appointment and duties of vehicle commanders and sentries.

(e) The action to be taken in the event of CT attack.

16. **Alertness.—** It must be impressed upon all ranks that a high degree of alertness is essential when moving along routes likely to be ambushed by the CT. Experience has shown that the idea of having different scales of alertness for different categories of road under the military classification scheme is not practicable. The policy will be, therefore, that on all roads other than those classified UNRESTRICTED the maximum degree of alertness will be maintained and EVERY MAN IN THE CONVOY MUST BE READY FOR INSTANT ACTION AT ALL TIMES.

17. **The preparation and loading of personnel carrying vehicles.**— Men travelling in a vehicle must be able to see all round them, fire their weapons or throw grenades without hindrance and debus in quick time—all with the minimum restriction of movement. For this reason the following points should be noted:—

(a) One ton or 3-ton vehicles should have canopies and canopy framework removed and tailboards down. Alternatively canopies can be rolled up to give overhead cover only but it should be remembered that the canopy framework does restrict the traversing of weapons, throwing of grenades or quick debussing over the sides of a vehicle.

(b) 14/15 is the maximum number of men which can be carried safely in the back of a 3-ton vehicle. If more than this number is carried men will be unable to use their arms effectively and in a sudden emergency are quite likely to become difficult for their vehicle commander to control. Similarly the number of men carried in other types of vehicle must be restricted to ensure freedom of movement.

18. **Vehicle Commanders.**— A commander must be detailed by name for each vehicle. His duties will be to ensure that all personnel in his vehicle are constantly on the alert and to assist in maintaining convoy formation by controlling the driver. The primary task of the vehicle commander is to command the troops in his vehicle should the convoy be ambushed and he must therefore travel in the back of the vehicle with the troops.

19. **Lookout Men.**— Although there is only one scale of alertness and all personnel travelling in a vehicle must be constantly on the alert and prepared for immediate action, it is obviously not practicable and is an unnecessary strain for everyone in a troop carrying vehicle to be scanning the road the whole time during a journey. In troop carrying vehicles, therefore, four men should be posted as sentries or look-out men. These men should be posted two at the front and two at the rear with arcs of observation covering the 90 degrees from the centre of the road to the side in each direction. Where possible these sentries should be armed with automatic weapons and grenades. In the event of an ambush it will be their duty to cover with fire from their positions the evacuation of the vehicle should this be necessary. They can also assist in the control of the convoy by informing the vehicle commander if the next following vehicle halts or drops back.

20. **Platoon weapons.**—LMGs, GF (EY) rifles and 2-in. mortars should be distributed throughout the length of a convoy. Detailed points to be considered in connection with these weapons are:—

 (a) *LMGs*.—The provision of an improvised mounting is recommended provided that this is so constructed that the gun can be taken off quickly. The Bren LMG on its bipod perched on the top of the cab of a vehicle is in a very insecure position and the gunner is very liable to be jolted off his feet should the vehicle swerve suddenly or the driver brake unexpectedly.

 (b) *2-in. Mortar*.—This weapon is rarely carried on patrol but can be carried easily in a vehicle and fired from it. Generally, there is overhead clearance along a road and a mortar can easily be brought into action from the roadside whilst troops move round a flank or the rear of the CT position.

 (c) *GF (EY) Rifle*.—This can be used in the same way as the mortar, firing '36' or '80' grenades.

21. **Smoke.**—The No. 80 Phosphorus Smoke Grenade, beside producing an immediate effective smoke screen, can inflict painful phosphorous burns and can be more useful as an anti-ambush weapon than the '36' grenade.

22. **The Scout Car.**—Two types of Scout car are on issue to units—the Ferret and the Daimler. Both vehicles have similar general characteristics although a different type of armament is carried. The principles governing the use are, however, the same

 (a) *Role*.—Scout cars are issued for use as convoy escort vehicles or as Commanding Officers' or Company Commanders' vehicles. In the latter role they provide an efficient and safe means of transport for commanders, and officers should regard them as personal chargers and interest themselves in their maintenance and appearance.

 (b) *Close Escorts*.—When small groups of vehicles move on BLACK roads the scout car should be posted centrally in the convoy. It has been found from experience that a vehicle posted at the front or rear of a convoy in these circumstances may be prevented from moving into the ambush area by other vehicles which have been halted or by dead or wounded lying on the road.

 (c) *Convoy Escorts*.—When large convoys move on main roads vehicles should be divided into blocks of about 5/6 and when sufficient scout cars are available one should be placed at the rear of each block. The reasons for this are:—

(i) Although the LMG mounting has a 360 degree traverse it is awkward for the firer to position himself in the vehicle so that he can fire accurately to the rear.

(ii) The particular role of the scout car in an ambush is to drive into it giving immediate fire support to those vehicles which are being attacked. Reversing or turning is a difficult and dangerous operation under fire and causes delay. Thus if the scout car is at the rear of a block of vehicles it can always move ahead and bring fire to bear forwards.

23. **Other Armoured Vehicles.**— Semi-armoured Vehicles. These are 1-ton or 3-ton GS vehicles which have been fitted with armoured cabs.

24. Armoured troop/load carriers 3-ton. These vehicles are issued on a scale of 6 per British/Gurkha infantry battalion and 5 to others. They are fully armoured and are capable of carrying ten equipped men or a maximum of 30 cwts. of stores and weapons, including the Bren LMG and GF rifle which can be fired easily through the ports. In view of their weight care must be taken when using estate roads and bridges.

25. **Convoy Control—Wireless..**— The WS No. 19 is always fitted in the scout car. The WS No. 88 can well be used as a link with the scout car and between other vehicles in a convoy. It must be remembered that in any ambush there will come a time when the CT will break off and retreat into the jungle. Personnel of the convoy may not themselves be able to follow up the CT and a quick wireless message to unit headquarters could well bring a follow-up party to the scene before the CT have moved far—or in some cases have moved at all.

26. **Precautionary Tactics.**— In some areas it may well be advisable for troops moving by road to stop and debus before approaching a likely ambush area in their vehicles and then to move forward on foot to clear the jungle on either side of the road. It is unlikely that such tactics will find the CT in position as they will probably move as soon as they see the troops moving towards them. Nevertheless, the very fact that troops are prone to get out of their vehicles and examine likely ambush positions on foot will become known to the local CT who will be less confident that they are going to secure easy victims without danger to themselves.

Section 5.—ACTION ON CONTACT

1. **Introduction.**—Whatever precautions are taken and preparations are made, the ambush when it is sprung, will always be an unexpected encounter. IA Drills are simple courses of action designed to deal with the problem of the unexpected encounter. They aim at IMMEDIATE, POSITIVE and OFFENSIVE action.

2. The CT springs his ambush on ground that he has carefully chosen and converted into a position from which he can kill SF by firing at them from above often at point blank range. The principle behind the IA Drill dealt with in this Section is that it is incorrect to halt in the area which the CT have chosen as a killing ground and so covered by fire—unless one is forced to do so. The drill, therefore, is to endeavour to drive on when fired upon, to halt only when through the ambush area or before running into it, and to counter attack immediately from flank and rear.

3. **Immediate Action Technique.**—The Danger Zone is the area in which effective CT fire can be brought to bear. In order that the CT may not have the advantage of operating on ground of their own choosing every effort must be made to get vehicles clear of the DANGER ZONE. Thus, when vehicles are fired upon:—

   (a) Drivers will NOT stop but will attempt to drive on out of the danger zone.
   (b) Look-out men/sentries will fire immediately to keep the CT heads down.
   (c) When vehicles are clear of the danger zone they will be stopped to allow their occupants to debus and carry out offensive action.
   (d) Following vehicles approaching the danger zone will NOT attempt to run the gauntlet of the ambush but will halt clear of the area, to allow their occupants to take offensive action.

4. Vehicles forced to halt in the danger zone. Where vehicles have not been able to drive clear of the area under fire, troops will debus under the covering fire of the look-out men, which should include smoke if possible, and will make for cover on the side of the road. The actual 'baling out drill' is dealt with in greater detail later on in this Chapter.

5. **Counter Attack:**—

   (a) *General.*—CT are always sensitive to threats to their rear or flanks. Offensive action to produce such threats can, however, only be carried out by those troops who are clear of the danger zone. If there are no such troops then a frontal attack under cover of smoke will have to be made.

(b) *Action when no troops have entered the danger zone.*—The convoy commander, or in his absence the senior vehicle commander present, will launch an immediate flanking attack on the CT position, leaving on the ground as supporting fire such weapons as LMGs, 2-in. mortars and GF rifles.

(c) *Action when all troops are clear ahead of the danger zone.*—In this case it will be difficult to put in an attack as quickly as in sub-para 5(b) above, because troops will be moving away from the scene of action. Nevertheless an encircling attack must be mounted as quickly as troops can be marshalled and brought back to a starting point. It is difficult to state categorically who should take the initiative in these circumstances and it must be made clear at the convoy commander's briefing whether the rearmost vehicle commanders are to act on their own initiative in this type of situation.

(d) *Action when some troops are clear ahead of the danger zone and others are halted short of it.*—With two parties one each side of the ambush confusion may arise as to which group should put in the attack against the CT and precious time may be wasted in getting the attack under way. If both parties attack at the same time without co-ordination, an inter unit clash may result. It is suggested therefore, that the party which has not yet entered the ambush should make the attack as in sub-para 5(b) above.

(e) *Scout Car tactics.*—Usually the best way in which a scout car can assist in counter ambush action is by driving right up to the danger zone to engage the CT at very short range. In this way it will probably be able:—

(i) to give good covering fire to the flanking attack.

(ii) to afford protection to any of our own troops who are caught in the CT killing ground.

(f) *Platoon weapons.*—The 2-in. mortar and GF rifle should be concentrated on the CT position or on his probable escape routes. In order that at least one of these weapons can be brought into play they should always be well spaced out in the convoy.

(g) *Command and control.*—It is always possible that the convoy commander may be killed or wounded by the CT initial burst of fire. He may be pinned down in the killing ground or be on the wrong side of the danger zone when the ambush is sprung. In order to ensure that there is always a nominated commander on the spot, whatever the situation, it is essential that vehicle commanders understand their responsibilities for organising a counter attack. This should be clearly laid down in unit convoy orders and stressed at the briefing before moving off.

(h) *Training*.—The technique outlined above should be practised again and again in varying situations until the natural re-action to a CT ambush is the application of an immediate action drill.

Section 6.—BALING OUT DRILL

1. **General.**— In springing an ambush the CT first of all tries to stop one or more vehicles in his killing ground by the use of mines or obstacles and/or by firing at the tyres and driver. He then tries to kill the entire vehicle load in the first moments of surprise. To do this he places an automatic weapon where it can cover the rear of our vehicles. It is therefore essential that when a soft vehicle is brought to a halt in a danger zone the troops debus instantly. This must be taught and practised as a drill.

2. **Vehicle loading.**— To ensure ease of debussing all packs and stores will be piled in the centre of the vehicle and excessive quantities of stores will not be loaded into vehicles which are also carrying troops.

3. **Alertness.**— The importance of alertness has already been stressed. Troops will be continuously on the alert holding their weapons at all times. Spare Bren magazines will be in the soldiers' pouches and NOT in boxes. Vehicle sentries will have primed grenades to hand ready to throw.

4. **Drill.**— When the vehicle is forced to stop :—

   (a) The vehicle commander will shout 'DEBUS RIGHT' or 'LEFT' to indicate the direction in which troops will muster.

   (b) Sentries will throw grenades and open fire immediately on the CT position.

   (c) Troops will debus over both sides of the vehicle and run in the direction indicated.

   (d) As soon as troops are clear of the vehicle sentries will debus and join the remainder.

(e) At this stage of the battle the aim must be to collect the fit men as a formed body for counter action. Wounded troops must be dealt with after counter action has been taken.

5. **Training.**—This drill must be practised frequently by vehicle loads, e.g. infantry sections and platoons. Where miscellaneous vehicle loads are made up before a journey, two or three practices must be held before the convoy moves off.

Section 7.—CONCLUSION

1. This Chapter has dealt basically with the problems of the road ambush and road movement generally as they affect sub-units of the infantry battalion. No attempt has been made to discuss problems peculiar to the protection of RASC supply convoys, civilian food convoys and the escorting of VIPs.

2. It is considered, however, that the principles are the same for all types of convoy. The following points, therefore, are reiterated:—

(a) The necessity for clear orders and detailed briefing by the convoy commander before moving off.

(b) The positioning and role of scout cars.

(c) The need for constant alertness on the part of all ranks.

(d) The need for security in planning road movements.

3. The danger of road ambush by the CT must not be allowed to become a bogey. Troops must be fully trained in IA Drills and should be taught that when well prepared they are more than a match for the CT under any circumstances.

4. The outward appearance of the road convoys of a unit is a good indication of its state of operational efficiency. The CT intelligence has its observers everywhere who can read and interpret the signs of a good unit as well as we can. Thus, the more prepared and aggressive our troops are, the less likely they are to be ambushed.

CHAPTER XIV

INTELLIGENCE

Section 1.—INTRODUCTION

1. Successful operations against the CT organization depend upon accurate and timely intelligence; without it the CTO can never be defeated. A first class intelligence organization, in which everyone plays their part is thus essential. All troops must realise the importance of reporting as accurately as possible every piece of information which they obtain, both about the CT and the topography of the country over which they are operating. In particular it must be remembered that though a piece of information may appear by itself to be of little or no importance, it can be of considerable value when added to other information already available.

2. Since there is no state of war in Malaya, the basic responsibility for maintaining law and order is still that of the Police. In the same way the responsibility for producing intelligence still rests with the Special Branch of the Police. In view of the size and importance of the problem, however, a special intelligence organization has been built up.

Section 2.—OWN ORGANIZATION

1. **The Special Branch of the Federal Police.**—This is the principal intelligence producing agency in Malaya. In the present Emergency, its main task is the collection, collation and dissemination of intelligence relating to the MCP. Special Branch Staff are located at Federal Police HQ, at all Police Contingent HQ and Police Circle HQ and at some Police District HQ.

2. **The Special Military Intelligence Staff (Malaya) SMIS.** The SMIS is an Imperial Military Intelligence unit, which works with the Police Special Branch. It consists of a GSO 1 (Int), GSOs 2 (Int), GSOs 3 (Int), and Mil Int Offrs (all known as MIOs) with a small clerical staff. The role of these officers, who are intelligence trained, is to work in the Special Branch of the Police at all levels, undertaking that part of Special Branch work which deals with tactical intelligence and the Order of Battle of the MCP (including the charting of all CT). This organization not only assists the Special Branch, by permitting its officers to concentrate more upon its normal counter-intelligence role, but establishes a

channel for the passing of operational intelligence to the Army. This organization has been built up in Malaya as a result of experience in the Emergency and has proved the best answer to the problem posed by the situation in which Special Branch remains responsible for obtaining, collating and disseminating intelligence, whilst the Army is the main operational user.

3. **Imperial and Federation Forces Intelligence Staffs.**—17 Gurkha Div/OCLF and Federation Army each have their respective Intelligence Staffs functioning on similar lines as follows:—

(a) *At HQ OCLF and HQ Federation Army level.*—The respective G (Int) Staffs carry out supervision of intelligence in their own commands and each is the military channel for reporting incidents and information concerning their own troops. Each HQ has a tactical Intelligence Staff, G (Int) (a) and a counter Intelligence Staff, G (Int) (b). On the G (Int) (a) side each staff works in close co-operation with the Special Branch at Federal Police level, primarily through the HQ SMIS (see paragraph 2 above).

(b) *At Bde and Bn level.*—Wherever it is possible to do so, Bde or Bn Int Staff jointly man Contingent, Circle and Independent District Operations Rooms with the Police in areas where military forces are deployed. This close integration ensures that the military commander for the Contingent or Circle has the up-to-date tactical information necessary for his day-to-day planning.

These operations rooms are responsible for collating information and transmitting it through Police channels to the Federal Joint Ops/Info Room at Police HQ in Kuala Lumpur.

Section 3.—INTELLIGENCE SOURCES

1. The main sources of intelligence are:—
    (a) SEP.
    (b) CEP.
    (c) Captured documents.
    (d) Identification of dead CT.
    (e) Information supplied by agents and informers and by the general public.

(f) Reports by SF patrols, particularly regarding:—
   (i) Wireless.
   (ii) Food cultivation.
   (iii) Food dumps.
   (iv) Camps.
   (v) Tracks.
   (vi) Arms and ammunition.
   (vii) Mines and explosives.
   (viii) Equipment.
   (ix) Tactics.
(g) Visual air reconnaissance.
(h) Air photography and interpretation.

2. **SEP.**— A surrendered CT is an extremely valuable source of information and can be of considerable use to Police Special Branch and for military operations. The following points must be borne in mind:—
   (a) *Secrecy.*—The fact that a surrender has taken place must be kept secret so long as it may be possible to turn it to our advantage.
   (b) *Handling.*—The fewer people who question a newly surrendered CT the better it is for his subsequent use. Interrogation will normally be carried out by a Police Special Branch Officer.

3. **Responsibilities.**
   (a) All SEPs are at all times the responsibility of the Police. The method of using them must be arranged mutually between the respective Military/Police Commanders.
   (b) The nearest Police Special Branch Officer will normally decide whether an SEP may be used on operations. If he is not available the military commander who takes the surrender is responsible for ensuring that the best immediate use is made of the SEP. He must always remember that an SEP must not be used on immediate follow-up operations if he is likely to be of use to Special Branch; e.g. a SEP who is willing to go back alone to gain information or to procure further surrenders.

4. It is possible that on occasions the time factor appears to be so vital that sufficient time is not available for a Special Branch Officer to get to the SEPs location in order to carry out the initial

interrogation. In this case the military commander may carry out the initial interrogation subject to the provisos in paragraph 3 above. A questionnaire is given at Appendix A.

5. **CEP.**— The principles of handling are the same as in the case of SEP, but a CEP may ONLY be used on operations for a period of 72 hours after capture. The time factor in this case is therefore of primary importance. A questionnaire for CEP is given at Appendix B.

6. No military personnel may promise immunity from prosecution of CEP to obtain their co-operation.

7. **Captured Documents.**— Any member of the SF who acquires CT documents will hand them over to the nearest Police Officer of the rank of Police Lieutenant or above. Where documents are found in CT packs care must be taken to see that they are not mixed but retained in the original packs as an aid to identification.

8. **Identification of Dead CT.**— The other sources of intelligence mentioned are of obvious value. On many occasions, however, (particularly in deep jungle) identification of dead CT, most of whom are now charted by Special Branch, will be the main, if not the only, means of establishing which MCP organization is in the area. It must therefore be borne in mind by SF at all times that whilst the killing of individual CT is in itself a worthwhile object, the identification of the body may be of even greater value.

9. The most reliable method of identification is by SEP already working with the SF. This can be done either by:—
   (a) A SEP with the patrol which kills the CT.
   (b) Bringing a SEP to the body.
   (c) Evacuating the body to the nearest Police Station.
   (d) Photographs or descriptions.

10. Methods (a) and (b) above will be rare; evacuation of the body will therefore normally be desirable. This can be achieved by one of the two following methods:—
   (a) By the patrol carrying the body out. Owing to the speed at which bodies decompose in this climate, ground evacuation will only be used when the carry is likely to take less than 8 hours.
   (b) By helicopter. Helicopters will only be used for this purpose when the carry by ground troops is unacceptably long or there is urgency in obtaining identification.

Requests for helicopters will be made in the normal way (see Appendix E to Chapter XVII) but should include:—
  (i) Index letter G (Load). Number of bodies to be carried.
  (ii) Index letter H (Time and Duration). Latest time at which the helicopter will be of use.
  (iii) Index letter K (Special Instructions). Whether additional wrappings are required (only one is normally carried). Place to which bodies are to be taken, normally nearest Police Circle HQ.

11. If evacuation should prove impossible photographs, fingerprints and a description of the body must be taken. The important points are enumerated below.

12. **Photographs:—**
  (a) If no camera is carried by the patrol one can be obtained through normal air supply channels.
  (b) For successful photography of the body:
    (i) The face should be washed and hair brushed.
    (ii) If "rigor mortis" has not set in, the CT's eyes should be forced open before photographing, to facilitate identification.
    (iii) A full face photograph should be taken.
    (iv) The photograph should be taken at short range.
    (v) A minimum of two photographs should be taken.

13. **Fingerprints.**— Fingerprint outfits are issued to units and full instructions are included in each box. The main principle to be observed is cleanliness, both of the equipment and of the fingers whose prints are being taken.

14. **Description.**— The following are the principle characteristics required for a description:—
  (a) Sex.
  (b) Race.
  (c) Apparent age.
  (d) Height, build and facial features.
  (e) Teeth, old scars and deformities.

Details should be as full as possible. The whole body must be examined.

15. **General.**— The body must be minutely searched and all documents and other articles carried by the CT must be recovered (see paragraph 7 above).

16. **Information from the public.**— All members of the public who have information to give should be passed on to the Police, who alone will handle agents and informers.

17. On no account will military units run their own agents or informers.

18. **SF Patrols.**— A great deal of tactical information is provided by SF patrols, whether sent out expressly for that purpose or acquired in the course of other duties.

19. The value of this source is immeasurably greater if:—
    (a) Correct briefing takes place beforehand.
    (b) Adequate training and thought has been given to the skills of careful observation and recording of important information.
    (c) Proper de-briefing and reporting takes place as soon after the patrol's return as possible (see Appendix C).

20. SF reports on all the subjects enumerated at paragraph 1(f) of this Section must be passed without delay to local joint operations rooms for onward transmission through Police channels where appropriate. Special notes on certain subjects are given in the succeeding paragraphs, and a form to assist in assessing the age of food dumps is at Appendix D.

21. **CT Wireless Activity.**— It is of great importance that all captured CT wireless equipment should be recovered for inspection. In addition it is essential that any information concerning the CT use or suspected use of wireless should be reported as quickly as possible.

22. Units finding a wireless set, either transmitter/receiver, transmitter, or receiver, will take the following action:—
    (a) Send a signal containing the following information:—
        (i) Type of set, i.e. transmitter/receiver, transmitter, or receiver.
        (ii) Make, name and number of set.
        (iii) Grid reference where found.
        (iv) Frequencies shown on dials at time of capture.
        (v) Direction in which aerial was running (including compass bearing if possible).

(b) This signal will be sent with priority OP IMMEDIATE and security grading of SECRET as follows:—
   (i) By Police Units.—Direct to Operation Information Branch at Federal Police HQ copy to SAC (E) Federal Police HQ.
   (ii) By Military Units.—Direct to Federal Police HQ marked for SMIS who will pass the Signal to SAC (E) Federal Police HQ.
   (iii) In both cases a copy will be sent to Brigade/Contingent HQ.
(c) Send a written report in quadruplicate in confirmation, with the following additional details:—
   (i) Signs of recent use.
   (ii) Description of the aerial (e.g. length, type and height).
   (iii) Description of the camp where the set was found.
(d) Send the equipment itself as soon as possible to SMIS (c/o Federal Police HQ). Care must be taken to ensure that the frequency dials are carefully read before the set is moved and if possible locked to prevent change during transit. The set must not be tampered with in any way.

23. **Wireless Interference.**— In order that wireless interference can be checked and identified the following action will be taken:—
   (a) An immediate report on the interference will be made if possible by phone or by OP IMMEDIATE signal. This will include frequency and call sign of the interference and will be sent as in paragraph 22 above. In both cases the telephone number is Kuala Lumpur 7771 Extension 200.
   (b) This initial report will be followed by a further report in writing as at Appendix E (4 copies).
   (c) Units will continue to monitor such interference until otherwise instructed.

24. **Documents Relating to Wireless.**— Documents relating to wireless activity and those found in close proximity to wireless sets, will be forwarded through the usual channels but must be passed as quickly as possible.

25. **Food Cultivation.**—With the improvement in Food Control CTs are being forced to carry out jungle cultivation as a source of food supply. Such cultivations can be divided into two types:—
   (a) *Aboriginal Cultivations.*—The CT in deep jungle make use of aborigines for cultivation work and it is difficult

to distinguish which cultivations are CT inspired. Experts such as Protector of Aborigines can usually say whether the amout of cultivation is just sufficient for the local aborigines, or if it is so large that CT must be living off it as well; but guidance can also be found in the type of crop grown e.g. Chinese types of vegetables, and the orderliness of the cultivation. If the crops are in neat rows and well tended they are probably destined for the CT.

(b) **Chinese Cultivations.**—These occur mainly away from the main mountain range and closer to the populated areas. The areas may be very small, but are usually orderly and may be surrounded with pig fencing.

26. It is clear that in order to deprive the CT of this source of food the destruction of the crops is of great importance. The means of destruction are:—

(a) Helicopter Spray.
(b) Pack Spray.
(c) By ground troops by hand.

27. Normally the crop will have to be destroyed by hand. Where the area is so large that the patrol will be excessively delayed, helicopter spraying can be requested. If this is impossible for topographical or other reasons, pack sprayers or XMU pellets may be dropped to the ground troops. Clearance for the destruction of crops in aboriginal areas must first be obtained from the Protector of Aborigines or District Officer.

28. Patrols discovering cultivations will report:—

(a) Grid reference.
(b) Size of clearing.
(c) Type, e.g. Aborigine, Chinese or undetermined.
(d) Condition, e.g. Stage 1—Just cut.
   Stage 2—Cut and cleared.
   Stage 3—Prepared and howed.
   Stage 4—Growing crops tended.
   Stage 5—Growing crops untended.
   Stage 6—Harvested.
   Stage 7—Disused and overgrown.

29. **Arms and Ammunition.**—SF recovering arms and ammunition from the CT will report:—

(a) Description of weapon and identification numbers.
(b) Quantity and calibre of ammunition.

(c) Date of manufacture of ammunition, and whether serviceable or not.

(d) Whether the ammunition has been refilled, i.e. whether it has been recapped or whether the cap shows that it has previously misfired and has been reconditioned. (In the case of grenades improvised fuses will be classified as refills).

30. All arms and ammunition recovered from CT will be handed over to the nearest Police Officer.

31. **Mines and Explosives.**—Where possible all mines and explosives should be recovered for technical examination. If this is not possible owing to danger in handling, a full report should be rendered stating whether the equipment was serviceable or not and quoting any identification marks or numbers. The method of disposal should also be given.

Section 4.—AIR RECONNAISSANCE AND PHOTOGRAPHY

1. **Introduction.**—The natural difficulties of Malayan topography make observation from the air of more than ordinary value, whilst the inability of the CT to prevent it makes it relatively easy.

2. Army Lt AC pilots have become expert at spotting traces of CT occupation in jungle and provide much intelligence for deep jungle operations.

3. In some cases the configuration of the ground, meteorological conditions, or the need for security, will prevent thorough visual reconnaissance. On such occasions PR, allied with photographic interpretation, is employed.

4. Apart from the normal use of PR for target study and briefing, it is used to provide a basic block cover of the whole Federation.

5. The detailed organization is explained in the succeeding paragraphs.

6. **Co-ordination.**—Air recce is co-ordinated by a GSO 3 (Int) Air Recce on the staff of HQ OCLF.

7. This GSO 3 works in the closest touch with:—
   (a) The Lt AC Sqn (visual reconnaissance).
   (b) The RAF squadrons employed on PR.
   (c) JAPIC (FE) and APIU (FE) (both in Singapore) and the APIS under command of HQ OCLF.

8. His task is to:—
   (a) Collate and disseminate intelligence derived from visual reconnaissance and PR.
   (b) Receive requests for PR, and give appropriate priorities.
   (c) Supervise photographic interpretation.
   (d) Issue air photographic material.

9. **Visual Reconnaissance.**— At present there is one Lt AC Sqn Army Air Corps in Malaya, with HQ at Kuala Lumpur and flights in various parts of the Federation.

10. The actual direction of flying for visual reconnaissance is controlled at the level of brigade HQ/flights. Flights are responsible for a stated area and carry out air reconnaissance on a general programme, to which are added specific requests from the Brigade, or Brigades, in the area. They also receive intelligence direction from MIOs.

11. Air reconnaissance reports are forwarded to the requesting unit or formation with a copy to G (Int.) Air Recce. This information is also plotted on maps at each flight HQ.

12. **Photographic Reconnaissance and Interpretation.**— PR in Malaya is used in order to:—
   (a) Provide "photo-maps" for ground forces and to bring old maps up-to-date or supplement existing maps, and to provide detailed information on topography, new estates, roads, etc.
   (b) Obtain new intelligence about clearings, cultivations, etc.
   (c) Provide briefing material about areas where operations are being considered.
   (d) Confirm or assist in pinpointing intelligence from other sources of CT activity in the jungle (e.g., visual air reconnaissance reports, ground forces reports and information from SEPs, CEPs and Special Branch sources).

13. **Organisation:**—
   (a) Co-ordination is carried out by G (Int.) Air Recce (see paragraphs 6-8 above).
   (b) Flying is carried out by the PR Squadron on the authority of HQ 224 Gp RAF on demand by G (Int) Air Recce.
   (c) Interpretation and mosaicing is carried out by an APIS, augmented by a detachment of JAPIC (FE).

14. **Requests:—**
   (a) Requests are made from State Operations Rooms through the military formation or unit concerned (normally brigade HQ) direct to G (Int) Air Recce on the proforma shown at Appendix F to this chapter. In cases of urgency, requests are submitted in signal form as at Appendix G, followed by the normal proforma request in confirmation.
   (b) Owing to the restricted opportunities for PR imposed by the meteorological conditions, requests have to be made as far ahead as possible.
   (c) On receipt of requests G (Int) Air Recce screens them and allocates priorities (under the direction of HQ SMIS and HQ 224 Gp RAF) and passes on the request for flying.
   (d) G (Int) Air Recce is responsible for following up the requests and altering priorities to suit changing circumstances.
   (e) On receipt of the photographs, G (Int) Air Recce passes them for interpretation to APIS and JAPIC (FE), again allotting any necessary priorities for work.

15. **Block Cover of Malaya:—**
   (a) The whole of Malaya is covered by basic block cover in the form of annotated mosaics each covering an area 20,000 yards by 10,000 yards.
   (b) Until June 1955, this block cover was flown at a scale of 1/10,000 and was used for intelligence and as photo maps.
   (c) Block cover is now flown at a scale of 1/20,000 primarily for use as photo maps, and is flown as and when it is required for specific areas.
   (d) The original mosaic together with a set of loose prints and sufficient photo copies for issue down to coy level are sent to the originator of the request for the photo cover. Photo copies of the mosaic are sent to other interested parties as required. Further copies may be supplied on request.

16. **Photographs for Intelligence Purposes:—**
   (a) When air photographs are required either to confirm intelligence from other sources, or to obtain fresh information, then the air cover will be flown at a scale of 1/5,000 or larger. Full photographic interpretation (PI) will be carried out on these photographs, which will be made up as mosaics and sent to originators of requests together with

a report of details of information found by PI. Areas to be covered by this scale of photography should not exceed the equivalent area of 25 x 1,000-yard map squares.

(b) Where required, verbal briefing from air photographs is carried out by the interpreter from the APIS/JAPIC.

17. **Photographs for Special Purposes:**—
    (a) Very large scale photographs of New Villages, estate lines and certain other areas are a valuable aid to Security Forces for the following purposes:—
        (i) maintaining a check on cultivations around villages.
        (ii) planning, briefing, and troop deployment.
        (iii) jungle/rubber edge patrolling.
    (b) Most New Villages in the Federation have now been photographed and enlargement at a scale of 20 inch to a mile issued to State Operations Rooms.
    (c) Requests for additional copies of New Village photography or for new flying where this type of cover is required should be made in the normal manner and item QUEBEC of the request proforma annotated "maximum enlargement."

18. **Conclusion.**—The fullest use is made of the potentialities of visual and photographic air reconnaissance to produce intelligence on CT camps, cultivations, routes, etc., in the jungle.

19. SWECs and DWECs obtain local help from the Lt AC flight in their areas and hold basic block photographic cover. Further specific information is produced by G (Int) Air Recce on request.

20. G (Int) Air Recce is responsible for co-ordination of work and the collation and dissemination of the product of air reconnaissance.

21. It is important to remember that, although the Army is the main user of intelligence from air reconnaissance, and the brigade/battalion IO is normally employed in joint operations rooms on this work, the intelligence material (including air photographs) is the property of the operations room, and must be left behind if the military unit or formation moves. This is essential in order to:—
    (a) Give the incoming unit the best possible intelligence take over.
    (b) Avoid wasteful re-flying and re-interpretation.

Section 5.—MILITARY SECURITY AND COUNTER INTELLIGENCE

1. As the MCP does not possess the normal organization of a first class enemy, it must exploit every resource of intelligence to redress the balance of inferior force. Thus, in addition to the direct screen of the Min Yuen, the MCP has established a network of agents and informers throughout the Federation whose task is to gather information and pass it quickly to the CT.

2. The G (Int) (b) staffs are responsible for the application of:—
   (a) Preventive measures to deny the CT all opportunity of gaining knowledge of our intentions.
   (b) Detective measures concerned with the investigation of breaches of security or covert activities detrimental to the security of the Armed Forces.

3. **Military Security.**— There is clear evidence that:—
   (a) Many successful ambushes against SF have been the direct result of lack of security.
   (b) CT movement out of an area due to be the scene of impending operations has taken place because of bad security, particularly careless talk.

4. In operational areas contractors and their employees, who are all vulnerable to CT pressure, quickly become aware of ration strengths, the units engaged, the names and personalities of senior officers and, unless great care is exercised in ordering rations, can forecast with some accuracy future unit changes of locations.

5. Security is many sided and the CT do not rely on one source only for information. All ranks are prone to careless talk, usually through vanity, thoughtlessness or ignorance. To counter innumerable instances of insecurity of material, loose methods of safeguarding secret papers, inefficient guards, unauthorised entry to WD premises and other breaches of security there is only one remedy: proper security training. The supervision of this training is the task of the Unit Security Officer, assisted by the G (Int) (b) staff, and the security agencies, to ensure that all ranks become security minded.

6. **Counter Intelligence.**— It is unfortunately only too true of the G (Int) (b) staff and security, as it is with the police and crime, that most of its time is taken up in the investigation of breaches of security that have already occurred.

7. The G (Int) (b) staff sets up certain standing controls, organises a system of passes and permits, and arranges with the help of Special Branch, for thorough vetting and verification of all employees but these merely limit the problem. They may make it difficult for an informer or agent to gain access to military establishments or, having got in, to be able to do much harm, but they cannot exclude the agent or nullify the work of those already inside.

8. The object of standing controls is, by a process of elimination, to throw into relief incidents or persons that seem to be suspicious and to make them the subject of investigation.

9. Properly trained, security minded personnel will not only prevent information from getting to the CT but, in adhering to standing security controls, will be quicker to observe any suspicious departures from them and assist the counter intelligence effort.

10. Military security and counter intelligence investigations within the Army are conducted by Field Security Sections, under the direction of the G (Int) (b) staff, and in certain cases other specialist organisations play their part. It can never be overstressed, however, that to be effective the work of the G (Int) (b) staff must be backed by sound unit security and an awareness of the issues involved, plus the need for prompt action by the units themselves as defined in current instructions on security.

Section 6.—CONCLUSION

1. The following points which are special to the Emergency in Malaya should be borne in mind when dealing with intelligence:—
    (a) The basic responsibility is still that of the Special Branch of the Federation Police, assisted by other agencies.
    (b) Intelligence material, whether SEP, CEP, dead bodies, documents or equipment, must be handed to the Police and dealt with in accordance with Police instructions.
    (c) Collation of intelligence takes place at Police Contingent, i.e. State Capital, level.
    (d) The role of the MIOs of SMIS is to undertake within Special Branch that part of Special Branch work dealing with tactical intelligence, thereby:—
        (i) Permitting Special Branch officers to concentrate more upon clandestine activity.
        (ii) Ensuring that the military units receive the intelligence they need in the appropriate form.

2. As the CT tend to thin out, and increase the security of their elements in contact with the masses, so the chances of contacting and eliminating them depends more and more on good intelligence, and in close co-operation between intelligence and operations staffs.

3. The topography of Malaya, combined with the increasing CT policy of withdrawing MRLA units and high level organisations from contact with the masses have made visual air reconnaissance, PR and Photographic Interpretation of even more than usual value to intelligence staffs.

4. Although their lack of speedy communications makes it difficult for the CT to take quick advantage of breaches of security, such as telephone conversations, unclassified correspondence and signals, careless talk, movements of troops, etc., it is certain that they do so in the end. For this reason, and because breach of the basic security rules is bad training for war, special attention must be paid to this problem. Deception and concealment of plans must also be practised to the fullest extent.

5. At Appendix H to this Chapter are details of the routine intelligence publications by which intelligence is disseminated.

Appendix A

SURRENDERED ENEMY PERSONNEL

INITIAL QUESTIONNAIRE

1. For convenience, this questionnaire is divided into two parts, Part I deals with the questions which it is suggested should be asked before deciding whether or not the SEP can be used on operations. Part II contains the questions which it is suggested should be asked to decide whether or not the SEP has any information of an operational nature.

PART I

Suggested questions are:—

(a) Name, race and dialect.
(b) Length of time SEP has been in the jungle.
(c) Rank and unit.
(d) Are there any CT who wish to surrender. If there are, is the SEP prepared to go back and persuade them to surrender.
(e) Is the SEP prepared to go back into the jungle to work for the SF.

Note:—If the SEP agrees to do either (d) or (e) above he will not under any circumstance be used on operations without permission from Special Branch. The SEP should be held as secluded as possible until he is handed over to Special Branch.

PART II

If the SEP does not agree to paragraphs (d) or (e) or if Special Branch have decided that he will be of no value, it is suggested that the SEP is asked the following questions to decide how he should be used on operations:—

(a) How many occupied camps does he know to which he can lead patrols. Are they occupied now, if so by whom. How long will it take to reach them.
(b) When does he think his absence will be noticed.
(c) When are the persons in the camps likely to know of his surrender.
(d) Any routes likely to be used by CT coming into, or leaving, the camps.
(e) Does he know of any arms dumps and the details.

Note:—The targets should then be selected in the order of priority.

(f) Further detailed questions on selected targets.

Appendix B

CAPTURED ENEMY PERSONNEL

INITIAL QUESTIONNAIRE

1. The following questions are suggested for an initial interrogation of CEP. In this connection it is pointed out that the CEP will not be promised a reward or immunity in any form, for information he may give.

2. Suggested questions: —
   (a) Name, race, dialect.
   (b) Length of time in the jungle.
   (c) Rank and unit.
   (d) Can CEP lead patrols to any occupied camps.
   (e) By whom are camps occupied.
   (f) When will CEP's absence be noticed.
   (g) Does CEP know of any arms dumps.

Appendix C

DEBRIEFING AIDE MEMOIRE FOR PATROLS

1. The purpose of this Aide Memoire is to guide those who have to debrief patrol commanders.

2. It suggests a number of questions but it must not stop 'debriefers' from asking other questions they may think relevant.

3. The proper channel of reporting answers is through the daily sitrep. Only in exceptional circumstances are supplementary reports needed.

4. **Hints on Debriefing:—**
   (a) Make the person who is being debriefed comfortable.
   (b) Do not make him write the answers. You must do the work while he relaxes.
   (c) Debrief as soon as possible while the knowledge is still fresh in his mind.
   (d) Avoid asking questions which suggest the answer.
   (e) Patrol Commanders will answer these questions better if they know what is needed before they go out.

5. **Topography:—**
   (a) Was the intelligence briefing accurate? If not, what inaccuracies were discovered?
   (b) Was the map accurate? If not, what were the inaccuracies?
   (c) If air photos were used, was the interpretation of use?
   (d) What was the state of tracks followed?
   (e) Did the tracks show signs of recent use?
   (f) Were any other tracks or game trails seen? Where?
   (g) Where rivers were crossed or followed, give location of:—
      (i) Bridges (include type).
      (ii) Fords.
      Were they in recent use?

6. If any aborigines or squatters were contacted out of their known locations, state:—
   (a) Name of ladangs.
   (b) Name of tribe and headman.
   (c) Number of aborigines.
   (d) Were they friendly?
   (e) Whether previous Government contact or not?
   (f) Have they moved recently? If so why?
   (g) Did they give any information?

7. **Contacts:—**
   (a) Where contacted? (Time, date, place, grid ref.).
   (b) How many CT. Of what races? Sex?
   (c) Any known persons? Can you describe any of them?
   (d) How were they dressed?
   (e) Were they carrying packs?

Appx C

Appendix C—*continued*

    (f) How were they armed? (weapons seen and estimated from volume of fire).
    (g) What were the CT doing? If moving, in what direction?
    (h) Any equipment or documents recovered? To whom have they been given?
    (j) Any casualties? To own troops or CT?
    (k) Have the CT casualties been identified? If not, what has happened to the bodies?
    (l) Any SEP, or CEP? What have you done with them?

8. **Camps:—**
    (a) Where and when was the camp discovered?
    (b) How was it sited, e.g. valley, hillside, hilltop?
    (c) How many huts or buildings?
    (d) What type were they?
    (e) Estimate their accommodation.
    (f) How long ago were they built?
    (g) When were they last used? By how many?
    (h) Were any defences constructed? Describe layout including sentry posts, warning signals, booby-traps, dugouts, etc.
    (j) How many approach or escape routes? Give their directions.
    (k) Any food dumps in the camp?
    (l) Any weapons, ammunition or armourers' tools?
    (m) Any signs of a printing press?
    (n) Any signs of wireless sets being used?
    (o) Any documents? If so, where were they found?
    (p) What was done to the camp?

9. **Cultivation Areas:—**
    (a) Give time, date and grid reference of place of discovery.
    (b) What was its size and shape?
    (c) Any steps taken to camouflage crops?
    (d) What kinds of crops?
    (e) How old were they?
    (f) When were they last tended?
    (g) Any signs of habitation in the area?
    (h) Any tracks?
    (j) What was done to the cultivation?
    (k) In the case of aboriginal ladangs can you estimate the food produced in excess of the aborigines own requirements.

10. **Supply Dumps:—**
    (a) Location time and date?
    (b) What was in it?
    (c) What was the condition of the store?
    (d) How was it concealed?
    (e) When was it last visited?
    (f) Estimate the age of the dump.
    (g) Has it been added to since it was first laid down?
    (h) What was done with the stores?

Appendix D

XIV
Appx D

NOTES ON COMMUNIST TERRORIST FOOD DUMPS

The principal methods of distinguishing between two types of dumps are:—

	Long-Term	*Short-Term*
(a)	Size and contents— Contain a considerable quantity of food and other stores, particularly tinned food. May include a high proportion of clothing or medical stores.	Will be quite small, perhaps one or two sacks of rice and a few tins of food. Unlikely to contain a preponderance of clothing or medical stores.
(b)	Method of storage and camouflage— Considerable care taken to preserve food, i.e., rice in sealed tins or acid jars, much tinned food. Dump buried in ground or on shelves with a proper roof. Much care taken to camouflage dump.	Not much care taken. Dump up a tree or hidden in a patch of lallang or belukar and covered with sacking or other covering.
(c)	Distance from source— Normally some distance into the jungle.	Fairly close to the jungle fringe.

The long-term dump is unlikely to be worth ambushing. The short-term may well be.

Definitions

The following definitions are used.

(a) *Etching.*—This is the effect of chemical reaction on the inside of a tin container. The inside of a tin is normally either straightforward tin plate or tin plate treated with lacquer; the latter produces a golden brown finish. On tin plate etching shows as dull streaks with a leaden look (streaking up to $\frac{1}{4}$ to $\frac{1}{2}$ inches wide). On lacquer the effect is to cause pitting of the lacquer.

(b) *Blown.*—A tin is described as 'blown' when decomposition has produced gases which swell out the ends of the tin. The end of the tin bulges out slightly, pressure removes the bulge but on release of pressure the bulge reappears.

(c) *Translucent and Opaque.*—Translucent means that light can partially pass through the article (e.g., a very old piece of celluloid which it is impossible to see through clearly), opaque means that no light passes through (e.g., the same piece of celluloid painted on one side).

Appendix D—*Continued*

ASSESSMENT OF HOW LONG FOOD HAS BEEN IN DUMP

SERIAL (a)	ITEM (b)	CERTAINLY LESS THAN SIX MONTHS IN THE DUMP (c)	PROBABLY MORE THAN SIX MONTHS IN THE DUMP (d)	CERTAINLY MORE THAN SIX MONTHS IN THE DUMP (e)
1.	Rice (in sealed containers).	(a) Grains slightly translucent-pearl coloured; (b) Grains not brittle; (c) Fresh smell; (d) No sign of larvae, grubs, weevils, cocoons, etc.	(a) Grains opaque yellowish white; (b) Grains brittle and some grains partially eaten by insects; (c) Weevils, larvae, grubs, cocoons, etc., present (alive or dead); (d) Musty smell.	Chemical and physical changes same as column (d) but much more advanced.
2.	Sugar (in sealed containers).	(a) Crystals separate easily; (b) No sign of stickiness; (c) No smell.	(a) Slight 'crust' starting to form around the edge of the container and just above the level of the sugar.	(a) Thick 'crust' on top; (b) Sticky; (c) Slightly sweet smell.
3.	Tinned Condensed Milk (with no cross on tin).	(a) White to yellow in colour; (b) Milk flows easily.	(a) Yellow to yellowish brown in colour; (b) Thick and difficult to pour; (c) Inside of tin dull and etched.	As for column (d) but in addition. (d) A deposit around side of tin just above milk level; (e) Heavy sediment at the bottom of the tin.
4.	Tinned Fish.	(a) Inside of tin clean and shiny.	(a) Inside of tin dull and etched; (b) Contents pulpy and not fresh to taste.	(a) Inside of tin dull, heavily etched; (b) Contents pulpy and almost unrecognisable as fish. (c) If in tomato juice, separation of juice into semi-clear liquid and thick deposit.
5.	Tinned Goods general:— (a) Labels; (b) Blown; (c) External surface;	Labels fresh looking and sticking well to the tin. Bright and shining.	Labels tending to lift and having blistered appearance. Dull with pronounced rusting around any dents and scratches.	 Blown tins. Extensive rusting.
	(d) Top or bottom of tin scored with a cross.	Little signs of rusting around cross.		

NOTE.—This table (1) Takes into account probable deterioration before food reaches a dump.
(2) Must be applied with common sense—the age must not be assessed purely on one particularly good or bad specimen.
(3) Applies only to long term dumps: contents of short-term dumps are almost certain to have been there for less than six months.

Appendix E

SECRET

To SPECIAL BRANCH FEDERAL POLICE HQ (3 copies)
Copy to SMIS

Subject: —

REPORT ON ENEMY WIRELESS TRANSMISSIONS OR INTERFERENCE

Further to my signal..

Herewith report in accordance with paragraph 11 (b) of Director of Operations' Instruction No. 22.

- A. When reported by a signal station, own frequency in kilocycles.
- B. Interfering stations' frequency in kilocycles or meters.
- C. Type of transmission, i.e. CW or Voice.
  If the latter, details of language spoken.
- D. Whether a permanent transmission or interference or whether spasmodic.
    - (i) If spasmodic, dates and times at which interference was experienced.
    - (ii) If permanent, date and time of start of interference.
- E. Strength of signal, i.e. strong, moderate, weak.
- F. Whether message is in cipher, code or clear. (This may not be known to the initiator of the report).
- G. Enclose copies of any intercepts recorded, with times of recordings.
- H. Any other information which may be of use in identification.

SECRET

XIV
Appx F

Appendix F

REQUEST FOR AIR PHOTOGRAPHS

To: G Int./Air Recce KUALA LUMPUR

Index letter key	Information required	Remarks
L	Demander's reference No.	—
M	Type of photo required.	i.e., Vertical or Oblique.
N	Map series and sheet No.	—
O	Air cover block No. or map references of the corners of the area.	Include identifying feature where possible, e.g., towns or mountains.
P	Purpose for which cover is required.	Include all possible detail, including local intelligence. AOP and sitrep detail is not required as it is already received by G (Int) Air Recce.
P	Type and extent of interpretation required.	e.g., Spot heights and all possible CT activity.
Q	Scale required.	Normally 1:20,000 for topographical purposes 1:5,000 or larger for intelligence purposes.
R	Number of copies required.	Original mosaics, photo—copies and loose prints should be listed separately in that order.
S	Delivery date and time.	State earliest date required.
T	Final date after which cover is not required.	—
U	Degree of priority requested.	—Operational Immediate. —Priority. —Routine. It is essential that an "honest" grading be given in order that priorities in the Federation as a whole can be accurately assessed.
U	Delivery address. Special Instructions for delivery.	— e.g., one set of loose prints to CPO, KEDAH, direct.

Appendix G

XIV
Appx G

URGENT REQUEST FOR AIR PHOTOGRAPHS

(to be written on normal message form)

SECRET

FROM: 28 Bde.
TO: G Int. Air Recce, KUALA LUMPUR
INFO: 2 Bde.
CPO, PERAK, (for SWEC).

PR DEMAND (.) LIMA (.) G 41 (.) MIKE (.) VERTICAL (.) NECTAR (.) RECCE GSGS 4690 SHEET 2E/11 (.) OSCAR (.) TOLAK QY 2095—2595—2590—2090—2095 (.) PAPA (.) EXTENT OF CT RECULTIVATION SUBSEQUENT TO OFFENSIVE OP JUL 57 (.) QUEBEC (.) 1/5,000 (.) ROMEO (.) ONE MOSAIC TWO LOOSE PRINTS (.) SIERRA (.) 9 DEC (.) TANGO (.) 20 DEC (.) UNIFORM (.) ONE SET PRINTS DIRECT TO CPO KEDAH

Appendix H

ROUTINE INTELLIGENCE PUBLICATIONS

1. **Daily Sitrep.—**

    A daily summary of events in the Federation issued down to units.

2. **Contingent Joint Police/Military Weekly Int Summary.—**

    Contains:—
    - Part I. Statistical Summary of Events.
    - Part II. Activity CT and Own by Police Circles.
    - Part III. Int Review by MCP areas.
    - Part IV. Comment.

    This summary is issued down to units in the Contingent and to higher Formation HQ.

3. **SF Weekly Intelligence Summary.—**

    Compiled at Federal Police HQ from daily Sitreps and Contingent WISUMs and contains:—
    - Part I. Comment.
    - Part II. Situation in the States.
    - Part III. Information.

    Once a month an extra section is issued which contains a general report on the situation.

CHAPTER XV

TRAINING FOR OPERATIONS

Section 1.—INTRODUCTION

1. Field-Marshal Slim's two remedies for the abnormal difficulties of the jungle were training and experience, because unless experience is based on sound and constant training it is apt to be costly.

2. Contacts with CT are sudden, rapidly fought encounters between small patrols, where the essential requirements for success are strong junior leadership and a high standard of individual shooting.

3. A high standard in these qualities can only be achieved and maintained by constant training. There can be no valid argument against the fact that training must take place throughout the whole year whatever the intensity of operations.

4. The aim of this Chapter is to show what training should be carried out before and during operations in Malaya.

Section 2.—INITIAL JUNGLE TRAINING

1. Battalions earmarked for Malaya from other theatres send advance parties on a Basic Jungle Warfare Course at the FARELF Training Centre Kota Tinggi. These advance parties help COs to train their battalions in jungle warfare on a four-week training course with assistance from FARELF Training Centre.

2. Instruction for basic jungle training must include the following subjects:—
   (a) CT background, methods and organisation.
   (b) The organisation and roles of SF, Police, Special Branch and the Home Guard. The Army's role in Malaya.
   (c) How to live in the jungle, including hygiene, health and first aid.
   (d) Jungle discipline and silent movement.
   (e) The establishment of jungle bases.
   (f) Patrol formations.
   (g) Jungle navigation.
   (h) IA Drills (including silent signals).

(j) The planning and laying of day and night ambushes in various types of country.

(k) Jungle shooting.

(l) Tracking.

(m) Dog handling.

3. It must be realised that this short four-week course aims to provide battalions with sufficient specialised knowledge of jungle warfare as applicable to the Malayan Emergency to enable them to be operational. Continuous training thenceforth is necessary for battalions to be fully effective.

Section 3.—TRAINING DURING OPERATIONS

1. **General.**— The following sections attempt to provide the answer to two questions:—

(a) What subjects should be taught to improve anti-CT technique.

(b) What proportion of time should be spent on training.

2. A large portion of this section will be devoted to shooting because:—

(a) It is not dealt with in other Chapters.

(b) The best plan, the best leadership and the most skilful fieldcraft will avail nothing if the men cannot shoot to kill when they meet the CT.

3. **Shooting.**— The best basis for a good shooting unit is that all officers and senior NCOs must be keen practical shots themselves.

4. **Shooting Cycle.**— It cannot be over-emphasised that the essential preliminary to success in jungle shooting is the ability to shoot in the standing position. To perfect the soldier for jungle shooting it is necessary to practise him in the kneeling, sitting and lying positions. He must be brought up to a standard where he can shoot accurately at the most fleeting targets from awkward positions.

5. The logical sequence of weapon training is:—

(a) Stage 1.—Pre-Classification training.

(i) Holding, aiming and trigger pressing lessons.

(ii) 30 yards Range Shooting.

(b) Stage 2.—Classification Course Instructional and Classification (Rifle and LMG).
(c) Stage 3.—Shooting on the Malayan Range. Practices to be fired on this range are shown at Appendices A and B to this Chapter.
(d) Stage 4.—Jungle Lane Shooting.
(e) Stage 5.—Competition shooting.

6. **Good Instruction and practice.**—The constant need for shooting practice cannot be overemphasised. It should be carried out at every available opportunity, on whatever form of range happens to be available. A little ingenuity will always provide a suitable range for some form of practice, whether it is for shooting at bottles floating down a stream or for shooting on a home-made Malayan Range. The standard of instruction and the degree of enthusiasm shown by the instructors is particularly important. Full use should be made, within the battalion, of instructors who have been Hythe trained or have attended one of the Platoon Weapons courses which are run in Malaya.

In this connection it is important that British battalions, when earmarked for Malaya, should send NCOs on Hythe weapons courses before coming out to Malaya.

7. **Short Range Shooting.**—The importance in Malaya of the quick deadly accurate shot has already been emphasised. Continual practise will be required on:—
  (a) The Malayan Range.
  (b) The Jungle Lane.
  (c) The Ambush Range.

8. **Malayan Range.**—The aim of the Malayan Range is to shoot in the standing position. To perfect the soldier for jungle the standing and kneeling positions at fleeting moving targets. Every company must have a range where firing can be carried out at ranges up to 100 yards. The range should be constructed under trees to reproduce the normal operational shooting light. Targets will be figure targets. In order to carry out timed practices at snap or moving targets, there must be a trench in which markers can move and present targets with safety. The alternative is a system of pull-up, and moving targets operated by wire. The trench system is by far the best, because it is a more reliable way of presenting targets, and because it allows more variation in placing them. Figure 1 shows a lay-out for a Malayan Range.

Figure 1.

X	X	X	X	A
X	X	X	X	B
100^X	75^X	50^X	25^X	

Such a lay-out enables two practices to be carried out simultaneously: one at stationary targets at A, and one at snap or moving targets at B. Both practices must be fired at the same range, and checking and pasting are done at the same time. The trench need not be straight but can zigzag in order to allow targets to appear in unexpected places. Details of the practices to be carried out are given in Appendix A (Rifle and M1/M2 Carbine) and Appendix B (Owen and L2A1 Carbine).

9. **Jungle Lane:—**

   (a) The aim of the Jungle Lane is to practise men in quick and accurate shooting, at targets representing CT, while the firers are on the move themselves down a jungle track.

   (b) A narrow winding track must be found, or cut, in jungle. The firer advances down this track at the ready position, as on patrol. At intervals, various types of targets appear. There is no need for any of these targets to be moved or controlled by hand. They can be placed so that as the firer turns a corner, or comes to a certain point, the target comes into his vision to his front or flank. If snap or moving targets are made to be controlled by hand, an instructor following behind the firer must operate the wire so as to present the target at the right moment.

   (c) The advantage of the first method is that the firer has to pick out a silent and stationary target; it is therefore a better test of his powers of observation than a pull-up target. The advantage of hand-controlled targets is that they can be made to appear for a definite timed exposure. The best solution is to have a proportion of static targets, with a variety of hand-controlled targets, appearing at ground level or at man height round the side of a tree, or moving at any angle desired. For scoring purposes, Figure 11 targets should have the "vital area" inscribed, as on the Malayan Range, and Figure 12 targets should have the circle inscribed in the centre. This is important, to bring out that only a killing shot is a good shot.

(d) CT fire can be simulated by firing a carbine or LMG in a pit near the target, firing it by means of a wire controlled by the instructor moving behind the firer. This is a good variation from static targets.

(e) It is vital that scores are properly marked and recorded, so that each man's progress can be assessed.

10. **Ambush Range.**— The object of having an ambush range is to practise fire control and shooting from an ambush position, in conditions representing, as nearly as possible, an operational ambush. The requirements, which are easy to fulfil are:—

(a) *Ambush Position.*—This should be large enough for about a section and needs careful selection. Natural cover will be required and therefore the position should be left untouched as far as possible.

(b) *Killing Ground.*—The killing ground should look as natural as possible from the ambush position, but trenches need to be dug in order that targets and markers can be moved about. If the ground allows, there should be several trenches at different angles, so that targets may approach and withdraw from different directions. A possible layout is shown at Figure 2.

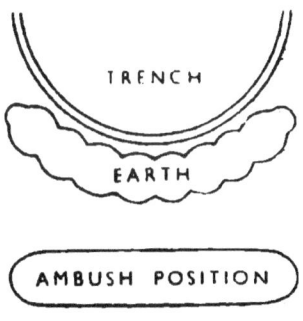

Figure 2

(c) *Safety Precautions.*—Care must be taken to ensure that sufficient earth is thrown up at the right places to give ample protection for the markers. If the ground does not favour natural protection, pulley-raised targets should be used.

(d) *Ingenuity.*—Exercises run on the ambush range depend on realism for success. The following points are useful:—

   (i) All movement by troops in the ambush position must be fully operational, e.g. position taken up silently; camoulflage, and clear orders.

   (ii) A wait should be imposed to introduce realism. Targets should appear without any warning. Once fire has opened targets must move rapidly.

   (iii) The range should be used by day and night.

11. **Post-Operational Shooting.**— After every operation a man should complete the following tasks:—

(a) His weapon should be inspected by the unit armourer.

(b) His weapon must be zeroed.

(c) He must group.

(d) He must fire rapid, snap and moving practices on the Malayan Range.

(e) If there is time he should be taken down a jungle lane.

12. **Conclusion.**—The standard of shooting required for success in Malaya can never be set too high. This standard can be achieved only by careful, continuous training. Time for this training can be found by battalions while on operations.

Section 4.—JUNIOR LEADER TRAINING

1. **General.**— Operations in Malaya largely consist of small patrols. The success or failure of these operations therefore depends on the standard of junior leaders. At the same time this form of operations is a first class training ground for junior leaders.

2. **The Requirement.**— The type of junior leader required is a mentally tough, self reliant hunter, determined to close with, and kill, the CT. He must be trained, and train his men, to be past masters in patrolling because this will be his constant task.

3. **Selection and Training.**—The company commander plays the major part in the selection and training of the junior leader. By operating with each platoon in turn he can give help and advice to junior leaders, earmark future leaders and can generally do more in a few days to improve junior leadership than a cadre could do in three weeks. This is particularly applicable to British battalions who have a high percentage of NS NCOs, with the attendant turnover. During retraining cadres should be run.

Section 5.—JUNGLE WARFARE TECHNIQUE

1. The following are the most important four subjects which must be practised and rehearsed constantly:—

 (a) *Ambushing*.—The laying of ambushes must be practised by day and night, in different types of terrain, e.g. jungle and rubber. CT and labourers must be represented. (Chapter XI gives full details of ambush methods).

 (b) *Immediate Action Drills*:—

   (i) The automatic and split second reaction to a chance encounter must continually be practised again and again under different conditions of terrain and varying circumstances. Details of IA Drills are shown in Chapter X, but it should be remembered that these are basic drills which should be improved upon, varied and interpreted according to conditions, terrain and individual commander's preference. IA Drills must never be allowed to deteriorate into stale formulae.

   (ii) CT must always be represented.

   (iii) The basis of all IA Drills is vigorous offensive action and this fact must be brought out on all training.

 (c) *Counter Ambush*.—Counter ambush drills are given in Chapter X. Counter ambush action when in MT is given in Chapter XIII. These must be practised with CT represented.

 (d) *Attack on CT Camps and Cultivations*.—These attacks come under two headings:—

   (i) The Immediate Attack. This is described in Chapter X, Section 3. It is in fact an IA Drill which requires good training if it is to be carried out at the necessary speed.

   (ii) The Deliberate Attack. This is described in Chapter XII. For complete success it requires careful preparation, training and rehearsal. CT must be realistically represented in positions which they would take up for their security.

2. **Other subjects.**—The following subjects require continual practise before and during operations. Improvements and variation of methods should be continually striven for in order to raise the standard.

(a) *Patrol Formations.*—The correct distance between individuals and groups will vary in accordance with terrain.
(b) *Observation.*—A vitally important subject. However tired a man may be he must never be allowed to plod along, eyes on the ground. This is a matter of training and discipline. A patrol which is not alert walks with death.
(c) *All round protection.*—The need for all round protection is more important in the jungle than anywhere else.
(d) *Silent movement.*—A vitally important subject because a noisy patrol will never achieve anything. British troops in particular require a lot of training before they reach the required standard, but once they have achieved it they can move as silently as any other troops in the world. Particular attention should be paid to halting, listening and observing.
(e) *Keeping direction,*—Chapter IX deals fully with navigation. Direction keeping comes with training and experience.
(f) *Tracking.*—Officers should be on the look-out for men who show a special aptitude for tracking. They should be earmarked for special training. Efforts should be made to train men to develop a 'tracker's eye.'

Section 6.—TIME FOR TRAINING

1. The question of how much time should be spent on training can best be answered by showing what must be done every time a company comes out of the jungle.

2. **Programme.**— At least four days are required for the following, in order of priority:—
   (a) zeroing and shooting;
   (b) rest;
   (c) administration;
   (d) jungle training.

3. These few days give the company commander his only real opportunity to improve the operational efficiency of his platoons and therefore these four items must be covered in a carefully balanced programme.

4. **Shooting.**— It is essential that each platoon should fire every day on the company's Malayan Range. The allotment of time for re-zeroing and shooting training on the Malayan

Range to sections or platoons will thus determine the times at which other, less important, tasks can be carried out. For example while one platoon is shooting in the early morning the other two will be carrying out some of the administrative tasks or jungle training. When necessary many administrative tasks can be carried out after dark.

5. **Administration.**— A considerable number of administrative points have to be covered, for example:—
   (a) Hot baths, haircuts and medical inspection.
   (b) Cleaning, inspection and checking of all arms, ammunition, wireless equipment and compasses, inspection and exchange of clothing and personal equipment.
   (c) Washing of clothes and application of DBP.
   (d) Miscellaneous items such as pay, reading of battalion orders, etc.

6. **Jungle Training.**— Although the company has just come out of the jungle, it nevertheless requires practice in jungle battle drills and IA. The best value will only be obtained from this practice if the CT are represented and the exercise is properly umpired and criticised.

7. **Games.**— Facilities for games will vary considerably in different company areas and because of different types of operational commitment. Every opportunity, however, should be taken to run inter-platoon football, cross-country and other competitions. Improvisation will usually provide facilities for basketball and badminton where no football fields exist. These games must be planned in advance as part of the programme.

Section 7.—COURSES AND CADRES

1. Throughout the year units should send a steady flow of students on courses. A list of courses available in FARELF is contained in the 'Brochure of All Arms Courses Available in FARELF' issued to all units.

2. Battalion cadres on the following should take place during the year.
   (a) Junior Leader.
   (b) MMG (less Malay Battalions).
   (c) 3-in. Mortar.
   (d) A tk Training.

(e) Weapon Training.
(f) Signals.
(g) Driver Operator.

Section 8.—CONCLUSION

1. The special nature of operations in Malaya emphasises the vital importance of quick deadly accurate shooting and the need for good junior leaders, on whom so much depends. These two essential pillars on which to build success can be acquired only by continuous training before and during operations.

2. Every unit has its quiet periods when investments may not appear to be paying large dividends, measured in terms of CT killed, but all of a sudden the ideal chance presents itself, and it is then that success hinges, not on luck, but on sound training and marksmanship.

Appx A

Appendix A

MALAYAN RANGE—PRACTICES

(Rifle and M1/M2 Carbine)

Practice 1

Grouping.—5 rounds. Fig. 11 target with 1-in. square patch as aiming mark. Standard required 4-in. group. HPS 25.

Practice 2

Timed.—5 rounds. Fig. 11 target with rectangles 2-in. x 4-in., 4-in. x 6-in. inscribed in centre of target. Time 15 seconds. Scoring 4, 3, 2. HPS 20.

Practice 3

Snap.—10 rounds. Five differently coloured Fig. 11 targets. Ten 4 second exposures timed at the Firing Point. (Reduced to 2 seconds as proficiency increases). Firer engages a colour as ordered by the instructor and fires one round each time a target is named. Scoring 3, 2. HPS 30.

Practice 4

Snap.—10 rounds. Fig 12 target with 6-in. circle inscribed in centre of target. Ten 4 second exposures (reduced to 2 seconds as proficiency increases). One shot each exposure. Scoring 3, 2. HPS 30.

Practice 5

Moving Target.—5 rounds. Length of run 15 yards. Target appears at walking speed. Firer engages with one shot and target breaks into running speed. Firer then fires 1 or 2 more shots. This process is repeated on the return run of the target. Scoring 3, 2. HPS 15.

NOTES

(a) Total number of rounds 35
    HPS 120

(b) Practices should initially be carried out at 25 yards, and increased up to 100 yards as proficiency increases.

(c) In practices 3 and 5, Fig. 11 targets will be marked with two lines 6-in. apart, forming a "vital area" 6-in. wide down the centre of the target from top to bottom. Scoring—3 points per hit in the vital area, 2 points per hit elsewhere on the target.

(d) Standing position will be used up to 50 yards range, and standing or kneeling at ranges over 50 yards.

Appx B

Appendix B

MALAYAN RANGE—PRACTICES

(Owen and L2A1 Carbines)

Practice 1

Grouping.—5 single rounds. Fig. 11 target with 1-in square patch as aiming mark. HPS 25. Standard required 4-in. group.

Practice 2

Timed.—12 rounds in 3-4 bursts. Fig. 11 target with rectangles 2-in. by 4-in., 4-in. by 6-in. inscribed in centre of target. Time:— 6 seconds (reduced to 4 seconds as proficiency increases). Scoring 4, 3, 2. HPS 48.

Practice 3

Snap.—15 rounds. Five differently coloured Fig. 11 targets. Five 3 second exposures (timed at Firing Point (reduced to 2 seconds as proficiency increases)). Firer engages a colour as ordered by instructor, and fires one burst each time a target is named. Scoring 3, 2. HPS 45.

Practice 4

Snap.—15 rounds. Fig. 12 targets with 6-in. circle inscribed in centre of target. Five 3 second exposures (reduced to 2 seconds as proficiency increases). One burst each exposure. Scoring 3, 2. HPS 45.

Practice 5

Moving Target.—15 rounds. Fig. 11 target. Length of run 15 yards. Target appears at walking speed. Firer engages with one burst, and target moves on at running speed. Firer then engages with another burst. This process is repeated on the return run of the target. Scoring 3, 2. HPS 45.

NOTES

(a) Total number of rounds 62
    HPS 208

(b) Practices should initially be carried out at 25 yards and as proficiency increases the ranges will be increased up to 100 yards.

(c) The grouping practice at 25 yards can also be utilised to "straighten up" the weapons for direction by tapping the foresight into the direction of error as shown by the MPI.

(d) In practices 3 and 5, Fig. 11 targets will be marked with two lines 6-in. apart, forming a "vital area" 6-in. wide down the centre of the target from top to bottom. Scoring 3 points per hit in the vital area, and 2 points per hit elsewhere on the target.

(e) Standing position will be used up to 50 yards, and standing or kneeling at ranges over 50 yards.

CHAPTER XVI

WIRELESS COMMUNICATIONS IN MALAYA

Section 1.—INTRODUCTION

1. This Chapter gives patrol commanders basic information about wireless communications in Malaya and some simple rules to follow when establishing communications in the jungle.

2. A more detailed outline of current techniques phrased in simple language will be found in the pamphlet "Some Notes on Wireless in Malaya" which was produced by the CSO Malaya and is issued to all units in Malaya. Further copies can be obtained from G (Trg) HQ 17 GURKHA Div/OCLF. If the best results are to be obtained by signal platoons it is essential that this pamphlet is thoroughly studied by all Regimental Signal Officers and NCOs.

3. The necessity for silence in the efficient conduct of operations in the jungle militates against the use of 'Voice' over patrol wireless sets. Morse Telegraphy is both silent in operation and often much more effective under the difficult wireless conditions in Malaya. It is therefore essential that the maximum number of signallers know the morse code at a speed of not less than eight words per minute.

4. **Communications for Air Support.**— See Chapter XVII Section 12.

Section 2.—WIRELESS SETS IN USE IN MALAYA

1. Units in Malaya are issued with the following sets:—
   (a) WS A 510 or WS 68T
   (b) WS 62
   (c) WS 19
   (d) WS 88
   (e) Receiver R 209

2. These sets are used as follows:—
   (a) *WS A 510.*—This is the patrol commander's set and is used to communicate with either battalion or company headquarters dependent on the signal layout. It is an Australian HF set specially designed for jungle operations. It operates on frequencies between 2 and 10 megacycles. It is crystal controlled which simplifies tuning. The receiver and sender, which are separate, fit into two basic pouches and the total weight of the complete station is

20 lbs. 9 oz. Its performance is much better than the WS 68T and is for most purposes as good as the WS 62. It can be used for Voice and Telegraph transmissions. The dry batteries with which it is powered will last for eight hours under normal conditions.

(b) *WS 68T.*—The set operates on frequencies between 3 and 5.2 megacycles and can be crystal controlled. It can be carried by one man but is bulky and uncomfortable. Together with his personal kit the operator has to carry a load of some 50-54 pounds and he should be assisted whenever possible. The set is designed for Voice and Telegraph. It is powered by a dry battery which, suitably conserved, can be made to last about 5 days on patrol.

(c) *WS 62.*—This is the set for company headquarters. It operates on frequencies between 2 and 8 megacycles and can be crystal controlled. The set is powered by wet batteries which require periodical recharging. This represents no difficulty at company headquarters. Although the set is light, the extra equipment required—batteries, charging engine, petrol, oil, distilled water—makes it unsuitable for patrol work. For deep jungle operations a number of WS 62 have been modified for working with dry batteries and may be made available on special authority.

(d) *WS 19.*—The WS 19 is a heavy, robust set designed to be operated in a static position or in a vehicle, and is normally used in battalion headquarters or in a scout car. It can be operated for long periods without wandering off frequency or requiring attention. It operates on frequencies between 2 and 8 megacycles and cannot be crystal controlled.

(e) *WS 88.*—This set is small, light, and easy to operate, but can only be used for Voice. It is a VHF set operating on 4-set frequencies about 40 megacycles and is therefore not of value for sky-wave working. Possible uses include short range links, convoy control and communication with aircraft. For the latter a WS 88 must be carried in the aircraft.

(f) *Receiver R 209.*—This is a receiving set only and provided at Battalion HQ as a general purpose receiver. Examples of its use are reception of broadcasts, listening in to wireless nets outside the Battalion and identifying interference. It is battery operated and covers frequencies from 1 to 20 megacycles.

Section 3.—AERIALS

1. The standard aerial for infantry wireless sets is a rod, from which is radiated a horizontal or ground wave. Due to the nature of the terrain and the vegetation in Malaya the ground wave is quickly absorbed or screened, or both.

2. It is therefore necessary to radiate a sky-wave which is reflected back to the distant station from the upper atmosphere. For efficient sky-wave radiation a wire aerial cut to a length proportional to frequency is required. A table of such lengths is at Appendix B to this Chapter. The simplest type of sky-wave aerial is in the form of the letter L, with the longer side horizontal and the shorter one making the lead into the set (see Appendix A Fig. 1). This is the type of aerial normally erected by the jungle patrol. The following points regarding this aerial must be borne in mind: —

- (a) The aerial must be of good copper wire.
- (b) It must be held clear of vegetation and all other matters by insulators.
- (c) Vegetation should whenever possible, be cleared from above and below the aerial (the earth acts like a reflector in an electric torch).
- (d) It must be cut to a length proportional to the frequency in use.
- (e) It should be about 20-25 feet off the ground.
- (f) Directional properties of the aerial are not critical but the required signal will be best received if the length of the aerial is at right angles to the direction of the required station.

3. The method of tuning this type of aerial with WS 68T is given in Appendix A to this Chapter.

4. Wire aerials for the WS A 510 are issued with the set kit. The length is varied by making or breaking connections across insulator chain links. The appropriate connections for different frequencies are printed on the aerial spools.

5. Other types of aerial are described in 'Notes on Wireless' and should be studied with a view to their use in special circumstances.

6. By far the most efficient aerial for short range sky-wave working is the JAMAICA. It is not practicable to erect this on patrol but it should be put up at every battalion and company Headquarters as it greatly improves the strength of the received signal. This is of considerable importance when patrol sets are

perforce poorly sited and are transmitting a weak signal to their control station. The JAMAICA aerial requires special stores for which separate indent must be made.

Section 4.—FREQUENCY ALLOCATION

Due to the large number of units using sky-wave in Malaya it is essential that units work only on their allotted frequencies to avoid interference with others. Control sets should therefore be set up accurately on the allotted frequency by crystal calibrator or wavemeter if they are not crystal controlled.

Section 5.—CONCLUSION

1. It is essential that intelligent men are selected for training as infantry company and platoon operators. They should also possess the necessary physique to carry their load for long periods over difficult country. Officers and NCOs should, by example, encourage operators in the use of correct procedure. Faulty procedure delays transmission and occupies time on the air.

2. Success of patrol communication depends, in the first instance on the training of signallers, secondly, on the preparation and checking of sets and batteries, and thirdly, on intelligent selection of sites by commanders. Once signallers are committed to a jungle operation they will be on their own without technical supervision from their signal officers.

3. Wireless communication in Malaya, although often difficult, is rarely impossible. With thorough training an operator soon learns to have confidence in his set and in his own ability to establish communications under the conditions and over the ranges involved.

Appendix A

METHODS OF TUNING SIMPLE SKY WAVE AERIAL FOR WS 68T

1. Normal methods of tuning for maximum rise on meter with meter switch at AE.

2. (a) Search for incoming signal with receiver.
   (b) Reduce to minimum with LF gain, and tune accurately.
   (c) Tune aerial for maximum signal.

3. (a) Meter switch to MA.
   (b) Aerial switch to 8.
   (c) Press pressel switch.
   (d) Rotate aerial tuning dial until slight but definite dip observed on meter.
   (e) If no dip is observed, put aerial switch to 7 and repeat.
   (f) Carry on until dip is obtained.
   (g) Net set in normal manner to tuning and netting call.
   (h) Retune aerial with new frequency.

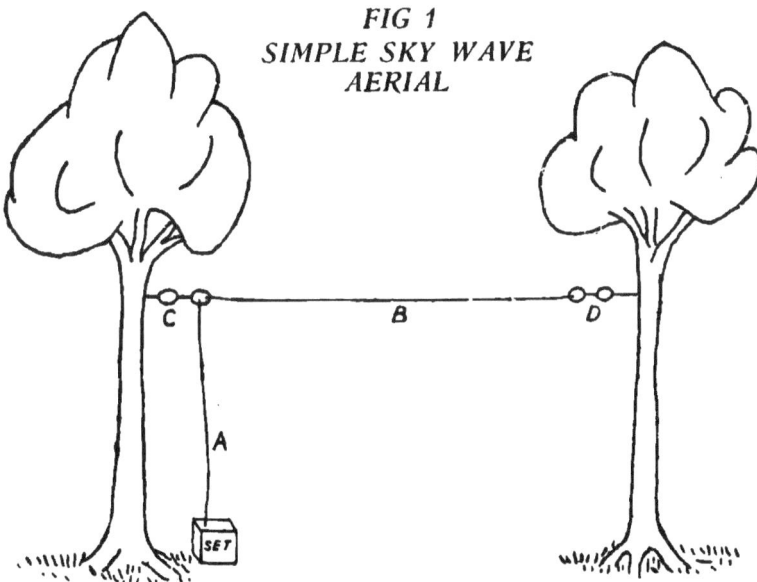

FIG 1
SIMPLE SKY WAVE AERIAL

A+B = LENGTH GIVEN IN APPX 'B'
C & D CHAIN LINK INSULATORS

XVI
Appx B

Appendix B

AERIAL LENGTHS

All lengths given are A plus B in Figure 1 to Appendix A

HALF WAVE AERIAL for use with WS A 510 and WS 68T

Formula for calculating $\dfrac{468{,}000}{\text{frequency in kilocycles}}$ = half wave length in feet.

Frequency in Kc/s.	Length A and B in feet.	Frequency in Kc/s.	Length A and B in feet.	Frequency in Kc/s.	Length A and B in feet.
3,000	156	3,800	123	4,600	102
3,100	151	3,900	120	4,700	100
3,200	146	4,000	117	4,800	98
3,300	142	4,100	114	4,900	96
3,400	138	4,200	111	5,000	94
3,500	134	4,300	108	5,100	92
3,600	130	4,400	106	5,200	90
3,700	126	4,500	104		

Note: The spool issued with the wire aerial for WS A 510 has aerial lengths appropriate to frequencies printed on it.

THREE QUARTER WAVE AERIAL for use with WS 62 and WS 19

Formula for calculating $\dfrac{702{,}000}{\text{frequency in kilocycles}}$ = three quarter wave length in feet.

Frequency in Kc/s.	Length A and B in feet.	Frequency in Kc/s.	Length A and B in feet.
3,000	234	5,500	128
3,500	200	6,000	117
4,000	175	6,500	108
4,500	156	7,000	100
5,000	140	7,500	94

CHAPTER XVII

AIR SUPPORT IN MALAYA

Section 1.—INTRODUCTION

1. **General.**— This Chapter is intended to give a working knowledge of:—
    (a) The support which the Royal Air Force can give to ground forces in Malaya.
    (b) The most important points to be considered in planning and executing joint ground/air operations.
    (c) The methods of submitting requests for air support.

2. **Types of Air Support.**— The following types of air support are available:—
    (a) *Offensive Air Support.*
    (b) *Transport Support.*
    (c) *Photographic and Visual Reconnaissance.*
    (d) *Psychological Warfare (PW) Support.*

3. **Planning:—**
    (a) *General.*—When operations are being planned for which any form of air support may be required, it is important that the Joint Operations Centre (JOC) in Kuala Lumpur is kept informed. If specialist advice is required an Air Representative is always available on request to assist at unit or formation planning conferences.
    (b) *Offensive Air Support.*—If offensive air support is to form part of a plan, the assistance of a representative from the JOC should be called for to attend at unit or formation planning conferences to advise on the type and weight of offensive air support. If support is required on a large scale a JOC representative should always be asked to attend.
    (c) *Transport Support.*—There is a limited force of helicopters, communication and supply aircraft available for essential air support. Immediate air transport support can be met only at the expense of normal operations. When large numbers of troops are to be moved or supplied by air, the JOC should be informed early of the date and duration of the operation and full details of the requirements.

(d) *Reconnaissance and Psychological Warfare.*—These types of air support are dealt with in detail elsewhere in this Chapter.

Section 2.—COMMAND, CONTROL AND LIAISON

1. **Command and Control.**— Command of the air forces allotted for support of ground forces engaged in the Emergency in Malaya is vested in the Air Officer Commanding, No. 224 Group, RAF; his operational control of these air forces is exercised through the JOC.

2. **Joint Operations Centre.**— HQ 17 Gurkha Division/Overseas Commonwealth Land Forces (OCLF) and Headquarters 224 Group RAF each contribute staff to the JOC which exercises centralised control of all air forces in Malaya. It is concerned entirely with direct support as there is no air opposition.

  (a) *The duties of the Army Staff* (GSO 2 (Air)) are to:—
    (i) Plan joint operations with the RAF Staff.
    (ii) Receive and assess demands for air support from the ground forces and to allot priorities when necessary.
    (iii) Inform the demanding units of the air effort allocated to them.
    (iv) Keep the RAF informed of projected ground operations and of the results of operations conducted with air support.
    (v) Provide GLOs (see paragraph 3 (b)) with briefing material and keep them informed on current and future operations.

  (b) *The duties of the RAF Staff* (Squadron Leader Operations and Intelligence Officer) are to:—
    (i) Decide on the suitability of tasks and allot priorities.
    (ii) Plan joint operations with the Army Staff.
    (iii) Allocate aircraft and issue RAF operation orders.
    (iv) Collect, collate and disseminate RAF Intelligence.

  (c) GSO 2 (Air) and Squadron Leader Operations are always on call. Units may communicate direct with GSO 2 (Air) on matters of urgency.

3. **Army/RAF Liaison** is maintained by RAF representatives from JOC (usually a Squadron Leader Operations) and Ground Liaison Officers (GLOs) at RAF units.

(a) *RAF Representatives, JOC.*—The RAF representative from the JOC is required to:—
   (i) Visit SF units and advise on air matters when required.
   (ii) Assist in joint planning of Army/Air operations.
   (iii) Form, with a GLO, an Air Contact Team (ACT) when required.
(b) *GLOs.*—GLOs are Army Officers specially trained in Land/Air Warfare. They are normally based at RAF airfields where their duties are to:—
   (i) Present the ground forces requirement to the RAF.
   (ii) Portray the ground situation to their RAF commander, pilots and aircrew.
   (iii) Assist in the interrogation of aircrews on return from missions.
   (iv) Report results of missions to the military commander concerned.
   (v) Position and operate air tentacles, and form an ACT with an RAF representative when required.
(c) In addition to their duties at RAF airfields, GLOs are in support of Army formations, the police and civil authorities. In conjunction with or in the absence of RAF representatives their duties are to:—
   (i) Keep in the operational picture and brief the JOC on the ground situation as necessary.
   (ii) Portray the air situation to the ground troops.
   (iii) Be available to give air support advice to formations and unit commanders.
   (iv) Check that the various aspects of Army/Air operations are functioning satisfactorily and inform the JOC of any difficulties.

4. **G Int/Air Recce.**—Co-ordination of PR demands, processing and interpretation, and of visual air reconnaissance is carried out by a GSO 3 Int /Air Recce, HQ 17 GURKHA Div./OCLF.

Section 3.—OFFENSIVE AIR SUPPORT

1. **Aircraft and Armament.**—The following aircraft types are available:—
   (a) *Medium bombers.*
   (b) *Jet fighter/ground attack.*

2. These aircraft are variously armed with 1,000 lb., 500 lb. and 20 lb. bombs, 60 lb. rocket projectiles (RP) and cannon or machine guns of 20 mm., ·5 in. or ·303 in.

3. **Types of Offensive Air Support.**—Offensive Air Support may take any of the following forms:—
   (a) *Air Strikes.*—Bombing, rocket and/or straffing attacks against known CT locations.
   (b) *Harassing Attacks.*—Bombing, rocket and/or straffing attacks against areas of CT activity.
   (c) *Close Support.*—Offensive air action in direct support of troops. (Available but rarely, if ever, usable in Malaya).
   (d) *Psychological Warfare.*—Consisting of both tactical and strategical use of Voice aircraft and leaflets (see Section 10).
   (e) *Crop Destruction.*—See Section 4.

4. **Aims of Offensive Air Support.**—Offensive Air Support operations aim to:—
   (a) Kill CT.
   (b) Induce CT to keep on the move, thereby increasing the chance of contacts and kills by ground forces.
   (c) Disrupt the CT base and command organisation.
   (d) Lower CT morale by inducing a sense of insecurity and to induce surrenders.
   (e) Assist in food denial by crop destruction.

5. **Air Strikes:—**
   (a) These are strikes against pin-point targets such as an occupied CT camp or a concentration of CT in a known location. In the case of occupied CT camps, the location of which is accurately known, the RAF should normally act in the primary role.
   (b) Targets in Malaya are rarely visible to the strike aircraft and because of the lack of a positive aiming point the most effective type of attack is one in which a formation of bombers drop a pattern of bombs designed to envelop the target area.
   (c) Accuracy of bombing is vital in every attack. The following methods are used to assist strike aircraft to engage targets effectively:—
      (i) Target marking flares dropped by Auster aircraft.
      (ii) Bearing and distance runs from flare or natural datum.

(iii) Radar control. Target Director Post (TDP).
(iv) Variations of the above methods.
(d) Ideal requirements for an airstrike are:—
   (i) Positive information regarding the presence of CT in the target area.
   (ii) The position of the target must be given with the highest possible degree of accuracy.
   (iii) Target screened from all ground and air action likely to compromise the effect of a surprise attack.
   (iv) Freedom of action to choose the time of the attack consistent with intelligence and weather information.
   (v) Immediate follow-up by ground forces whenever possible.

6. **Harassing Attacks.**—These are area air strikes against broadly defined targets and are usually in the supporting role:—
   (a) *Aims of Harassing Attacks are to:*—
      (i) Maintain pressure on CT.
      (ii) Induce movement of CT and so increase the chances of contacts by ground forces.
      (iii) Lower morale and induce CT to surrender.
      (iv) Deny selected areas to CT.
   (b) *Air Requirements are:*—
      (i) Reasonable assurance that CT are in the area.
      (ii) An area of not more than 4 x 1,000 yard map squares.
      (iii) Follow-up by ground troops whenever possible.
      (iv) The use of voice aircraft and leaflet dropping whenever appropriate.

7. **Selection of Target.**— The following factors should be considered:—
   (a) The aim of air support.
   (b) Type and size of the target.
   (c) Accuracy of the target position.
   (d) Timing and duration of attack.
   (e) Position of own troops in relation to target.
   (f) Police clearance.

8. **Safety Areas.**— The normal danger areas within which there are to be no troops, civilians, habitations or legal cultivations, are:—
   (a) *By Day, on the line of attack:*—
      1,500 yards on each flank.
      1,500 yards on the undershoot.
      3,000 yards on the overshoot.

(b) *By Night, on the line of attack*:—
   2,000 yards on each flank.
   2,500 yards on the undershoot.
   3,500 yards on the overshoot.

9. **Safety Precautions.**— As an additional precaution, requesting units are to give the positions of any of our own troops, civilians, estate labour and habitations within 500 yards of the safety areas as defined in sub-paragraphs 8 (a) and (b) above.

10. **Police Clearance.**— Police clearance must be obtained by the formation or unit requesting the air support, for all targets and signalled to the JOC. Such clearance must relate to the ground position at the time of issue and thereafter until the airstrike is complete. It is important that the area cleared is stated precisely and that no changes will occur due to troop movements, etc. The minimum area required can be found in the preceding paragraph 8 on Safety Areas. Normally clearances must be passed to JOC at least four hours prior to the "time on target" of the strike force.

11. **Requests for Offensive Air Support.**
   (a) Offensive Air Support requests will be submitted direct to JOC 224 Group RAF in accordance with the guide to the preparation of requests given in Appendix A. Copy of all requests will be sent to higher formation HQ, who have the right of veto or amendment, and to GLOs Tengah and Butterworth.
   (b) Requests will normally be given precedence 'OP IMMEDIATE.'

12. JOC will pass acceptances and refusals direct to units, copy to formation HQ concerned.

13. Immediately aircraft return from a strike the GLO will obtain a quick debrief from the crew and will signal a snap report to the JOC and the unit and formation HQ concerned. Snap reports will include the following information:—
   (a) RAF Operation Order number and target number if applicable.
   (b) If all armament fell in target area. If not, grid reference of area hit outside target area.
   (c) Time on and off target.
   (d) Additional information, including grid reference of anything seen in target area, e.g. unexploded bombs.

Reports of unexploded bombs should include approximate location, direction of bombing run, number of bombs in the stick which failed to explode and any other information likely to assist a demolition party.

14. **Follow-up Report.**— Follow-up reports should be prepared as soon as circumstances allow, giving more detailed information in accordance with Appendix P. These reports should be submitted by the unit concerned to its formation HQ for forwarding to JOC, copy to HQ 224 Group. JOC requires two copies. Copies of unit reports should be sent to GLOs concerned.

Section 4.—AIR TRANSPORT SUPPORT—GENERAL

1. **General.**— Air Transport Support in Malaya includes:—
    (a) Air supply by both air-dropped and air-transported methods.
    (b) Paratroop operations.
    (c) Air transported movement of operational units and their equipment, known more generally as troop-lifting operations.
    (d) Casualty evacuation flights.
    (e) Communication flights.
    (f) Crop destruction.
    (g) Reconnaissance, in certain special circumstances.
    (h) Air-to-ground broadcasting by loudspeaker (Voice operations).

2. **Air Transport Forces Available.**— The following air transport forces are available in support of emergency operations:—
    (a) A force of medium range transport aircraft. Their main tasks are air supply, paratroop operations, leaflet dropping, and air-transported troop movements.
    (b) One squadron of medium helicopters whose main tasks are troop lifting, paratroop operations, and crop destruction.
    (c) One squadron of light helicopters whose main tasks are casualty evacuation and communication flights.
    (d) One flight of fixed-wing communication aircraft.
    (e) One flight of light air transport aircraft whose main tasks are troop lifting, communication flights, air-transported supply and casualty evacuation.
    (f) One flight of Voice aircraft (see Section 10).

(g) Communication flights are provided also by aircraft on charter from the Federation Air Service.
(h) Communication flight facilities are available also from one Army Air Corps Squadron of light aircraft. These facilities are controlled by the Army formation to which the flights are allocated.

3. **Roles and Priorities.**— The allotment of fixed priorities to the various roles for which the air transport forces can be used is neither practicable nor desirable. It is necessary to adopt a flexible system, based on control by a staff which is aware of the importance of each current operation and which understands the problems and priorities of the civil, police, army and air force users. As a guide to the JOC and those requesting air transport support, the following priorities are applicable to light air transport aircraft and helicopters:—

(a) *Light Air Transport Aircraft.*
  (i) Provision of regular air service to specified police posts and jungle forts.
  (ii) Exchange of garrisons from specified police posts and forts.
  (iii) Communication flights for commanders and their staffs.
  (iv) Casualty evacuation.
  (v) Air-transported supply to specified police posts and forts.

(b) *Helicopters.*
  (i) Casualty evacuation.
  (ii) Tactical movement of troops including paratroop operations.
  (iii) Movement of commanders, staff officers, and special intelligence material; reconnaissance and communication flying for security forces and civil authorities in connection with the Emergency.
  (iv) Movement of guides, aborigines, SEP and CT dead when required for interrogation or identification in connection with Emergency operations.
  (v) Exchange of police garrisons at jungle forts not equipped with an airstrip, when marching or river movement is operationally undesirable.
  (vi) Aerial spraying of illegal cultivations.
  (vii) Supply or salvage, for security forces or civil authorities, directly connected with Emergency operations.

(viii) Reconnaissance, supply, or evacuation, for security forces or civil authorities in the event of floods or serious disaster. This might take over-riding priority.

4. **Detachment of Air Transport Forces.**— Detachments of aircraft and crews from the main Air Transport Forces' Base will from time to time be ordered by the AOC No. 224 Group. Such detachments will only be ordered in those few special cases when the operational advantages gained outweigh the technical, supply, and domestic difficulties inherent in detaching aircraft (particularly helicopters) away from their primary maintenance base facilities.

5. **Planning of Air Transport Operations.**— All forms of air transport are expensive and in short supply. To enable the most efficient use to be made of the forces available formations and units must take the following factors into consideration when planning operations involving the use of air transport support:—

(a) Helicopters are far more expensive to operate than equivalent fixed wing aircraft.

(b) Helicopter performance is adversely affected to an increasingly large degree at altitudes over 2,000 feet. High temperature, and LZs below the minimum specifications, also affect performance to a large extent.

(c) As a general rule, all air transport operations should be mounted from the nearest possible suitable airstrip/LZ to the operational area.

(d) Any tactical routing of aircraft involves a greater air effort.

(e) In order to achieve a good utilisation rate with communication aircraft, communication flights must be planned with a high degree of flexibility.

(f) Because of the daily tendency for build-up of clouds, air operations over the central mountainous area of Malaya are difficult (and often impossible) after about 1300 hours.

(g) Commanders should make maximum use of the advice of the RAF in the initial stages of contemplating and planning an operation involving air support. This is the only way to ensure that the commander will get the maximum advantage from the air effort available.

(h) To enable the JOC to co-ordinate air transport support tasks, requests should be submitted with as much prior warning as possible.

(j) Once a task has been agreed and accepted by the JOC, details of Avgas requirements, routes to be flown, and number of aircraft/crews required are resolved, and the RAF Operation Order is issued. Any last minute changes to the task invariably change these planning details and are often difficult to arrange.

(k) Once he is given a task, the aircraft captain is ordered to adhere rigidly to the RAF Operation Order which covers the task. Pilots may only diverge from an operation order without prior reference to JOC for reasons of emergency, that is:—

   (i) Casevac.
   (ii) Reinforcement of patrols in contact with CT.
   (iii) Replacements of essential radio which has become unserviceable.
   (iv) Supply of emergency rations.
   (v) To provide aid to ground forces or civil authorities thought to be in imminent distress (e.g. cut off by flood waters).

6. **Aircraft Details.**— Brief details of aircraft performance, use of equipment, emplaning drills and safety precautions will be found in the Appendices to this Chapter.

7. **Helicopter Landing Zone (LZ) Requirements.**— Details of the requirements for helicopter LZs for normal and emergency use are contained in Appendix L.

8. **Transport Aircraft Airstrips.**— A list, periodically revised, of airstrips which are cleared for use by various air transport aircraft is contained in Joint Army/Air Instructions.

Section 5.—AIR TRANSPORT SUPPORT—AIR SUPPLY

1. **General.**— There are two methods of air supply:—
   (a) Air drop by parachute or free drop.
   (b) Air transportation on to an airstrip or LZ.

2. **Air Supply Drops.**— Air supply by the air drop method forms the major part of air supply operations. The majority of air supply drops are carried out by a small force of medium range transport aircraft. Small supply drops can be made from light aircraft, and, when special conditions warrant their use, from helicopters.

3. **Air Transported Supply.**— When a suitable airstrip is available and the light air transport aircraft effort can be allocated, the air supply of jungle bases will be carried out by the air transported method. When special conditions warrant their use, helicopters may be used to air land supplies at jungle LZs. Special instructions relating to demands for operational airtransported supply are contained in paragraph 12.

4. **Procedure for Requesting Air Supply:**—
  (a) *Army.*—All requests for supply by air will be addressed by units direct to:
    (i) GLO RAF KUALA LUMPUR, and to
    (ii) 55 Company RASC (AD), and
    (iii) with information copy to "JOC for attention G2 Air."

When Engineer, Medical or Ordnance stores are required, Engineer Branch of the Formation concerned, 39 Field Ambulance Unit, or 21 Air Maintenance Platoon as appropriate will be included as action addressees. A copy of each request will also be sent to the immediately superior formation.

  (b) *Police.*—Requests by the Civil Police for air supply to jungle forts, police patrols, etc., will be forwarded as per paragraph 4 (a) above by COMPOL (Q). When an abnormal quantity of supplies is required COMPOL (Q) should consult the GSO 2 (Air), Headquarters No. 224 Group, who will be able to obtain RAF advice as to how and when the particular operation can best be handled.

5. **Method of Requesting.**— Requests may be given the signal precedence of OP IMMEDIATE if necessary and will be submitted on normal signal message forms. Text will open with the words "AIR SUPPLY" and the code letters V (VICTOR), W (WHISKEY) and Y (YANKEE) will be used as detailed below.
  (a) *V—Supplies Required:*—
    (i) This paragraph will give full details of supplies and stores required, including NAAFI supplies; the latter will, when it is considered there may be a non-availability of any item, show alternatives to be issued in lieu. The number of men being supplied through the DZ will be shown at the beginning of the text which will be laid out as follows:—
    RASC Supplies.
    ORD Supplies.
    MED Supplies.
    RE Stores

NAAFI Requirements.
Unit Stores, mail and papers.
- (ii) Unit stores will be accepted for dropping only if the unit is able to deliver to 55 Company RASC (AD). Weight signalled must be the accurate weight of stores otherwise no guarantee can be given that they will be despatched. *Stores must be delivered to 55 Company RASC (AD) by 0900 hours on the day before the drop.* Packages will not exceed 3' x 2' x 2' and must be clearly labelled with the name of the unit and DZ letter for which it is intended.
- (iii) When the requirements of other forces/units/sub-units are included in the signal they will be given after those of the unit making the request and in the order given in paragraph 5 (a) (i) above (this includes such units as Sarawak Rangers, Police, (including Home Guards and SEPs) and Aborigines (Sakai)).

(b) *W—DZ Grid References.*—The map sheet, the two grid letters and the six-figure grid reference of the DZ will be given. If special considerations require that the message should be encoded, the encoding will be repeated once. On no account should requests be delayed for want of a grid reference. If a grid reference is not available when a request is forwarded, the map sheet must be included to enable tasks to be planned. The grid letters and the six grid figures can follow later. Out of office hours this latter information should be telephoned to the Operations Room, RAF, Kuala Lumpur (Telephone: Kuala Lumpur 7711).

(c) *X—Recognition Aids:—*
- (i) A DZ letter and a horizontal bar will be shown on the ground by means of fluorescent panels. Extra horizontal bars may be used to differentiate between sub-units using the same DZ letter. They will be placed alongside the DZ letter.
- (ii) Any aid to facilitate recognition of the DZ from the air will be noted on the request. It should also be stated what recognition aids are being used to guide the aircraft to the DZ, for example, "White smoke—Marker balloon."
  Note. Marker balloons have proved particularly satisfactory as DZ markers, and will be used whenever possible.
- (iii) Wireless frequency will be given by quoting the current serial number of the frequency in use.

(d) *Y—Time and Date Drop Required.*—As far as possible a margin of time will be given to coincide with the times the RAF normally undertake their sorties, i.e. 0900 to 1100, 1130 to 1330, or PM. Other times will be accepted only under special circumstances. GLO RAF Kuala Lumpur will notify the unit concerned only if the planned time of the drop differs from that requested. If on the day of the supply drop there is a change of timing, GLO RAF Kuala Lumpur will notify the unit by the quickest means possible. This paragraph YANKEE will also include the appointment and telephone number of the unit's contact, e.g. "CONTACT IO KLUANG 204."

(e) A specimen air supply request is given at Appendix B. Units will note that:—
  (i) Types of ration (BRITISH, GURKHA or MALAY) are written in full.
  (ii) Ordnance clothing is demanded by item, size and quantity—in that order.

6. Notice Required:—

(a) *Air Supply Requests.*—Air supply requests will reach addressees by 1800 hours at the latest on "D" minus 2, D-Day being the day of the actual drop. Additions to requests will not be made after this time unless subsequent justification can be made to HQ 17 GURDIV/OCLF, Q (Maint). 55 Company RASC (AD) will report all late requests to HQ 17 GURDIV/OCLF.

(b) *Ammunition and Petrol Demands.* Demands for abnormal quantities of ammunition and petrol will reach addressees by 1400 hours on D minus 2.

(c) *Emergency Air Supply.*—Genuine emergency air supply demands will be accepted outside the above time limit and may, for speed of delivery, be passed by telephone to GLO RAF Kuala Lumpur during normal working hours, or duty G 2 (Air), JOC after office hours. If the request is accepted, 55 Company RASC (AD) should be contacted by telephone (Kuala Lumpur 7372) without delay giving details of items required, and this will be followed by the unit's confirmatory signal to addressees listed at paragraph 4 above. Units must appreciate that after 1100 hours on "D" minus 1 all Army and RAF arrangements for the next day's supply drops have been settled. The supply drop commitment is generally heavy compared with aircraft availability and therefore late demands are a serious complication. When an emergency air supply drop is required, units will, if possible, use their AAC/Light Aircraft Flight to drop in one day's supply, thus enabling their normal bid to follow the correct procedure.

7. **Preparation of DZs.**— To ensure an accurate drop, the pilot should be able to concentrate solely on adjusting height, speed and alignment before dropping. Any hills on the approach to the DZ or obstructing the escape route after dropping, will adversely affect his concentration on the DZ and the drop will consequently be less accurate. A second factor affecting accuracy is identification of the DZ location. The further away the pilot can recognise the DZ the more time he will have to make the adjustments necessary to ensure an accurate drop. To ensure maximum accuracy, the pilot should be able to sight the DZ position at least 400 yards from the dropping point. This means that an observer on the ground, should be able to see the aircraft when it is at least one quarter of a mile away on its dropping run. To give a reasonable guarantee that all packs will fall into the DZ, it should be cleared to a minimum of 40 yards diameter. Inaccuracies must be expected if the above conditions cannot be provided by troops on the ground. Units will follow the directions at Appendix "J" in selecting and marking DZs.

8. **DZ at Map Reference Differing from Briefed Position.**— If the aircraft finds a DZ marked with the correct letter and smoke at or near the grid reference given in the request, the pilot will carry out the drop even if he has no wireless contact with the DZ.

9. **Safety Precautions During Air Drop.**— The DZ must be clear of personnel during a drop. Free dropping in particular can be dangerous to personnel on the ground.

10. **Debrief After Air Drop.**— On completion of a supply task the pilot is debriefed by the GLO RAF Kuala Lumpur; any observations on DZ siting, marking, etc., will, if of practical value, be forwarded by signal to units concerned. Conversely, units' observations of assistance to the crews of supply drop aircraft should be passed to GLO RAF Kuala Lumpur, copy to JOC, through normal channels.

11. **Tactics.**— If for operational reasons aircraft are required to avoid any particular areas during a drop, to make diversionary dummy runs, or to give to the ground troops their position as a fix, this should be stated in the air supply request at paragraph 'Y', giving reasons for the request.

12. **Special Operational Airlifts.**— Under exceptional circumstances it may be necessary to request supplies to be air-transported. On these occasions, requests for air-transported supply

will be submitted with as much warning as possible and in the same way as air supply drop demands, except that paragraph 'VICTOR' will be preceded by the words "AIR-TRANSPORTED SUPPLY" and paragraph 'YANKEE' will give the location of the airfield where delivery is to be made together with the last date by which stores, for operational reasons, must arrive; e.g.: —

"............................YANKEE. KUANTAN. essential by 19 mar."

GLO RAF Kuala Lumpur will notify units direct of ETA of aircraft.

13. **Provision of Marker Balloons:**—
   (a) *Normal Supply of Balloons:* —
       (i) Army units will place demands for normal supply on ADOS 17 GURKHA Div/OCLF.
       (ii) Police units will place demands for normal supply on Police Federal Stores Depot.
   (b) *Supply of Balloons by Air:* —
       Marker balloons required to be air-supplied to Army and Police units in the field will be demanded as, or included in, a normal demand for air supply (see above).

Section 6.—AIR TRANSPORT SUPPORT—PARATROOP OPERATIONS

1. **General.**— Under certain conditions, the use of parachute troops in an airborne operation may be advantageous. Operations in which the use of parachute troops may be justified are as follows: —
   (a) Jungle search and rescue.
   (b) Direct assault on CT camps in areas where there are no helicopter LZs.
   (c) Patrols or ambush parties either independently or in conjunction with other troops, under similar conditions to (b) above.
   (d) To cut helicopters LZs in inaccessible operational areas where no LZs exist, as a preliminary to a helicopter trooplift operation.
   (e) Widespread reconnaissance patrols in large areas of deep jungle inaccessible to air-transported troops.

2. **Planning Paratroop Operations.**—When formations and units are considering paratroop support, it is important that, whenever possible, an officer of the paratroop squadron and an officer of

the RAF be brought in on the initial stages of contemplation and planning, so that expert attention may be given in the earliest stages to the selection of a practicable DZ.

3. **Paratroop Forces Available.**— 22nd Special Air Service Regiment (22 SAS) consists of troops specially trained and equipped for operations in deep jungle and for parachuting. The majority of 22 SAS is normally employed in the jungle and not more than one squadron (a maximum of 60 men) is likely to be available for parachute operations at short notice.

4. **Paratrooping Aircraft.**— The Air Transport Force for paratroop operations consists of medium range transport aircraft and/or medium helicopters. These aircraft are normally continuously employed on air supply, route transport, and trooplifting operations. To allocate the air effort required for paratroop operations invariably means diverting aircraft from other tasks.

5. **Paratrooping from Helicopters.**— Where a paratroop operation is mounted with medium helicopters it will be necessary to position the aircraft and the parachute troops at a suitable RV LZ within 30 nautical miles of the DZ. A force of six medium helicopters can drop 18-24 paratroops in a compact group. Normally speaking, operations involving more than one troop (about 16 men) of paratroops are not possible using medium helicopters, unless a slow build-up of paratroops on the DZ is acceptable.

6. **Timing.**— Parachute troops can normally be ready to emplane for operations within the following times of a request for their use being agreed:—

    (a) One troop (10-15) ... ... 6 hours
    (b) One squadron (maximum of 60 men) ... 24 hours

However, a paratroop operation requiring the employment of more than one squadron of paratroops may take some days to mount, as additional men may need to be withdrawn from deep jungle operations, and the necessary air transport force would need to be earmarked and equipped for the task.

7. **Capabilities.**— 22 SAS can carry out parachute descents into:—

    (a) Primary jungle.
    (b) Padi or clearings free of logs and stumps.
    (c) Matured rubber.
    (d) Oil palm, coconut, and other plantations.

8. **Unsuitable Surfaces and Terrain.**—The following types of surface are not suitable for paratroop descents:—
    (a) Thick bamboo (scattered clumps of young bamboo in primary jungle are acceptable).
    (b) Clearings with logs, stumps, etc.
    (c) Dead or wild rubber.
    (d) Rocky ground.
    (e) Stream beds—dry or flowing.
    (f) Areas which have been subjected to air attack.

9. **Rallying after Descent.**—After descent, paratroops may need from 20 minutes to 2 hours in which to re-organise for operations in a formed body. The time varies according to the surface of the DZ. Slopes offer no special obstacles to parachute landings, but very steep slopes and ridges do present special flying/parachuting problems and slow up rallying. Early information on this point will assist the mounting of the operation.

10. **Characteristics.**—The chief characteristics of parachute troops are:
    (a) They can be introduced into areas not readily accessible by surface travel or where there are no helicopter LZs.
    (b) Their use can achieve surprise, especially where the local inhabitants are acting as a CT intelligence screen.
    (c) They can provide an immediate follow-up after an air attack, but the DZ must be clear of the bombed area.
    (d) The individual paratrooper is vulnerable during descent until he has reached the ground and until he has shed his harness; particularly when the abseil equipment is being used, this process may take up to 10 minutes.
    (e) The paratroop force as a whole is vulnerable until it has formed into a body.

11. **Requests.**—Requests for the employment of parachute troops will be submitted to JOC (for attention G 2 Air) by formation HQ, giving as much as possible of the information required by the guide and example given at Appendix C.

12. **Command and Control:**—
    (a) In all paratroop operations the senior available officer of 22 SAS will be present at the take-off airfield/LZ until it is confirmed that all paratroops have dropped or that the paratroop operation is cancelled.

(b) When parachute troops operate independently the senior officer 22 SAS will be in command of the operation. With him will lie the responsibility for the cancellation, postponement, or execution of the operation.

(c) When JOC places parachute troops in support of another commander, that commander will command all troops engaged in the operation.

(d) If the senior officer 22 SAS considers that circumstances have made the parachute operation unduly hazardous or otherwise inadvisable, he will be responsible for advising the superior commander. The ultimate responsibility for the cancellation, postponement, or execution of the parachute operation will then lie with the superior commander.

13. **Liaison.**— 22 SAS will provide a liaison officer with the superior commander.

14. **Communications.**— 22 SAS will be responsible for establishing communications between the following:—

(a) The senior officer 22 SAS at the take-off airfield/LZ,

(b) the liaison officer with the superior commander, and

(c) the parachute troops after they have dropped.

Section 7.—AIR TRANSPORT SUPPORT—TROOPLIFTING

1. **Introduction.**— Troop lifting operations are the movement of forces in formed bodies in tactical and semi-strategic roles. The forces are air-transported onto secured airstrips/LZs.

(a) Semi-strategic movements are normally initiated and planned at Command level and will normally be carried out by medium range transport aircraft.

(b) Tactical movements are generally initiated at SWEC/Brigade or DWEC/Battalion level and, owing to lack of suitable airstrips, will normally be undertaken by medium helicopters. In the event of a suitable airstrip being available, tactical air-transported operations may be undertaken by light transport aircraft.

2. **Planning.**— The following general factors should be taken into consideration when planning operations involving the air transport of troops:—

(a) Air transport is expensive and should not be used if the tactical/strategical situation allows the use of surface transport.

(b) In order to achieve the most rapid build-up with the minimum use of air transport, the distance from the rear airstrip/LZ to the forward airstrip/LZ should be the absolute minimum.

3. **Airstrips/LZs.**—To assist formations and units in planning air transported operations, the minimum LZ requirements for helicopters are outlined in Appendix L to this Chapter. Fixed wing transport aircraft will only be operated into those airstrips listed (appropriate to aircraft type) in Joint Army/Air Instructions.

4. **Organisation on the Airstrip/LZs:**—
   (a) *Rear Airstrip/LZ.*—An English-speaking officer or NCO will be detailed as the unit emplaning officer and is responsible for supervising the emplaning of his unit in accordance with RAF instructions. He will remain at the airstrip/LZ until the last lift.
   (b) *Forward Airstrip/LZ.*—An English-speaking officer or NCO (where possible the force commander) will be detailed as the unit deplaning officer at the forward airstrip/LZ and will travel on the first lift. He should be prepared to discuss with the pilot on the aircraft inter-communication system the selection where necessary of an alternative LZ should the original selection be not suitable. Once on the ground he becomes the airstrip/LZ commander with the following duties:—
   (i) To act as the link between aircraft pilots and the ground troops.
   (ii) To recce the airstrip/LZ and brief pilots accordingly.
   (iii) To improve the LZ where necessary by cutting down trees, bushes, lallang, etc.
   (iv) In conjunction with the pilot, to select the best point of touch down on the LZ and to mark it with a letter "T" in fluorescent panels.
   (v) To marshal aircraft into the LZ after the first lift, paying particular attention to tail and under-fuselage clearance.
   (vi) To supervise deplaning.
   (vii) To organise the ground defence of the airstrip/LZ whilst the lift is in progress, and to arrange the orderly dispersal of troops from the airstrip/LZ to their task.

5. **Marshalling.**—Details of hand signals to be used to helicopters are contained in Appendix M.

6. **Aircraft Security.**— When operating into an unprotected and insecure airfield/LZ, at least two aircraft will always be used, one of which if necessary will act as air escort.

7. **Requests.**— All requests for air-transported operations will be submitted to JOC in accordance with the specimen at Appendix D. This Appendix also contains a guide to the preparation of requests.

8. **Importance of Detailed Request.**— It is important that full details are included in the request in order that:—
   (a) Priorities can be allotted.
   (b) Flight planning can be completed.
   (c) Aircraft can be used economically.
   (d) Fuel requirements can be estimated.
   (e) The task can be co-ordinated with other air transport tasks.

9. **Availability of Aircraft.**— Requests often exceed the availability of aircraft, which may need to be diverted from other roles and fitted with special equipment. When requests cannot be met on the date/time required, the JOC will suggest alternatives.

10. **Load for a Particular Flight.**— The load carried on each particular flight is at the discretion of the pilot of that particular flight. Under no circumstances will aircraft be loaded in a manner other than that authorised by the pilot.

Section 8.—CASUALTY EVACUATION BY AIR

1. **Introduction.**— The following facilities exist in Malaya for the evacuation by air of casualties.
   (a) Light helicopters on standby during daylight hours for the evacuation of casualties from jungle operational areas.
   (b) Although not on standby, fixed wing transport aircraft and medium helicopters will be used to evacuate casualties when suitable airstrips/LZs are available.
   (c) A routine flight is carried out once each week by a medium range transport ambulance aircraft to facilitate the transfer of casualties from military hospitals in Malaya to Singapore.

2. **Factors Affecting Requests for Evacuation.**— The following factors will be considered when requesting or authorising air evacuation of casualties:—
   (a) The casualty's need for urgent medical attention.

(b) Availability of other means of evacuation, and time involved.
(c) Effects of the air journey on the patient.
(d) Possibility of making a suitable LZ in time. If the casualty occurs some days' march into deep jungle it may be quicker to clear a new LZ than to go to an existing one.
(e) It should always be possible to find a LZ near the point where the patrol carrying the casualty emerges from the jungle.

3. **Procedure for Evacuation by Helicopter.**—The following procedure, although designed primarily to achieve speedy evacuation of casualties by helicopter, may also be adapted for use when the casualty is situated at an airstrip:—

(a) *Action by Patrol Commander.*—The patrol commander will pass to unit HQ:—
   (i) Personal details of the casualty.
   (ii) Description of injuries.
   (iii) Grid reference and full details of proposed LZ.
   (iv) Time by which casualty will be at LZ.
   (v) Time by which the LZ is expected to be ready.

Note:—The patrol commander will inform his unit HQ immediately the casualty has arrived at the LZ.

(b) *Action by Unit HQ.*—Immediately information has been received that a casualty requires air evacuation, the unit HQ will forward a request for an aircraft to the JOC by the fastest means. The following is the minimum information required:
   (i) Nature of casualty and whether sitting or lying.
   (ii) Grid reference of LZ with description if possible.
   (iii) Time the LZ is expected to be ready.
   (iv) Time casualty is expected to be ready for evacuation.
   (v) Destination of casualty.

Unit HQ will then place a request, through formation HQ, for an Army Air Corps light aircraft to reconnoitre the proposed LZ for suitability. The result of this recce will be reported by the fastest means to JOC and to unit HQ.

(c) *Method of Evacuation:*—
   (i) The aircraft will be detailed to RV at the airstrip/LZ nearest to unit or Tac HQ. The RMO of the unit will

be picked up there and taken in by the aircraft to see the casualty, whenever the seriousness of the injury or illness appears to make that desirable.

(ii) If the LZ is found to be unsuitable, an Army Air Corps light aircraft will search for a better one. The pilot will inform the patrol commander either by RT or message drop. Troops will not move until told to do so by the pilot, otherwise contact may be lost and much time wasted.

(iii) The final decision on the suitability of the LZ and the load to be carried will be made by the helicopter pilot.

(iv) If for any reason the aircraft cannot undertake the evacuation, the patrol commander will be told as soon as possible and the next quickest method of evacuation begun immediately.

(d) *Fitting of Helicopter Stretcher Equipment.*—Light helicopters used on casualty evacuation tasks are equipped to carry up to two stretchers. Details of this equipment and method of stowing the stretcher are given at Appendix O.

4. Procedure for Evacuation by Fixed Wing Aircraft.— On occasions when the distances involved are great and/or the casualty is close to an airstrip, a suitably equipped fixed-wing aircraft may be used for all or part of the task. The decision to use a fixed-wing aircraft will be made by the JOC, and depends largely upon the availability of a suitably equipped aircraft. Requests for AAC light aircraft will be made to the Army formation concerned.

5. Routine Evacuation by Medium Range Transport Ambulance Aircraft.— Routine evacuation of casualties is carried out once per week by medium range transport ambulance aircraft from Butterworth, Taiping, Ipoh and Kuala Lumpur to Singapore. Requests for the use of this service will be passed through medical channels to HQ FEAF.

6. Evacuation by Air of Dead Bodies.— The evacuation of dead bodies will normally be carried out using surface travel. However, where the carry is expected to exceed one day's march, or special circumstances exist, a request may be submitted for evacuation by helicopter. The following procedure will be used when air evacuation of dead bodies is required:—

(a) *Requests.*—Requests should be submitted to the JOC in accordance with the specimen outlined in Appendix D. The following points should be included in the demand:—

(i) The requests should be headed "Bodyvac."

(ii) Paragraph G.—Number of bodies to be carried.

(iii) Paragraph H.—Latest time at which bodies are to be taken.

Note: This request will normally be forwarded either by the unit HQ, or by the nearest Police Circle/District HQ.

(b) *Action by Patrol Commander.*—The patrol commander will take the following action:—
   (i) Pass to unit HQ information based on that outlined in sub-paragraph 3 (a).
   (ii) Prepare the body by completely covering it and binding it securely to a length of bamboo or timber to keep it rigid. It is important that the bamboo or timber must not protrude beyond the length of the body.

(c) *Action by Unit HQ.*—Immediately information is received that air evacuation of a dead body is required, a request will be passed by the quickest means to JOC. Where necessary, the unit will request an AAC recce of the LZ.

(d) *Method of Evacuation.*—Bodies will normally be evacuated by one of two methods, the first method being used whenever the equipment is available and when not more than one body is to be evacuated:—
   (i) By light helicopter using a bodyvac cylinder attached to a stretcher frame which slides into the normal stretcher rails in the aircraft. The lid of the cylinder is taken off or put on by a "turn-and-pull" or "push-and-turn" action respectively. Before being put into the cylinder, the wrapped body will be encased in a polythene bag which will be carried in the helicopter. The unit to whom the body is delivered will take it away in the bodyvac cylinder; that unit is then responsible for returning the cylinder, cleaned and disinfected, to the RAF as quickly as possible.
   (ii) By carriage in the normal passenger or luggage compartment of an aircraft. When this procedure is used, the body will be wrapped as at 6 (b) (ii) above, and encased in a polythene bag which will be carried in the aircraft.

Section 9.—AIR TRANSPORT SUPPORT— COMMUNICATION FLIGHTS

1. **Definition.**— A communication flight means the movement by air to secured airstrips or LZs of personnel other than formed bodies of troops or police.

2. **Aircraft Resources.**—Communication flights are undertaken by the following aircraft types:—

(a) RAF medium and light transport aircraft and AAC light aircraft.

(b) RAF light helicopters.

(c) Federation Air Service aircraft on charter.

3. **Aircraft Allocation.**—The JOC will decide which type of aircraft to employ on a particular communication flight task, depending upon:—

(a) Availability of suitable airstrips/LZs.

(b) Number of passengers and amount of baggage.

(c) Time required for the task.

(d) Aircraft availability.

4. **Use of Scheduled Services.**—Before a request is submitted for a communication flight, every effort will be made to fit the movement into civil airways or RAF scheduled air services.

5. **AAC Light Aircraft.**—Communication flights by light aircraft of the Army Air Corps Squadron will normally be arranged through the formation controlling the AAC Light Aircraft Flight concerned. On occasions, however, the JOC will arrange such flights direct with the AAC Light Aircraft Squadron HQ.

6. **Airstrips.**—A list of airstrips (appropriate to aircraft types) to which communication flights may be flown is contained in Joint Army/Air Instructions.

7. **Helicopter LZs.**—Except for visits by commanders and staffs to units actively engaged on operations, communication flights by helicopters will be confined to recognised permanent LZs. Under no circumstances will communication flights be undertaken into LZs below the standard of minima specified at Appendix L.

8. **Requests.**—Requests for communication flights (other than by affiliated AAC Flights) will be submitted to JOC in accordance with the guide and example shown at Appendix E. Where airstrips are not available, full details of all helicopters LZs to be used are required under paragraph "M". The JOC will decide which type of aircraft is to be employed and will inform applicants of acceptance or refusal.

Section 10.—PSYCHOLOGICAL WARFARE

1. **Voice Aircraft:—**
    (a) *Availability.*—Medium and short-range aircraft specially fitted for broadcasting messages from the air are available to support the Federation Government PW policy. These aircraft are known as Voice Aircraft and are based at RAF Kuala Lumpur.
    (b) *Method of Operating:—*
        (i) Messages can be broadcast over area targets by 'square search' methods; on flying lines; and over pin-point targets by orbiting.
        (ii) The average target is about 30 squares. Where more than one target is given in a request, the total number of squares should not normally add up to more than 100.
    (c) *Employment.*—See Chapter III, Section 12.
    (d) Voice Aircraft should not be used in an area where there is to be an air strike in the near future.

2. **Control.**—The operational control of Voice Aircraft is exercised by HQ 224 Group, RAF.

3. **Requests for Voice Aircraft:—**
    (a) *Normal Requests:—*
        (i) Requests for Voice Aircraft will be submitted through police signal channels to Federal Police HQ, Kuala Lumpur (abbreviated address COMPOL OPS) for HPWS. Army signal channels will not be used.
        (ii) Each request will be in respect of one exploitation only. The text of the signal request will be prefixed by the words "VOICE ROUTINE." The signal must contain the information outlined at Appendix F to Chapter III.
        (iii) Providing a special date has not been specified, requests are flown as soon as possible subject to weather and serviceability of aircraft.
        (iv) For the planned exploitation of a tactical target as part of a specific operation a date should be booked in advance. Details of the task should then be submitted as soon as possible.
        (v) It is essential that the officer who is named as the person to be contacted in the event of any query

arising shall be conversant with the request and know all the details connected with it. Failure to observe this provision may lead to delay, and could necessitate cancellation of the desired Voice Aircraft operation.

(b) *Urgent Requests*:—

(i) In special circumstances, where users consider that they have a target which should be given the highest possible priority, requests should be prefixed "VOICE BLITZ" (NOT "VOICE ROUTINE") and despatched by IMMEDIATE signal. Subject to weather conditions, Voice Aircraft may then be recalled from other tasks in the Federation in order to meet such demands, but misuse of this system will lead to unfair and uneconomic use of the aircraft and requests will only be made in exceptionally urgent cases.

(ii) Providing a "VOICE BLITZ" signal is received at Federal Police HQ, before 2100 hours, the message can be accepted, translated and tape recorded that night and the sortie flown at first light the following morning. Requests received after 2100 hours cannot be dealt with until the following day as there is insufficient time to prepare and translate the material before the Radio Malaya studios close.

Note: An IMMEDIATE signal containing a "VOICE BLITZ" request will reach Federal Police HQ within one hour of its despatch by a DWEC.

(iii) Telephoned requests for Voice Aircraft sorties will not be accepted, unless the circumstances are most exceptional, e.g. when the operational situation requires that a Voice Aircraft sortie be flown at first light the following morning, and it is too late for the DWEC to despatch an IMMEDIATE "VOICE BLITZ" signal in time to reach Kuala Lumpur by 2100 hours. In these circumstances a "VOICE BLITZ" signal may be telephoned to the Duty Officer at Federal Police HQ *and* at Contingent Police HQ. Confirmatory signals will be despatched immediately to Federal and Contingent Police HQ. These signals will be prefixed "VOICE BLITZ CONFIRMATORY."

(iv) Telephoned "VOICE BLITZ" requests will not be made to Army HQ, HQ 224 Group, RAF, or the Joint Operations Centre. These HQ are not authorised to accept them.

4. **Leaflets.**—Leaflets are divided broadly into two categories. First, strategic leaflets, dealing with themes of general application to any CT unit throughout the Federation; secondly, tactical leaflets, devised to exploit specific events or grievances. Leaflets are usually distributed by medium or short-range aircraft at the rate of 5,000 leaflets per 1,000-yard map square or flying line. Small quantities are also distributed by ground forces and by the field units of Information Services.

5. Requests for leaflets to be dropped will generally be made by or through State Information Officers. In cases where supplies of leaflets have been sent in bulk to State or Area Information Officers drops may be carried out by arrangement with local AAC Flights without further reference to HPWS.

Section 11.—LIGHT AIRCRAFT SQUADRON ARMY AIR CORPS

1. **Command and Control:**—
    (a) The Lt AC Sqn Army Air Corps is under command of 17 GURKHA Div/OCLF.
    (b) Recce liaison flights are detached in support of formations and are under operational control of these formations.

2. The main tasks of the Lt AC Sqn are as follows:—
    (a) *Reconnaissance.*—Most of the air recce for CT cultivations and camps is undertaken by light aircraft. There are five types of recce:—
        (i) *Visual Recce.*—This is a continuous process carried out by detached flights in areas chosen usually as a result of existing intelligence reports. In large areas over which flights have permanent or semi-permanent clearance the recce is done square by square. One 10,000-yard map square can be completed in $1\frac{1}{2}$ hours' flying (not counting positioning time). In smaller specially selected areas the recce may be more concentrated, using up to 3 aircraft for the task. This type of recce produces the best results but increases the chance of compromise and should therefore only be undertaken when the aircraft are operating in close support of ground forces. Priorities for recce are arranged by SWECs and formations. Security is not necessarily prejudiced by the presence of aircraft over a certain area.

(ii) *Topographic Recce.*—This enables commanders to look at the area in which they are operating. Unless they are accustomed to flying, map reading will at first be difficult and passengers will be well advised to mark obvious landmarks on the map before take-off. Commanders should not expect too much from these flights. It is only after considerable practice that signs of CT activity can be seen. These flights should be limited to one hour. Passengers should always take a map with them.

(iii) *Contact Recce.*—Contact recces are carried out for the following reasons:—
  (aa) To pin-point a lost patrol and give it its grid reference.
  (bb) To guide a patrol to a given point.
  (cc) To act as a wireless relay station. When a contact recce has been requested the patrol should send out a tuning and netting call as soon as it hears the aircraft and, in the case of (aa) and (bb) above, be prepared to put up smoke when the pilot orders it. All AAC light aircraft carry a 62 set and when required can also use an 88 set. The satisfactory range of the latter set is limited to about 2,000 yards.

(iv) *Photographic Recce.*—The light aircraft can only be used to take air photographs with a hand-held camera of a particular point, generally only obliques and low obliques. Vertical runs and mosaics cannot be undertaken.

(v) *Helicopter LZ Recce.*—This task is undertaken to clear newly cut or re-activated landing zones for both casualty evacuation and troop lifting. For the evacuation of casualties it is advisable to request AAC light aircraft recce as early as possible to avoid the construction of an LZ in an unsuitable place (see Section 6 paragraph 8). In connection with casualty evacuations this type of sortie will be given highest priority.

(b) *Target Indication.*—On suitable targets an AAC light aircraft is sometimes required to mark the target with a smoke marker to give an aiming point for bombers.

(c) *Air OP.*—With guns and mortars and for shore bombardment by HM ships.

(d) *Supply Drops*:—
  (i) Free or parachute drops can be made of single loads weighing up to 50 lb. Maximum weight per sortie is 200 lb., in four 50 lb. loads. Supplies should be packed after consultation with the flight concerned or delivered to the flight for packing.
  (ii) The deciding factor in requesting a light aircraft air drop as opposed to an Air Transport Support Force supply drop is the time factor and the weight and nature of the stores. A light aircraft air drop can very often be laid on at shorter notice than a supply drop by a larger aircraft. Light aircraft can either free drop or parachute drop, though the latter cuts down the weight of stores that can be carried and increases the time needed for preparation.
  (iii) By arrangement with the Flight Commander it is possible for a unit to store, ready for dropping, a number of the particular kind of rations that the unit uses, in his Flight location. This enables an emergency supply drop to be carried out almost at once.
  (iv) The drill for the troops on the ground accepting a light aircraft air drop is the same as for a full supply drop.
(e) *Message Dropping*.—The first man to recover a message bag dropped by an aircraft should wave the message round his head so that the pilot can see that the message has been received.
(f) *Air Search*.—Search for crashed aircraft.
(g) *Communication Flights*.—Communication flights will be arranged only when other means of transport cannot reasonably be used and will be subject to the requirements for aircraft for operational purposes.

3. **Requests for AAC Flights.**— Requests for AAC light aircraft flights will be passed to the Army formation which a particular flight supports giving as much warning as possible. Flight Commanders will usually affiliate a pilot to a particular battalion. The best results will be obtained by the unit in close liaison with this pilot.

4. The following information is required when making a request:—
  (a) *For Pilot Recce*:—
    (i) Area.

(ii) Particulars of task.
(iii) Intelligence background.
(iv) Latest time information required.

(b) *For Topographical Recce:—*
  (i) Time and place for passenger.
  (ii) Passenger's rank and name.
  (iii) Area.
  (iv) Task.

(c) *For Contact Recce:—*
  (i) Time and place for passenger, if any.
  (ii) Passenger's rank and name.
  (iii) Approximate grid reference of patrol.
  (iv) Task (including whether English speaking operator is available with patrol).
  (v) Intelligence background and position reports.
  (vi) Frequency and call sign of patrol.

(d) *For Communication Flights:—*
  (i) Time of departure.
  (ii) Place of departure.
  (iii) Destination.
  (iv) Passenger's rank and name.
  (v) Time of return if necessary.

(e) *For Supply Drops:—*
  (i) Grid reference and identification of DZ (if any).
  (ii) Time required.
  (iii) Type and quantity of supplies—whether required or provided.
  (iv) Location of supplies and time available.
  (v) RT frequencies and call sign.

5. Requests for air observation of gun or mortar fire should be originated by a representative of the fire unit.

6. There are generally insufficient aircraft to meet all demands. By varying the time of take-off, it may be possible to get considerably more flying time into each day. Aircraft are often required for other sorties and should not be kept waiting.

7. **Passengers.**— Intending aircraft passengers should note that:—
  (a) They must wear long trousers.
  (b) They must carry a weapon and ammunition.
  (c) The total weight of a passenger's baggage, including personal weapon, must not exceed 30 lb.

Section 12.—COMMUNICATIONS AND VISUAL SIGNALS

1. **Methods of Communication.**— The following are used to pass messages concerned with air support:
    (a) Command wireless nets, telephone or teleprinter. These may be either Army or RAF.
    (b) Air Support Signal Troop (ASST).
    (c) Ground/Air visual signals.
    (d) Ground/Air voice wireless links.

2. **Air Support Signal Troop (ASST):—**
    (a) The ASST provides a wireless net reserved for messages concerning air support. It consists of a number of tentacles each in a truck containing the following wireless sets:—
        (i) VHF Set.—For an Air Contact Team (ACT) to communicate with aircraft.
        (ii) WS 19 HP.—To communicate with the JOC.
        (iii) No. 19.—For local liaison with the formation or unit which the tentacle is supporting.
    (b) Tentacles will be deployed to formations/units as ordered by the G (Air) staff. One tentacle cannot be split to form two detachments.

3. **Auster Relay.**— Auster aircraft can act as relay stations between ground troops using HF and striking aircraft using VHF.

4. **HF Communication to Aircraft:—**
    (a) Valettas and Bristol Freighters are fitted with crystal controlled HF on 3710 and 5925 kilocycles per second. When troops wish to communicate by wireless with these aircraft, requests will include the net identification sign and call signs and which of the two frequencies is to be used.
    (b) Austers are fitted with WS 62 and can therefore net to any frequency between 2 and 8 megacycles per second.
    (c) Other aircraft and all helicopters are fitted only with VHF wireless but lightweight wireless sets such as WS 88, WS A 510 and WS 68T can in exceptional circumstances be carried in them to communicate with ground troops. The pilot of the aircraft will not normally be able to speak over a link established in this way.

5. **Call Signs.**—Aircraft use call signs as follows:—

   (a) Call sign 96 FOX, reserved for Austers.

   (b) Call sign 96 GEORGE, reserved for other aircraft using 3710 or 5925 kilocycles per second except during supply drops, when the DZ letter of the supply drop on which they are engaged will be used as a call sign.

6. **Ground/Air Visual Signals.**—Ground/air visual signals are provided in the following ways:—

   (a) Verey light or Aldis lamp code, details of which are given in Appendix G to this Chapter.

   (b) Ground/air panel system, details of which are contained in Appendix H.

Appendix A

XVII
Appx A

GUIDE TO PREPARATION OF REQUEST FOR OFFENSIVE SUPPORT

Index letter (incl. in msg.) (a)	Detail (incl. in msg.) (b)	Remarks (c)
A (TASK)	(i) Unit. (ii) Map Sheet. (iii) Grid refs of tgt. (iv) Background to op and info on which based. (v) What the strike is expected to achieve.	(i) To allow direct comn on queries. (iv) The more and better the info, the bigger the air effort likely to be put on. (v) On this depends type of ac and armament and tactics employed.
B (TIME AND DURATION)	(i) Time required on tgt. (ii) Duration of strike. (iii) Time after which no air action acceptable.	(i) Alternative time if possible. (ii) Short sharp attack or is tgt required to be occupied for a period. (iii) In case of unavoidable delays, ac on other tasks, bad weather.
C (POSN OF OWN TPS)	(i) Grid refs or at least distance and direction from tgt. (ii) Intentions of own tps after strike.	(i) Affects direction of attack and armament. (ii) Affects tactics and armament.
D (SPECIAL INSTRS)	(i) Sigs to indicate tgt or own tps. (ii) Action by ac at end of strike. (iii) Police clearance. (iv) Any other special requirements. (v) Frequency S e r i a l No and if required NIS and any special call signs. (vi) Appt and tele No of unit contact.	(i) Usually not necessary, unless own tps close to tgt. Sigs may be requested by RAF on certain tgts. (ii) Lt sigs or 'flag wag' over given area. (iii) Whether given or requested. W h i c h OCPD responsible. (iv) If rubber, huts, etc. in area, whether clear for attack. (v) Direct communications required as safety precaution. (vi) e.g. "Contact I.O. KLUANG 204."

Appendix B

XVII
Appx B

SPECIMEN REQUEST FOR AIR SUPPLY

Specimen air supply request is shown below. The following points should be noted:—
  (a) Figures followed by full stops are spelled out in words.
  (b) Types of ration (BRITISH, GURKHA or MALAY) are written in full.
  (c) ORD clothing will be demanded by sizes.
  (d) See also Section 5, paras 12-15.

Precedence-Action Op Immediate	Precedence-Info Routine	Date-Time-Group 191800 GH APR
From 2/7 GR		
To: GLO RAF Kuala Lumpur 55 AD COY RASC 39 FD AMB COMPOL Q	Security Classification Unclas	
	Originator's Number Q 7	
Info: JOC (attn G2 Air)	Special Instructions	

AIR DROP (.) VICTOR (.) GURKHA fd ops 50 for 2 days (.) GURKHA compo 49 for 3 days (.) BRITISH 24 hr 1 for 3 days (.) rum cigs matches to scale (.) tommy cookers one hundred (.) insect repellant 2 pints (.) ORD (.) jungle boots size 7-ten (.) 6-four (.) ponchos three (.) Kukris three (.) jackets bush size 3-two (.) 4-twelve (.) MED (.) adhesive plaster 1 roll (.) NAAFI (.) duty free rum 10 bottles (.) for SARAWAK RANGERS (.) RASC (.) MALAY Compo 2 for 5 days (.) cigs matches to scale (.) FOR ABOS (.) rations 12 for 5 days (.) FOR 3 MALAY (.) RASC (.) MALAY fd ops tea 15 for 2 days (.) MALAY 2 men 15 for 3 days (.) rum cigs matches to scale (.) ORD (.) socks size 2 prs five (.) trousers size 3-two (.) MED (.) bandages 2 in qty twelve (.) NAAFI (.) orange crush 5 bottles (.) FOR POLICE 5 FF (.) MALAY (.) 2 men 30 for 5 days (.) sock size 2 prs ten (.) on repayment ikan bilis 1 kati (.) FOR ABOS WITH POLICE (.) rations 40 for 5 days (.) gifts sponsored by BILES of PAHANG SWEC (.) 2 piculs salt (.) 20 small hand mirrors (.) WHISKEY (.) map 3 18 reference later (.) XRAY (.) DOG 3 bars white smoke and balloon freq No. 364 (.) YANKEE (.2) 220900 to 221100 GH MAY (.) Contact I.O. KLUANG 204.

Appendix C

GUIDE TO PREPARATION OF REQUEST FOR PARATROOP OPERATION

Index letter (incl. in request) (a)	Detail (b)	Remarks (c)
A (INFORMATION)	(i) Map Sheets. (ii) Summary of information on which request is based.	
B (OWN TPS)	(i) Location of other troops. (ii) Intentions of other troops. (iii) Controlling HQ and locations.	
C (TASK)	(i) Area of paratroop descent. (ii) Aim to be achieved by parachute troops. (iii) Earliest and latest dates/times of descent. (iv) Estimated duration of operation for parachute troops. (v) Size of paratroop force required.	(i) Including type of country.
D (SPECIAL INSTRS)	(i) Ground troops frequency. (ii) Prevailing weather conditions. (iii) Any special requirements. (iv) Appt. and tele. No. of unit contact.	(ii) Particularly cloud to be expected at the relevant time of day (iv) e.g. "Contact I.O. KLUANG 204."

Appendix D

GUIDE TO PREPARATION OF REQUEST FOR TROOP/FREIGHT LIFT

Index letter (incl in msg) (a)	Detail (incl in msg) (b)	Remarks (c)
E (INFORMATION)	(i) Unit. (ii) Map sheets. (iii) Background to operation and info on which based. (iv) Own troops locations.	(i) To allow direct communication on queries. (iii) Priorities will be decided on this information. (iv) Other troops involved in the operation.
F (TASK)	(i) Purposes for which aircraft is/are required.	
G (LOAD)	(i) Details of load. (ii) Distances of lifts.	(i) Number of troops, weight and nature of cargo. (ii) To permit planning of fuel loads and number of lifts.
H (TIME AND DURATION)	(i) Time aircraft required. (ii) RV. (iii) Duration of requirement. (iv) Alternative times and dates.	(i) Make allowance for loading time. (ii) Grid reference and description.
J (LZs/AIRSTRIPS)	(i) Grid references of LZs. (ii) Dimensions. (iii) Approaches. (iv) Type of country. (v) Height above mean sea level. (vi) If LZ secure. (vii) Names of Airstrips.	(i) If recorded LZs give serial number, other details not required. (iv) If LZ NOT secure air escort will normally be arranged.
K (SPECIAL INSTRS)	(i) Local command frequency. (ii) Any other special instructions. (iii) Appt. and tele. No. of unit contact.	(iii) e.g. "Contact I.O. KLUANG 204."

XVII
Appx D

Appendix D—Continued

SPECIMEN TROOP/FREIGHT LIFT REQUEST

Precedence-Action Op Immediate	Precedence-Info Op Immediate	Date-Time-Group 241200 GH
From 1 GORDONS		Security Classification *
To JOC (attn G2 Air)		
Info Gurdiv 26 Bde GLO KUALA LUMPUR		Originators Number OPS 5

TROOPLIFT (.)

ECHO (.) 1 GORDONS and 3 FF (.) 3H/9 (.) OCCUPIED CAMP FOR 30 FOUND VK 950430 240800 GH (.) ONE CTK IDENTIFIED AS 8 PL 3 REGT (.) CT FLED NORTH (.) CAMPS IN AREA VK 9651 TO WHICH CT HAVE MOVED AFTER PREVIOUS CONTACTS (.) ONE PL FOLLOWING UP FROM SOUTH (.) ONE PL MOVING EAST FROM KEPOH 9253 (.)

FOXTROT (.) TO MOVE TPS FROM LABIS TO AMBUSH CAMP AREA VK 9651 (.)

GOLF (.) 20 EQUIPPED BRIT TPS (.) 400 LB RATIONS AND AMN (.) EACH LIFT NINE MILES (.)

HOTEL (.) 270930 GH (.) FOOTBALL FIELD LABIS 844417 (.) ONE DAY (.) NOT LATER THAN 1200 GH (.) NO ALTERNATIVE DATE (.)

JULIET (.) VK 952521 (.) 75 YDS DIAMETER (.) APPROACHES 30 DEGREES (.) PRIMARY JUNGLE (.) 670 FEET (.) LZ USED FOR TRG 04 JAN (.) NOT SECURE (.)

KILO (.) CALL SIGN 43 (.) TAC HQ VK 844417 (.) CONTACT I.O. KLUANG 204.

* *Note:* Originator will insert appropriate security classification.

Appendix E

GUIDE TO THE PREPARATION OF REQUEST FOR COMMUNICATION FLIGHT

Index letter (incl in msg)	Detail required	Remarks
L	Time of departure.	
M	Place of departure and destination.	Include interim stops, Grid References and details of LZs.
N	Details of passengers between each pick-up point.	Rank and name required.
P	Time of return.	If necessary, otherwise omit.
Q	Purpose of journey.	In order that priorities can be arranged.
R	Weight of passengers and luggage.	If night-stop required, or more than three passengers.
S	Special Instructions, incl. appt. and tele. No. of unit contact.	e.g. "Contact I.O. KLUANG 204."

XVII
Appx F

Appendix F

GUIDE TO THE PREPARATION OF REQUEST FOR VOICE AIRCRAFT

(A) **Information to be Signalled.—** ...

    Note: (i) "Action" addressee will be:
             "COMPOL OPS for HPWS."

          (ii) "Info" addressee will be requesting unit's next superior formation in Malaya.

Index letter (incl in msg)	Detail (incl in msg)	Remarks
A (TASK)	(i) Name, appt. and tele. No. to whom enquiries can be addressed.	(i) May be originator of demand, JOR or other official.
	(ii) Map sheet.	(ii) Map sheet number.
	(iii) Map ref. of target.	(iii) Nature of the target should be given, i.e. area targets, flying line or pin-point. Map ref. should be given. (a) For area targets as four figure co-ordinates, starting at the left hand bottom corner of the target area and proceeding in a clockwise direction. (b) For flying lines and pin-points, as either four or six figure co-ordinates.
	(iv) CT eliminations for exploitation.	(iv) Names of eliminated CTs who are to be exploited, using best known alias. Sex of eliminated CT if name is not known.

Index letter (incl in msg)	Detail (incl in msg)	Remarks
	(v) Points to be exploited.	(v) Designation of local CT unit if known. Any detail which would help to induce surrenders or break morale, such as details of recent kills or surrenders, sickness, food shortages, locally hated leaders. It is essential that in (iv) and (v) above Chinese Commercial Code Nos.* and Contingent Wanted List No. of all terrorists mentioned are given.
B (TIME)	(i) Time required on target (TOT).	(i) If time is not specially important put SOONEST.
	(ii) Time after which broadcast is not acceptable (NAA).	(ii) If time is not specially important, put DO NOT CANCEL; messages will be flown for three to five days, depending on availability of aircraft.
C (SPECIAL INSTRS)	(i) Police clearance.	(i) Clearance to be obtained from local Special Branch.
	(ii) Language and dialect.	(ii) e.g., Chinese Mandarin or Malay Kelantan.
	(iii) Public targets in neighbourhood.	(iii) e.g., Villages or towns in vicinity of target or en route to target which could be hailed with strategic message, if time permits. Language and dialect should be given.

* Chinese Commercial Code Numbers (CCC Nos.) are numbers, each denoting a particular Chinese character.
See (B) over for specimen request.

XVII
Appx F

Appendix F—*Continued*

(B) **Specimen Request.**—

From: JOR KUANTAN
To: COMPOL OPS for HPWS
Info: CPO PAHANG (OPS)

Originator's No.	Date	Addressee's Ref. No.	Date

Voice routine (.)

ALPHA (.) ONE (.) Mr. SMITH police circle SB officer KUANTAN 222* (.)

TWO (.) sheet 3 D/1-5 (.)

THREE (.) area enclosed by WM 3278 (.) WM 3283 (.) WM 3683 (.) WM 3678 (.)

FOUR (.) BCM CHENKOW CCC 2582 5384 WL 0054 (.) Surrendered 17 Aug. (.)

FIVE (.) AH KEONG CCC 0068 1730 WL 1760 surrendered 8 Aug. (.) RAMIAH WL 2345 and LAU YAP CCC 5071 5509 WL 0486 surrendered 19 Jul. (.) all 9 platoon (.) RAMIAH sick in hospital (.) suggest section leader LIEW MIN KEONG CCC 0491 3046 1730 WL 2475 brings out known waverers AH KAM CCC 0068 7002 WL 1729 and LEONG KWAI CCC 2733 1145 WL 789 (.)

BRAVO (.) TOT soonest (.) NAA do not cancel (.)

CHARLIE (.) clearance SB KUANTAN (.) Chinese dialect MANDARIN (.) strategic message to SUNGEI AMPAT New Village WM 370925 CANTONESE.

Originator's Signature Rank/ Appointment	Security Unclassified	Priority Routine	Date Time Origin

* If AIO is available he should deal with enquiries at Police Circle or DWEC level.

Appendix F—Continued

(C) **Guide to the Preparation of Request for Search and Rescue by Voice Aircraft.—**

1. The procedure for requesting a 'Search and Rescue' Voice Aircraft operation is in general the same as that set out in Appendix "F" (A) and (B). The following additional points should be noted:—
    (a) the request should be prefixed "VOICE SEARCH AND RESCUE." This will ensure that it receives priority over all other requests and that if necessary Voice Aircraft already airborne will be recalled;
    (b) the last known position of the missing individual or unit should be given;
    (c) wherever possible some indication should be provided of the missing individual or unit's instructions;
    (d) the suggested message should cover the following points:—
        (i) if possible it should be addressed by rank and name to the officer, NCO or senior in the missing unit;
        (ii) specific instructions should be given in the Voice Aircraft Message, e.g., "Make smoke", "Stay where you are", "Proceed NORTH to large river";
        (iii) if search operations have begun the message should indicate the fact and should, if necessary, state means of identification of ground forces involved.

2. The following is a specimen 'Search and Rescue' demand:—

Specimen Demand for Voice Search and Rescue.

From: I.O. 2/10 GR
To: COMPOL OPS for HPWS
Info: GURDIV/OCLF
       63 Bde

Voice search and rescue (.)

ALPHA (.) ONE (.) Capt. TROLLOPE KULAI 232 extension 99 (.)

    TWO (.) Sheet 3L/7 (.)

    THREE (.) Area enclosed by VP 6253 (.) VP 6258 (.) VP 6758 (.) VP 6753 equals 25 squares (.)

    FOUR (.) Four man patrol three days overdue (.)

    FIVE (.) Message to Cpl- TRUBSHAW (.) suggest he should not move but should make smoke if possible (.) AUSTERS and troops are searching (.) troops have yellow hatbands (.)

BRAVO (.) TOT soonest (.) NAA do not cancel (.)
CHARLIE (.) English.

XVII
Appx G

Appendix G

LIGHT SIGNAL CODE

Ground/Air and Air/Ground

Airstrikes, Air Supply and Helicopters

1. **Ground to Air:—**
   - (a) Single RED ... ... 'Short delay.'
   - (b) GREEN ... ... 'Carry on' or 'Land here.'
   - (c) Series of REDS ... 'Cancel drop' or 'Cease attack and return to base if no instructions being received on RT' or 'Do NOT land.'
   - (d) WHITE ... To attract attention, or 'Your message understood.'

2. **Air to Ground:—**
   - (a) Single WHITE and Single GREEN ... 'DZ or LZ unacceptable.'
   - (b) Single WHITE ... 'Short delay.'
   - (c) Series of GREENS ... 'Starting attack' or 'Starting drop' or 'Landing.'
   - (d) Series of WHITES ... 'Operation abandoned' or 'Strike or drop completed.'
   - (e) Single GREEN ... 'Acknowledged.'
   - (f) AMBER downward identification light (Lincolns at night) ... 'Am on my bombing run.'

Air Escort to Convoys

3. **Ground to Air:—**
   - (a) RED ... ... 'Cease Attack.'
   - (b) GREEN ... 'Convoy being attacked please strafe in direction this light.'
   - (c) WHITE ... To attract attention or 'Your message understood.'

4. **Air to Ground:—**
   - (a) Series of WHITES ... 'Abandoned escort'
   - (b) Series of GREENS ... 'Road clear ahead.'
   - (c) Single WHITE ... 'Road Block or obstruction ahead'
   - (d) Single GREEN ... 'Acknowledged.'

Any Aircraft
   Three REDS ... DISTRESS.

XVII
Appx H

Appendix H

GROUND/AIR PANEL CODE FOR USE IN MALAYA

Notes:—(i) This code may be used throughout the 24 hours of any day. During daylight hours panels will be used. During hours of darkness lights will be used.

(ii) Messages which are common to this code and to the International Ground Air Emergency Code are marked with an asterisk (π).

(iii) In order to avoid confusion between the following code and the letter code used to designate supply dropping DZs, all letters used for DZs should have at least one horizontal bar alongside the DZ letter; further bars alongside can be added to differentiate between sub-units using the same DZ letter (see Serial 34 below).

Serial	Message	Signal
	REQUIREMENTS	
1.	Require Doctor; serious injuries.	I π
2.	Require Medical supplies.	II π
3.	Helicopter required for casevac here. (Signal to be displayed at best touch-down point for helicopter).	H
4.	Require Boots and Clothing.	III
5.	Require Wireless Set complete with battery.	⊽
6.	Require Wireless Battery.	V
7.	Require Fuel and Oil.	L π
8.	Require Map and Compass.	□ π
9.	Require Firearms and Ammunition.	⋁⋁ π
10.	Require Small Arms Ammunition.	⋁⋁
11.	Require Food and Water.	F π
	TACTICAL	
12(a).	Ground party in action with enemy. or	
(b).	Enemy attacking or preparing to attack from direction of arrow.	⟂
13.	Target of opportunity in direction indicated.	⇞
14.	Request direct air support. (Enemy in direction of arrow. ALL own tps behind. Arrowhead, and vertical bars, denote distance of enemy, one bar for each 1,000 yards).	⇑ ∧III

XVII
Appx H

Appendix H—*Continued*

Serial	Message	Signal
15.	Enemy in possession of landing ground.	+॥
16.	Enemy attack has failed.	L×
17.	Enemy concentrating in direction indicated and NOT in contact.	⌐_
18.	Am proceeding in this direction.	↑ ✱
19.	Unable to proceed.	× ✱

VOCABULARY

20.	I have a message for you.	××
21.	Message received.	××I
22.	Nothing more to communicate.	×N
23.	Are you receiving my signals?	×I×
24.	I have NO means of communication.	×⊔
25.	Repeat message. or NOT understood.	⌐L ✱
26.	All's well.	LL ✱
27.	YES.	Y ✱
28.	NO.	N ✱

INSTRUCTIONS TO AIRCRAFT

29.	Helicopter to touch down here.	T
30.	Aircraft is *NOT* to land here.	× ✱
31.	Cancel Air Strike or Supply Drop.	×L
32.	Indicate direction to proceed.	I< ✱
33.	Probably safe to land here.	△ ✱
34.	Position and identification of dropping zone (DZ) for air supply drop or paratroop operation. (i.e. "KILO" or "KILO ONE BAR")	K —
		K≡
		(i.e. "KILO THREE BARS")

Appendix J

AIR-DROPPED SUPPLY

Selection and Marking of DZs

1. **Introduction.**—The following notes outline the methods by which the ground forces can assist in reducing for aircrews the hazards inherent in supply dropping operations in Malaya.

2. **Limitations Imposed on Pilot.**—In addition to conditions imposed on the pilot by the weather, he has to give the following factors the closest attention during the comparatively short period he is within the drop circuit, at which time the aircraft is operating at its extreme limits:—

   (a) *Instruments*, to ensure that the aircraft speed does not fall dangerously low.

   (b) *Aircraft controls*, to put the aircraft where he wants it at the right speed and altitude, both of which are critical to the success of the air-drop.

   (c) *Surrounding country*, which is frequently very close to and higher than his aircraft—always a dangerous situation.

   (d) *"Escape" route from the DZ*, from which there is often only one way which leaves no margin for error.

   (e) *Crew drills*, covering his instructions to his crew and army despatchers.

   (f) *The DZ*, keeping it in sight and following the circuit pattern which he has selected for the drop. Excessive attention to a poorly marked DZ, for the fear of losing it, leaves the pilot less time for close attention to other essential details.

3. **Ground Force Aids.**—The safety margin for the aircraft can be improved by:—

   (a) Good siting of DZs, particularly in hilly country.

   (b) Good DZ marking.

   (c) Establishing early contact with the aircraft.

   (d) Giving the RAF greater date and time latitude for delivering air-drops, so that they are not asked to operate in marginal weather conditions more often than is absolutely necessary.

4. **Selection.**—The selection of a suitable DZ in the first instance is of the greatest importance, and the following points should be specially noted:—

   (a) The line of flight must be considered, as supply dropping aircraft cannot climb or descend steeply. A gradual downhill run both approaching and leaving the DZ is desirable.

   (b) Whenever possible a DZ should be sited where there is no hill within a mile radius which is 300 feet higher than the DZ. Therefore the DZ should be selected on high ground in relation to the surrounding terrain. Sites on top of a knife-edge ridge or on a steep slope should be avoided.

   (c) The DZ should be as large as possible. If the DZ is less than 40 yards diameter, ground troops must accept that there will not be a reasonable guarantee that all packs will fall into the DZ.

Appendix J—*Continued*

5. **DZ Description.**—When a DZ is used for the first time by a unit a brief description of the surrounding country will be included in the air supply request. In hilly country the direction of approach and the circuit should also be suggested; e.g. "approach from NORTH and circuit to WEST."

6. If the DZ is likely to be difficult to find, or if the troops are not sure of their location, an Auster Reconnaissance will be flown to establish the proposed DZ location and description. The Auster Pilot will report details to the unit and to GLO RAF KUALA LUMPUR.

7. **DZ Marking.**—The following action will be taken to mark a DZ:—

   (a) The DZ identifying letter, with at least one horizontal bar alongside it, must be displayed in fluorescent panels on the most conspicuous point in the DZ, usually the centre. It must be clearly visible from the air. (See Appendix H).

   (b) Where other sub-units are using the same identification letter, then each sub-unit must be identified by a different number of bars following the letter. These bars will be set horizontally, one above the other, alongside the DZ letter. (See Appendix H).

   (c) A marker balloon will be anchored to the centre of the DZ, and will always be flown clear of the trees and kept in position until the drop is completed. The aircraft crew uses the balloon as a wind indicator and as an aiming point.

   (d) A short while before the aircraft is due or when it is first heard or seen (whichever is the sooner), the ground troops will put up smoke. When the aircraft has found and identified the DZ the ground troops will stop making smoke unless the pilot specially asks for the smoke to continue.

8. For DZs in regular use at Jungle Forts and Police Posts the procedure given in sub-paragraphs 7 (c) and (d) may be modified in that marking may be by fluorescent panels only.

9. **Signals:—**

   (a) A short while before the aircraft is due or when it is first heard or seen (whichever is the sooner), the ground troops will attempt to contact it by wireless.

   (b) If wireless contact fails then the Verey light code will be used. (See Appendix G).

10. **Date and Time of Supply Drops.**—To reduce the necessity for air crews to press forward with supply drops when weather conditions are marginal, units will be prepared to accept 48 hours' delay from the date and time requested in their supply drop bids. It is the responsibility of the GLO KUALA LUMPUR to notify the date and time of any postponed drop direct to the requesting unit.

11. **Request for Air Supply.**—See Appendix B for specimen Air Supply Drop Request.

Appendix K

SINGLE-ENGINED PIONEER AIRCRAFT—DETAILS OF PERFORMANCE AND EMPLANING/DEPLANING DRILL

1. **Load and Performance.**—The angle at which the Pioneer aircraft is required to climb away from the ground governs the load that can be carried. The maximum angle at which a fully loaded aircraft can be taken off is 30°, and any increase in this figure will result in a substantial reduction in load, e.g. 40° equals a reduction of 25% of the load. The length of take-off run is as follows:—

    (a) 250 feet under stable conditions.

    (b) Up to 450 feet under turbulent conditions.

Under conditions of nil wind, the landing run is about 250 feet.

2. **Fuel Consumption.**—Rate of fuel consumption is 18 gallons per hour under cruising conditions, with a tank capacity of 60 gallons.

3. **Speed.**—The Pioneer cruises at 90 knots.

4. **Freight Carrying.**—The maximum weight load which can be carried is 800 lbs. excluding the pilot and fuel. The loading doors limit the size of individual packages to the following dimensions:—

    3 ft. 6 ins. x 3 ft. 6 ins. x 4 ft.

Important: When units prepare packages for carriage in aircraft, it is important that each package is clearly labelled with its packed weight and its destination.

5. **Casualty Evacuation.**—Pioneers can be equipped to carry a single stretcher with an attendant. The stretcher is loaded into a hatch in the port side of the fuselage.

6. **Emplaning and Deplaning Drills for Trooplifts. Emplaning:**—

    (a) Four men with packs and firearms report to the port side (left side) door of the aircraft. Firearms will have been previously unloaded, and grenades defused.

        Note: **Grenades No. 80 are prohibited** for carriage on the person or in personal packs in aircraft.

    (b) No. 1 man leaves his firearms and kit on the ground, climbs into the aircraft, and sits in the rear seat furthest from the door.

    (c) No. 2 man leaves his firearms and kit on the ground, climbs into the aircraft, and sits in the other rear seat.

    (d) No. 3 man leaves his firearms and kit on the ground, climbs into the aircraft, and stands facing the door.

    (e) No. 4 man then passes *three packs only* to No. 3 man who passes them to No. 1 and No. 2 men who stow them on the floor at their feet.

    (f) No. 3 man sits down in the right hand front seat.

    (g) The pilot then emplanes if he is not already in the aircraft.

    (h) No. 4 man then passes the last pack to No. 3 man.

    (j) No. 4 man emplanes.

Appendix K—*Continued*

(k) Emplaning supervisor hands firearms to No. 4 man, who holds them upright with butts resting on the floor.

(l) All passengers then fasten their safety straps.

7. **Deplaning Drill.**—The deplaning drill is the reverse of the emplaning drill:—

(a) No. 4 man hands out firearms to deplaning supervisor.

(b) No. 4 man deplanes.

(c) No. 3 man hands out his pack, stands up and hands out the other packs.

(d) No. 3 man deplanes.

(e) Nos. 2 and 1 men deplane.

8. **Prevention of Damage to Aircraft.**—When handling kit and firearms and when loading freight, personnel must take great care to prevent projections from damaging the perspex, the seats, and the aircraft fittings.

9. **Action in the Event of Crash Landing.**—In the event of a crash landing, the following will be the procedure:—

(a) Pilot warns passengers: "Crash Landing", and passengers acknowledge.

(b) Passengers tighten their safety harnesses.

(c) Passengers disconnect inter-comm plug and tuck lead in clothing.

(d) At about 100 feet from the pround the pilot shouts: "Brace! Brace!", and passengers acknowledge.

(e) Each passenger than braces his body and shields his face in the crook of his arm as follows:—

   (i) Passenger in front port (left) seat braces foot against cross-tube at back of pilot's seat, with right arm crooked across his face and right hand grasping the hand-hold above the port (left) door.

   (ii) Passenger in front starboard (right) seat braces and holds as at (i) above, but with left foot, and with left arm and hand grasping the hand-hold above the starboard (right) door.

   (iii) Passenger in rear port (left) seat braces feet against base of seat in front of him, with left arm crooked across his face and left hand grasping the metal strut which is above his right shoulder.

   (iv) Passenger in rear starboard (right) seat braces and holds as at (iii) above, but with right arm crooked across his face and right hand grasping the metal strut which is above his left shoulder.

(f) As soon as the aircraft has come to rest, passengers release their harnesses and leave the aircraft, standing off at a safe distance in case of fire and/or petrol tank explosion. Before going away from the aircraft, however, passengers should ensure that the pilot is assisted from the aircraft if he has been injured.

Appendix L

XVII
Appx L

MINIMUM SPECIFICATIONS FOR HELICOPTER LANDING ZONES

1. **General Requirements.—**

    (a) *Dimensions.*—The following are the minimum dimensions for helicopter LZs:—

     (i) An area of 30 yards in diameter completely cleared to ground level.

     (ii) A further area beyond this, surrounding the cleared area, 10 yards wide and cleared to within 2 feet above the ground.

     (iii) The completed LZ will thus be a minimum of 50 yards in diameter (see diagram at sub-paragraph 3 (a)).

     (iv) There must be no branches over-hanging this cleared 50 yards area.

    (b) *Ground:—*

     (i) For Landing. Ground will be level and firm. The surface will be cleared of all loose rubbish, tree stumps, etc. This is most important as the fuselage of the Whirlwind helicopter, for instance, has a ground clearance of only 10½ inches.

     (ii) For Hovering. Helicopter air transport operations can be done without the helicopter actually landing. The same 50 yards clearing is required and the helicopter will hover 2 feet above the ground obstruction(s) which are preventing it landing. However, because of the abnormally high engine power required during hovering, loading and unloading must be carried out as quickly as possible; and every effort will be made by ground troops to improve the LZ surface until it is fit for the aircraft to land.

     (iii) The ground should not be cleared by burning, nor should fires be lit on the LZ other than a small smudge fire for wind direction, and then only at the request of the pilot; this fire should then be alight whilst the helicopter is approaching, landing, or hovering.

    (c) *Approaches:—*

     (i) For permanent and operational LZs at sea level, angles of approach and exit will not be greater than 30° measured outwards from the edge of the clearing. Any trees at the edge of the clearing higher than about 20 feet, and trees which protrude above the required angle of approach, must be removed to clear an approach and exit lane of at least 40 yards in width.

     (ii) In an extreme emergency it may be possible to use an LZ when the approach angle is up to 45°

     (iii) Permanent LZs (e.g. police posts, jungle forts, base camps) should be of the same dimensions as at paragraph 1 (a) above, but approach angles should be a maximum of 10° for at least 500 yards, if possible, so that maximum loads can be carried in and out by the helicopters.

(iv) Helicopter performance deteriorates with increased altitude, and the maximum angles of approach to clearings that helicopters are permitted to use are as follows:—

Sea Level to 3,000 feet	...	30°
3,000 feet to 4,000 feet	...	20°
4,000 feet to 5,000 feet	...	10°

Altitudes of 5,000 feet and above require a completely flat approach.

Note: Failure by ground troops to achieve these requirements may result in the clearing being refused by the helicopter pilot, with whom the final decision always lies.

(d) *Marking:*—
  (i) LZs will be marked with the letter "T" at the best touch-down point.
  (ii) If the helicopter is not required to land, the "T" will be replaced with the letter "X".
  (iii) On hearing the first helicopter in the area of the LZ a smoke grenade will be ignited to indicate to the pilot the LZ position and wind velocity. When further sorties are to be made to the same LZ, and on the same operation, a smoke fire may be requested by helicopter pilots to enable them to gauge any change in the wind strength or direction; this fire must be as small as is practicable, and on one side of the probable approach path of the helicopter, so that the smoke drifts down the side of the LZ rather than across the LZ; excessive smoke will obscure the vision of the pilot who may be unable to land until the smoke has dispersed.

2. **Platform LZs.—**
  (a) *Platforms.*—When it is not possible to find ground which meets the requirements at paragraph 1 (b) above, a platform LZ will be constructed. The size of clearings with platform touch-down points are exactly the same as given at paragraph 1 (a) above, plus the following additional requirements for the platform itself:—
    (i) The platform will be at least 25 feet square
    (ii) The platform must be capable of supporting a weight of 8,000 lbs.
    (iii) If logs or bamboos are used, the top layer of poles must be at right angles to the touch-down direction.
    (iv) The platform must be of firm construction that will not move when the helicopter touches down and rolls forward slightly.
    (v) The platform surface must be level and undamaged.
    (vi) No materials may be used in the platform which show signs of rotting or damage by insects.
    (vii) There must be no sign of ground erosion beneath the platform.
  (b) *Inspections.*—Whenever possible, and before a request is submitted for a helicopter to use a particular platform, the platform will be inspected by the Unit/Patrol Commander who will satisfy himself on the following points:—
    (i) That the platform is able to withstand the weight of the loaded helicopter.

Appendix L—*Continued*

- (ii) That there is sufficient all-round clearance.
- (iii) That the platform is able to withstand the effects of the undercarriage splaying out.
- (iv) That there is no sign of wood rot in the platform or ground erosion beneath the platform.
- (v) That the platform surface is level and undamaged.
- (c) *Requests by Units for use of Helicopter Platform LZ.*—All requests to use helicopter platforms must contain the last date on which an inspection of the platform was made, and the condition of the platform at that time.
- (d) *Landing on Platform LZs.*—Helicopter pilots will not land on a platform unless an all clear signal is given by the Unit/Patrol Commander on the ground. When the platform is an old one in a clearing no longer occupied, the first lifts will be roped in from the helicopter, to check the platform for serviceability and to renovate it as necessary.

3. **Illustrations.**—A diagram of a LZ and sketches of platform types are added to illustrate the above specifications for helicopter LZs and platforms.

(a) *Diagram of a LZ.*

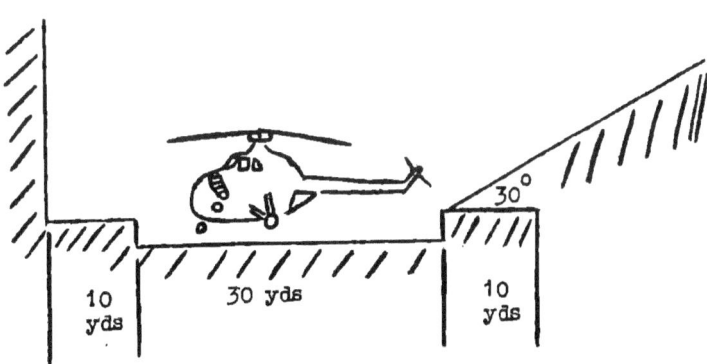

Appendix L—Continued

(b) *Examples of Platform LZs.*

SURFACE PLATFORM.

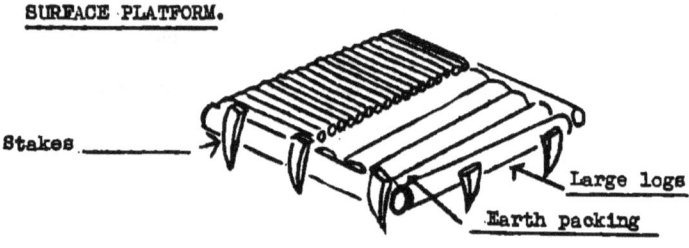

Stakes

Large logs

Earth packing

ROUGH GROUND PLATFORM.

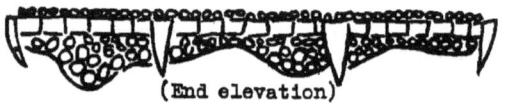

(End elevation)

PLATFORM OVER SWAMP OR SHALLOW WATER.

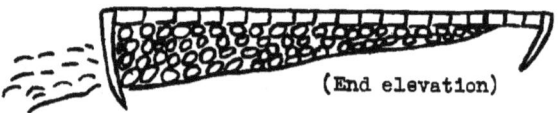

(End elevation)

BAMBOO PLATFORM AREA.

(Bird's-eye view)

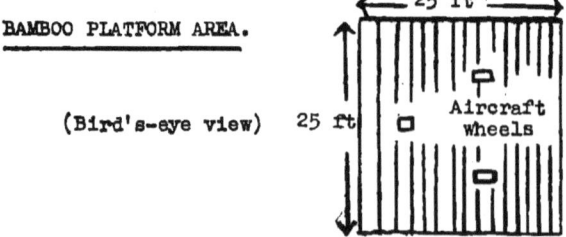

25 ft

25 ft

Aircraft wheels

XVII
Appx M

Appendix M

MARSHALLING AND RECEPTION OF HELICOPTERS AND HAND SIGNALS FOR HELICOPTERS

1. **General.**—Marshalling officers must be able to distinguish between the types of helicopter when they are airborne. This is particularly important insofar as approach to the aircraft is concerned as it nears or touches the ground; **the main and tail rotor blades of the helicopter may well be so close to the surface as to constitute a positive danger to personnel** unless they are fully conversant with the correct approach and exit paths for each particular type of aircraft (the Sycamore helicopter, for example, is particularly dangerous at all times in this respect, and all helicopter rotors are likely to become a danger whenever the helicopter is operating near or on sloping ground). Therefore **personnel will carefully study the characteristics of particular helicopters,** as given at the Appendices to this Chapter.

2. **Position of Marshaller.**—The Marshaller should stand well away and to the pilot's right side front, keeping both the pilot and tail rotor in view. At the same time he must stay well clear of the main rotor blades, bearing in mind that, whenever possible, the helicopter may roll forward a few feet immediately after landing to reduce the outward force working on the undercarriage. Because the pilot is sitting on the starboard side of the aircraft his range of vision to his port (left) and rear is strictly limited. The position of the Marshaller is illustrated as follows:—

MARSHALLING

Marshaller to stand well out of rotor disc range, with the aircraft to his right. Remember, if you cannot see the pilot's face, he cannot see you.

3. **Marshalling Signals.**—The hand signals which will be used always for marshalling helicopters are listed below at paragraph 5.

4. **Approaching and Leaving the Aircraft.**—Personnel will **approach and leave the helicopter only along the approach paths detailed for the appropriate helicopter type,** and therefore personnel will study closely the Appendices which deal with particular helicopter types. In addition, the following rules will be strictly observed:—

    (a) An Officer, Senior NCO, or police official, will always be at the LZ to meet the aircraft. He will control all personnel, civil and military, on and adjacent to the LZ; this control is particularly important on town padangs and the like.

XVII
Appx M

Appendix M—*Continued*

(b) Personnel on the ground will not approach the aircraft until called forward by the pilot or crewman, and then will only approach along the approach path detailed for the particular helicopter type (see relevant Appendices).

(c) Vehicles will not approach the aircraft.

5. **Hand Signals for Marshalling Helicopters** are as follows:—

(a) 'GO UP'.

(b) 'GO DOWN'.

(c) 'STEADY'.

(d) 'MOVE TO PORT' (hands pushing to the side).

(e) 'MOVE TO STARBOARD' (hands pushing to the side).

(f) 'COME FORWARD' (hand beckoning).

(g) 'MOVE BACK' (hands in motion of pushing aircraft away from Marshaller).

(h) 'CANCEL—LANDING PROHIBITED' (waving of arms).

Appendix M—*Continued*

6. **External Load Signals.**—When an external load is being lowered onto or lifted from the ground, the marshaller will indicate progressively to the pilot the distance of the load from the ground:—

   (a) *Back View of Marshaller—Load being Lowered:—*

When a load is being lifted, the marshaller will give signals in the sequence (iv) to (i).

   (b) The load must never be dragged along the ground, and therefore it is vitally important that the pilot is given a clear indication of the distance of the load from the ground, so that he may gain forward speed and therefrom lifting power as soon as possible.

   (c) The marshaller must endeavour to ensure that his arm signals are not obscured against his body. The sketches above show the ideal of the marshaller facing full bodied towards the pilot, with signals being given at right angles across the pilot's line of sight.

   (d) 'QUICK RELEASE—CARGO SLING' (throat cutting motion).

Appendix N

WHIRLWIND (MEDIUM) HELICOPTERS

DETAILS OF PERFORMANCE, EMPLANING DRILLS, AND SAFETY PRECAUTIONS

1. **Recognition.**—The Whirlwind helicopter is classed as a medium helicopter. Points of recognition are that it has a four-wheeled undercarriage (the two front wheels are smaller than the rear wheels), and the tail rotor is on the port (left) side of the tail boom.

2. **Loads and Distances.**—The following table gives the planning figures for the Whirlwind medium helicopter:—

Distance Flown Between LZs	Pay Load
30 nautical miles	800 lbs.
16 nautical miles	850 lbs.
50 nautical miles	720 lbs.

Notes:—These figures are for LZs up to 2,000 feet above sea level; above this altitude loads decrease by at least 100 lbs. per 1,000 feet. Under turbulent wind conditions the tabulated figures would be still further reduced.

When the take-off is from an airstrip or full-sized football field, with no surrounding obstructions, a greater load may be carried. Nevertheless, notwithstanding any figures which are given in this Appendix (which figures are provided only for guidance in planning), the actual load to be carried will always be detailed by the particular pilot concerned and his order is final.

3. **Fuel Consumption** rate is 40 gallons (290 lbs.) per hour under cruising conditions.

4. **Speed.**—For planning purposes, the Whirlwind medium helicopter is reckoned to travel at one nautical mile per minute.

5. **Rate of Effort.**—For flights of longer than 30 minutes' duration, the aircraft will refuel for each flight. Maximum flying time to be expected from one aircraft in one day is 9 hours. This is not a sustained rate.

6. **Casualty Evacuation.**—Two stretchers can be carried at any one time.

7. **Paratrooping.**—Three paratroops plus one dispatcher can be carried for distances up to 30 nautical miles.

8. **Spraying.**—Four helicopters can be fitted with spray equipment, at 24 hours' notice.

9. **Emplaning and Deplaning:—**
   (a) *Seating.*—Seating is not usually fitted unless asked for: the maximum seating is for three; each set of three seats weighs 10 lbs. Travelling positions for trooping (nil seats) are as follows:—

Appendix N—*Continued*

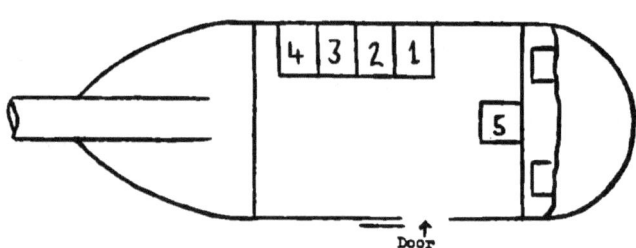

Passengers take up positions in numerical order, with their kit at their feet, against the numbers which are marked as above on the inside of the aircraft.

(b) *Ropes*.—Scrambling ropes are carried by all aircraft. Troops are able to deplane using the rope when the helicopter is up to 30 feet from the ground (the figure of 30 feet, which is for sea level, decreases with increasing LZ altitude).

10. **Paths of Approach.**—Diagram showing paths of approach to and departure from a Whirlwind (medium) helicopter:—

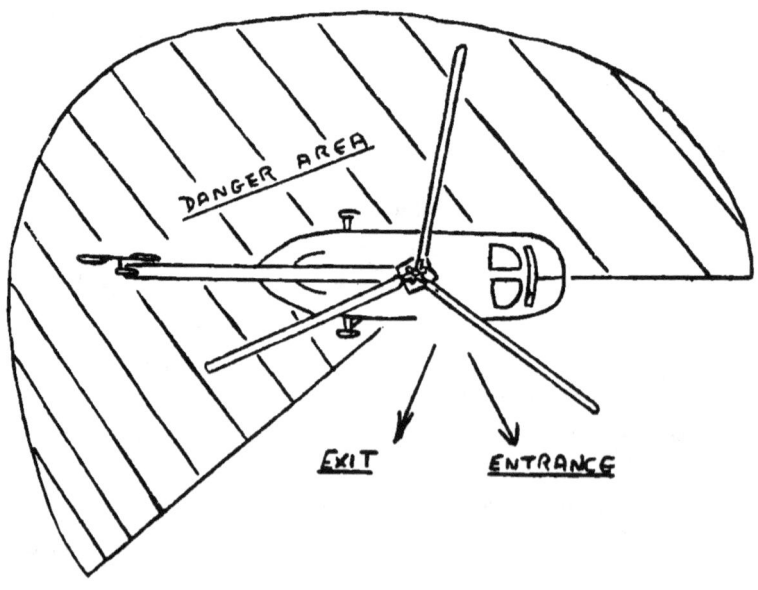

Appendix N—*Continued*

11. **Notes:**—
    (a) Door will remain open during flight.
    (b) No smoking during flight.
    (c) Handles marked with yellow and black paint will not be touched, except in emergency.
    (d) Heads should be lowered whilst deplaning.
    (e) Weapons and equipment will be placed between the legs during flight.

12. **Marshalling and Reception.**—See Appendix M for marshalling instructions and general reception arrangements.

XVII
Appx O

Appendix O

SYCAMORE (LIGHT) HELICOPTER

DETAILS OF PERFORMANCE, EMPLANING DRILLS, AND SAFETY PRECAUTIONS

1. **Recognition:**—The Sycamore helicopter is classed as a light helicopter. Points of recognition are that it has a three-wheeled undercarriage (the single nose wheel is smaller than the two rear wheels), and the tail rotor is on the starboard (right) side of the tail boom; the position of the tail rotor may be easily remembered by thinking "Sycamore = Starboard."

2. **Dangerous Characteristics.**—The main rotor blades and the tail rotor sweep unusually close to the ground; therefore an approach to the aircraft whilst the rotors are spinning will have tragic results unless the approach and exit instructions at paragraph 9 (b) are strictly obeyed.

3. **Load and Performance.**—The following table gives planning figures for the Sycamore light helicopter:—

Distance Flown Between LZs	Pay Load
75 nautical miles	540 lbs.
50 nautical miles	600 lbs.
25 nautical miles	'700 lbs.

Notes:—(i) These figures are for LZs up to 1,500 feet above sea level; above this altitude, deduct 170 lbs. per 1,000 feet.

(ii) The above figures will be amended according to conditions at the particular LZ; the load to be carried will always be detailed by the particular pilot concerned, and his order is final.

4. **Fuel Consumption Rate** is 24 gallons (173 lbs.) each hour under cruise conditions.

5. **Speed.**—For planning purposes over relatively short distances, the light helicopter is reckoned to travel at one nautical mile per minute.

6. **Use of Stretchers:**—

(a) The Sycamore is equipped to carry either one or two stretcher cases, according to conditions at the LZ. The stretcher will be loaded from the port side and the pilot or crewman will always supervise the loading. The feet of the stretcher fit into slides and are locked on the starboard side by self-locking catches and on the port side by manually operated bolts. The port door (Ambulance Blister) is made of perspex and care must be taken to prevent it swinging back and being damaged. If, for any reason, it is necessary to use the starboard (right) door, care must be taken to prevent the door from hitting and damaging the exhaust pipe.

XVII
Appx O

Appendix O—Continued

(b) The following illustrations show how the stretcher is loaded into the Sycamore:—

No. 1. This photograph shows the stretcher support runners. It is viewed from the loading (Port) door.

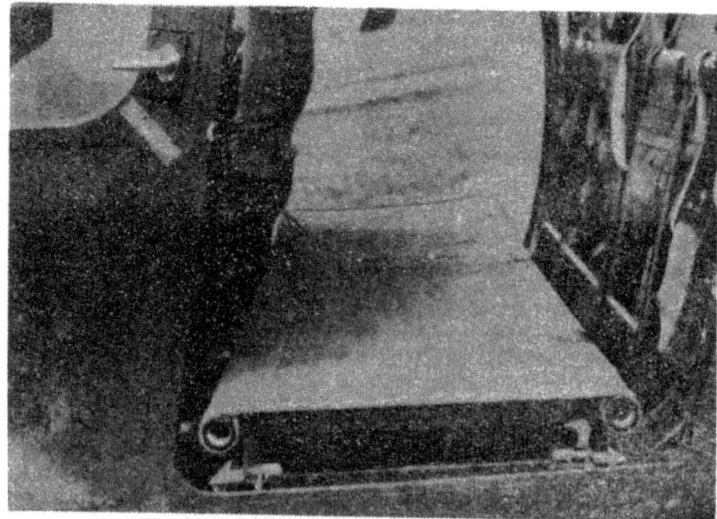

No. 2. The stretcher is now in position. It will be noted that the handles have been removed to prevent damage to the perspex door when it is closed.

Note that the retaining bolt on left is unlocked, that on right is locked.

Appendix O—*Continued*

XVII
Appx O

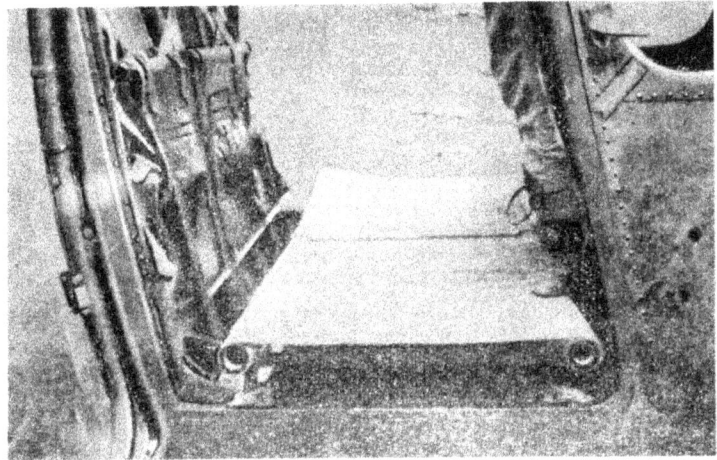

No. 3. View showing starboard side of aircraft and stretcher feet locked in runners.
Note the self-locking catches on this side.

No. 4. View showing starboard side of aircraft with stretcher in position and doors closed

Appendix O—*Continued*

7. **External Loads:—**
   (a) Loads, can be carried externally up to a weight of 300 lbs. in a net suspended from the underside of the fuselage. The equipment comprises three sections:—
      (i) *Slings.*—These are permanent fixtures and are joined together at a quick release box, on top of which is a button which, when pressed, jettisons the cable and net.
      (ii) *Cable.*—This is either 3 ft. or 6 ft. in length and is held at one end by the locking device of the quick release box and, at the other end, by a large hook with spring clip.
      (iii) *Net.*—The rectangular net is of rope mesh, having at each corner a 3 ins. ring. The net mesh is 9 ins. square.
   (b) The load can be released either from the ground, by pressing the button on the quick release box, or from the cockpit by means of the pilot's control.
   (c) *Operation of Net.*—The net containing equipment can be picked up from a LZ and delivered to any required place. The pilot must never allow loads to be dragged along the ground. Lifting and delivery must always be in the vertical plane.
      (i) *Picking-Up.*—The pilot will hover over the load and must be marshalled vertically downwards until the loop of the net can be attached to the cable hook. When this is done the marshaller will signal the pilot to climb vertically and will indicate when, and by how much, the load is clear of the ground. (See Hand Signals at Appendix M).
      (ii) *Delivery.*—The helicopter will arrive over the marker panels and be marshalled vertically down until the load is on the ground. The freight net may be released by:—
         (aa) operating the quick release box or
         (bb) signalling the pilot to operate his release or
         (cc) by unhooking the net rings from the cable.

XVII
Appx O

Appendix O—*Continued*

(iii) *Attachment of Load.*—The following illustrates the external load hook being lowered, and a load being attached and lifted:—

Appx O
XVII

Appendix O—*Continued*

8. **Winching.**— Winching facilities are available, at 24 hours' notice, for weights up to 300 lbs.

9. **Emplaning and Deplaning:**—
   (a) The pilot is responsible for the briefing of all passengers, and approach will not be made to a Sycamore helicopter unless this briefing has been carried out, and then only in the direction shown in the sketch below.
   (b) Approaching the Aircraft. Because of the low sweep of the main rotor blades and the nearness of the tail rotor to the ground, an approach to the helicopter whilst the rotors are spinning will have tragic results unless the following instructions are obeyed:—
      (i) Ground personnel will not approach the aircraft until called forward by the pilot or crewman.
      (ii) If the rotors are turning, the approach will be made only from the port side, i.e. the pilot's left, as follows:—

Sketch shows:—
   Danger area (shaded).
   Position of marshaller.
   Approach path.

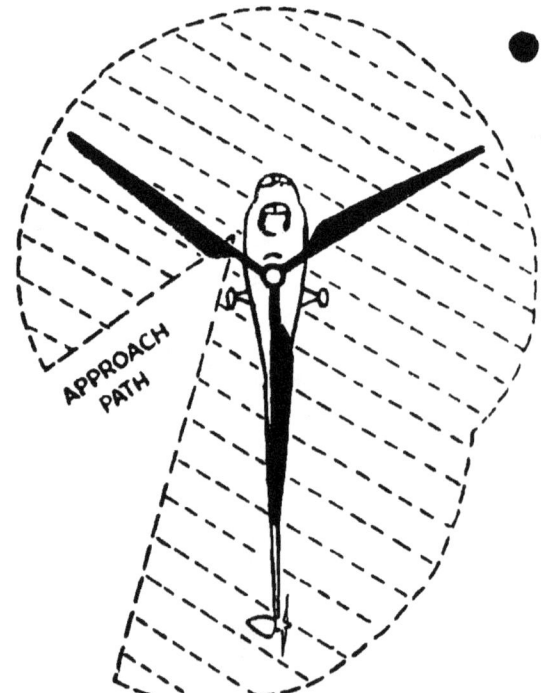

Appendix O—*Continued*

(iii) On sloping ground the rotor clearance can be less than 5 ft. from the ground. This is especially the case in front of the aircraft. Therefore all approaches will be in a stooping attitude, as follows:—

Approaching sycamore aircraft with engine running.— Approach from the rear port side in a crouched position. Open port door. Do not allow the door to swing back.

Warning.— If the aircraft is resting on sloping ground or on a LZ platform cut into sloping ground, it is obvious that the clearance between the rotor and the ground will be less than if standing on flat ground. Therefore when preparing a LZ, think carefully and—keep your heads.

(c) *Marshalling.*— Whenever possible, the Sycamore will roll forward a few feet, immediately after touching down; the marshaller must be prepared for this in his positioning of himself and the aircraft during marshalling. See Appendix M for general instructions on receiving and marshalling helicopters.

XVII
Appx P

Appendix P

GROUND FORCES FOLLOW-UP REPORT ON AIRSTRIKE

1. Fill in this form after every airstrike which your formation/unit has received.

2. Parts A, B, C and D must be completed in all cases. The first section of Part E must be completed when troops enter the area after a strike. The remainder of Part E should be completed if time permits observation.

3. The completed form is to be forwarded without delay to JOC.

4. If delivery of this completed form is likely to be delayed more than 48 hours, a FLASH report will be sent to JOC at the first opportunity. Part D is a guide to the information required in a FLASH report.

Date of Strike   Operation Order Number

PART A—TARGET LOCATION, TYPE, AND TIME OF ATTACK

Target	Pin-point Map Ref. or Boundaries of area	Terrain (Primary/secondary jungle swamp, lallang, etc.)	Day/Night attack
No. 1			
No. 2			
No. 3			
No. 4			

PART B—TARGET APPRECIATION

How many CTs were believed to be in target? How important were they?

Were CTs believed to enter area after a contact?
If so, when was the contact?

If CTs did not enter area after a contact, what was source and date of target information?
General intelligence appreciation?
Auster recce?
SEP/CEP information?
Other sources?

Appendix P—*Continued*

PART C—OBJECTS OF STRIKE

Was the object of the strike:—
(1) to kill CTs?
(2) to move CTs towards own troops positions?
(3) to encourage surrenders?
(4) to prevent CTs escape in a particular direction?
(5) other objects?

PART D—EFFECT OF STRIKE

Did any contacts occur after the strike? Do you consider any of these were caused by the strike?

Did any CTs surrender who were in the area when the strike took place. Do you consider any of these surrenders were caused by the strike?

Is it since known to have driven CTs out of target?

Is it known to have produced, killed or wounded CTs? State how many and source of information?

If troops entered target after strike did they find any damage to CT property? (Describe briefly).

General Appreciation of Effect of Air Strike:

Appendix P—*Continued*

PART E—DETAILS OF BOMB BURSTS
(To be completed only if troops entered area after strike)

When did troops enter target?

How many craters were noticed?

How many signs of bombs bursting high up in trees?

Approximate dimensions of craters ...	Depth .... ft. Diameter .... ft.	COMPLETE
Approximate extent of damage round craters	Yards from crater	ONLY IF TIME
Approximate extent of damage round airburst bombs ...	Yards from burst	PERMITS OBSERVATION

Date..   Unit...

CHAPTER XVIII

EMPLOYMENT OF THE ROYAL ARTILLERY IN ANTI-CT OPERATIONS

Section 1.—ARTILLERY RESOURCES

1. There are three types of artillery available:—
   (a) *25 per Gun.*—A highly mobile and accurate weapon with a maximum range of 11,400 yards firing Charge 3. No super charge is issued in Malaya. The terrain in Malaya, however, restricts this weapon to areas served with roads or motorable tracks.
   (b) *5·5 inch Guns.*—A mobile, accurate and hard hitting weapon with a maximum range of approximately 16,000 yards. A maximum axle weight of $7\frac{1}{2}$ tons presents bridge load problems particularly when estate roads are used.
   (c) *3·7 inch AA Guns.*—A useful long range gun giving a maximum range of 18,600 yards. Its great weight demands care when siting it in wet weather on ground likely to become soft. Ammunition shifting also makes heavy demands on troop personnel.

Section 2.—ALLOTMENT

To obtain the best results from the limited artillery available in Malaya, the most careful consideration of the allotment is necessary. When brigades receive information that guns, or searchlights will be available, battalions should, whenever possible, be invited to submit bids in advance, showing what operations are to be mounted together with the proposed employment of artillery. It is most important that a decision as to allotment is made early enough for the artillery task to be decided in the preliminary planning.

Section 3.—THE ADVANTAGES

1. The type of support offered by artillery in anti-CT operations is, in many ways, similar to that given by the RAF. Often however, there are many advantages in using guns or mortars as opposed to aircraft:—
   (a) The use of guns is not restricted by bad weather.
   (b) They can operate equally well by day or night without the give away sign of a searchlight.

(c) Artillery is better able to achieve surprise as shells can be brought down on a target without warning.
(d) Artillery support can be used much closer to our own troops than support by air bombing.
(e) Artillery support is generally more accurate than air attack.
(f) Artillery is capable of a more sustained effort and when required can give round-the-clock support over several days.
(g) Better communications tend to make liaison between the gunner and the infantryman more intimate and in consequence, artillery support is more flexible. Guns can be called down and lifted in a matter of minutes.

Section 4.—LIMITATIONS IN MALAYA

The nature of the country and the characteristics of the CT modify the normal capabilities of artillery in the following ways:—

(a) Observation of fire is very restricted and is usually impossible without the aid of an Air OP.
(b) Owing to the difficulty of observation, predicted fire is normal and observed fire the exception. In Malaya predicted fire is less accurate than normal, owing to the inaccuracy of maps in some areas and the absence of an organisation to provide up-to-the-minute meteorological information.
(c) In view of these factors, fire should not be brought closer to our own troops than:—

25 pr	500 yards
5·5 inch	1,000 yards
3·7 inch ...	550 yards

Extra allowance may be required if observed fire is not possible and survey and meteorological information is unreliable.
(d) The difficulty of observation limits the possibility of using artillery in a destructive role.
(e) Restrictions on firing within 1,000 yards of the rubber/ jungle edge (predicted shooting) have given the CT a degree of immunity which he has been quick to exploit. Patrolling by ground troops within the corridor thus created inside the jungle/rubber fringe should be carried out rigorously in order to deny the CT the comparative sanctuary of this strip of country.

Section 5.—TYPES OF SUPPORT

1. Artillery can offer the following types of support to infantry in anti-CT operations:—
   (a) *Flushing.*—CT in thick or difficult country can be flushed by artillery fire on to troops waiting in ambush.
   (b) *Harassing.*—Harassing fire can be used to keep CT on the move when their whereabouts is known or to harass them generally by methodical searching of an area. Harassing is most valuable during the hours when CT are normally resting and when operations by infantry have to be halted. To be successful it should be carefully planned in conjunction with infantry operations and must be maintained over long periods. Unless this type of fire is carefully planned and controlled it can result in an enormous expenditure of ammunition with little tangible result.
   (c) *Destructive Shoots.*—The disadvantage of using artillery to attack CT camps is the requirement for ranging and the relatively small scale of attack possible with the weapons available in Malaya. Methods which can achieve surprise and casualties are:—
      (i) Ranging on a datum point, then switching on to the target with maximum fire.
      (ii) Preliminary registration of a camp for future destructive shoots. In areas where there are a number of located camps and cultivations it may be worthwhile to register them all (with AOP observation) and then carry out, at a later date, a HF programme on a 'milkround' basis, both to cause casualties and to lower CT morale.
   (d) *Blocking Escape Routes.*—When troops are engaged in follow up operations, i.e. aften an incident, artillery can be used to dissuade the CT from using certain of the likely escape routes. This is more likely to be effective in steep hilly country or swamp where movement is canalised within fairly narrow limits. By use of this technique CT may be driven into ground of our own choosing.
   (e) *Deception.*—Artillery fire in an area away from that in which troops are operating, may deceive CT as to our intentions giving them a false sense of security and covering the noise of movement made by our own troops.
   (f) *Illumination.*—Areas can be illuminated for short irregular periods at night by firing star shells. This may prove a

deterrent to food suppliers. The searchlight section can give movement light to assist SF by illuminating the boundaries of operational areas e.g. railways, roads and perimeter wire.

(g) *Searchlights.*—The searchlight can provide beacons as datum points for bombing aircraft operating at night and as rallying points for surrendering CT, to be used in conjunction with psychological warfare. It is not necessary to ask for searchlights when demanding night air support. This is included by the JOC in the planning of the strike.

2. The value of artillery in 'showing the flag' must not be forgotten. Guns located in populated areas and firing in view of villagers can have a marked effect on civilian morale. It may also have a deterrent effect on CT supporters. Mortars should not, however, be used for this purpose unless very stringent safety precautions are observed.

3. The proven principle of using artillery in strength is just as applicable in Malaya as elsewhere. Dispersal in sections and even troops causes little or no damage and results in a great waste of ammunition. Guns in mass not only cause great damage but have a considerable effect on CT morale, and what is more important, increases the area hit and consequently the chances of a kill.

Section 6.—ORGANIZATION AND ADMINISTRATION

1. Artillery units in Malaya are organized along normal lines, capable of operating in mass or as detached troops.

2. Survey is available. It is usually possible to put all guns on one grid but owing to the nature of the country it is rarely possible to survey the target. Accurate predicted fire is, therefore, not always possible.

3. A troop is self contained for technical purposes and has its own REME and ACC personnel. It can carry ammunition as follows:—

25 pr: 132 rpg, 5·5 inch: 100 rpg, 3·7 inch: 40 rpg.

Additional transport is required to lift administrative stores if the period of detachment is to be a long one, and for the cartage of ammunition.

4. If the unit is to be away from base for a long period special arrangements have to be made for medical attention, POL and REME services beyond the capacity of the unit fitter.

Section 7.—AMMUNITION

1. When artillery is to be allotted, the G staff of the formation concerned should discuss the ammunition requirement with the battery or troop commander, so that the artillery officer is able to arrange for the dumping of the required amount of ammunition.

2. The ammunition is delivered to the nearest railway station or to the gun position by RASC transport. Normal 3-ton loads are:—

25 pr	184 rounds
5·5 inch	50 rounds
3·7 inch	80 rounds

Additional transport may be required for the lifting of ammunition from the railway station to the gun position.

3. For planning purposes it should be taken that normal expenditure of 25 pr ammunition should average 100 rounds per day per troop. Rates may be much higher when intensive effort is required for a short time. Staff control is imposed from time to time on natures which are in short supply. Release may have to be obtained from the appropriate HQ. It must be remembered that extravagent use of ammunition and, in particular, high rates of fire, cause excessive wear of guns and fatigue of gun detachments.

Section 8.—AIRCRAFT SAFETY

1. Attention must be paid to the danger to aircraft from artillery firing. Air sentries must be posted on gun and mortar positions and warning signals must be sent out in accordance with Joint Army/Air Instruction No. 7.

2. It is essential that every assistance is given to ensure that control orders from ACC Kuala Lumpur are passed to the guns with the minimum delay.

Section 9.—INTELLIGENCE REPORTS

When any known casualties or surrenders of CT occur as a direct result of artillery support, brigades and battalions should make particular note of this fact in their intelligence reports.

CHAPTER XIX

HANDLING OF ABORIGINES BY SECURITY FORCES

Section 1.—BACKGROUND

1. **General.**—During the Japanese occupation the MPAJA (i.e. the MCP) was forced to operate from the jungle, and became largely dependent on the aborigines for foodstuffs, guides and porters. In 1948, when the Emergency started large groups of the MCP withdrew to the jungle and were again in contact with the aborigines. For about thirteen years, therefore, virtually the only people who have been in almost constant contact with the aborigines are the (Chinese) MCP. During this period the CT have dominated some groups of aborigines and are using them to assist the 'Revolution.'

2. **MCP Policy towards the Aborigines.**—The 1951 Directives of the Central Politburo of the MCP laid down that there would be a partial withdrawal of MCP forces into the deep jungle for re-indoctrination and re-training. This withdrawal denied to the party their former sources of supply from the inhabited area and resulted in a greater degree of dependence on the aborigines for their basic fresh food requirements, and for intelligence on SF activities in the deep jungle. The MCP therefore formulated a policy towards the aborigines which set out how they were to be handled and organised. This policy aimed at educating them in matters of health and hygiene; giving them simple remedies; improving their planting methods to give a greater yield of produce; introducing them to the affairs of the world (as seen through Communist eyes); and finally the political training of selected aborigines and the arming of them to assist the MRLA.

3. The organisation which educates, indoctrinates, and generally administers the aborigines for the MCP is the 'ASAL Organisation.'

Section 2.—GOVERNMENT COUNTERMEASURES

1. The further the MCP withdrew into the deep jungle, the further removed they became from Special Branch sources of information and the more difficult they were to dislodge. As a first step in countering their policy it was decided to extend protection and administration to the main aborigine areas in the form of Jungle Forts manned by the Police. As a second step, the Department of Aborigines was placed on an emergency footing and greatly expanded. Trained teams from the Department were located

in these Forts and in the natural outlets where the aborigines normally come out of the jungle to contact civilization. One of the main tasks of these teams is to win over the aborigines and obtain intelligence from them on CT dispositions and activities.

2. Since the reorganization of the Department of Aborigines the vast majority of formerly CT dominated groups have been brought under Government control. There now remain under 300 who are actually co-operating with the Communists. Most of these are to be found along the main mountain range in the northern half of the Federation. The MCP is still very largely dependent on these aborigines for foodstuffs, tactical intelligence etc. in the area in which they are operating.

Section 3.—HANDLING OF ABORIGINES

1. Appendix D of 'An Introduction to the Malayan Aborigines' by P. D. R. Williams Hunt, which is issued to all units in Malaya, gives full notes on the handling of aborigines by SF. This Appendix should be read by all those who are liable to have any contact with aborigines. It should, however, be borne in mind that the Department of Aborigines is responsible for the Civil and Emergency administration of the aborigines and where possible officers of this Department should accompany SF units operating in known aborigine areas.

2. **Rations.**— The weekly ration issued to an aborigine who is working for the SF is :—

Item	Amounts
Rice	4½ katties
Salt	2 tahils
Coconut Oil	4 tahils
Ikan Bilis	8 tahils
Tobacco	2 tahils
Coffee Powder	4 tahils
Sugar	10 tahils
Duan Puckok	1 Bundle

3. **Wages.**— The daily wage issued to an aborigine working for the SF is $2 (plus rations as 2 above) or $2.50 less rations. This is paid from unit imprest account. For simplicity, it is always desirable that aborigines employed by SF should be rationed by SF.

4. **Guides.**— Section 3 paragraph (viii) of Appendix D of Williams Hunt's book refers to the positioning of aborigine guides within a patrol formation. The actual positioning of guides is the patrol commander's responsibility. Section 7 of Chapter VIII of this pamphlet deals fully with the position of guides with a patrol.

CHAPTER XX

THE EMPLOYMENT OF DOGS ON OPERATIONS AND THE ADMINISTRATION OF WAR DOGS

Section 1.—GENERAL

1. To obtain the maximum value from trained war dogs, it is essential to have an understanding of the conditions best suited for their employment. Dogs, like the rest of the animal kingdom are subject to outside influences which have a direct bearing on their behaviour. It follows, therefore, that the performance of any dog, no matter how highly trained, is not constant and it cannot be expected to work efficiently under every type of condition. This is often not fully appreciated, and instances have occurred where adverse criticism has been levelled against a dog simply because the person responsible for its employment was ignorant of its limitations. Full value will only stem from a full knowledge and better understanding of the capabilities of the dogs.

2. War dogs are a valuable weapon, which properly used, give us an advantage over the CT. The fullest use should therefore be made of them.

3. Only two types of operational dogs are in use in Malaya :—
   (a) Tracker Dog (see Chapter XXI).
   (b) Infantry Patrol Dog.

The two breeds most commonly employed are the Labrador, especially the black variety, for tracking, and the Alsation for patrol.

Section 2.—CONTINUATION TRAINING

The standard of efficiency of operational dogs, after issue to user units, can only be maintained and improved upon by regular continuation training. The importance of this fact cannot be too strongly stressed. If neglected the dog will quickly lose is usefulness as an operational weapon. RAVC NCOs are attached to all dog sections and, included in their duties, is careful supervision of continuation training. In this matter they should be given full support and facilities to enable them to carry it out expeditiously.

Section 3.—INFANTRY PATROL DOG

1. **General.**—A patrol dog works by air scent and hearing, and is trained to give silent warning, by pointing, of any individual or

group. He is not taught to attack and should not be used as a tracker. As he is required to work silently he must never be encouraged to bark. The patrol dog is therefore useful for giving silent warning of ambushes, attempts at infiltration and the presence of any 'foreign body' before such presence can be detected by a human.

2. The distance at which warning is given depends upon the following factors:—
    (a) Wind direction and velocity.
    (b) Prevailing weather conditions.
    (c) Density of vegetation.
    (d) Individual ability.

3. **Operational Employment.**— The infantry patrol dog can be employed in two ways:—
    (a) On a lead.
    (b) Loose.

In both cases the dog is under the direct control of its handler.

4. As vegetation impedes the movement of air and thus reduces the distance at which the dog can indicate 'foreign presence' it is customary in this theatre, during daylight, when moving along tracks, to work the dog loose. Depending on the nature of the track he is allowed to range up to about 30 yards in front of his handler. This procedure should always ensure the patrol receives adequate warning.

5. The dog normally 'points' by one or a combination of the two following ways:—
    (a) Freezing—the most definite indication.
    (b) Raising the head with ears pricked.

6. **Limitations.**— The success of a patrol depends on its ability to locate a CT without itself being detected. In all cases a trained patrol dog will detect a hidden CT before the patrol. He can be worked either by day or night in most kinds of weather and country; and is not disturbed by the noise of battle. Certain limitations must, however, be stressed.
    (a) His performance usually deteriorates in heavy tropical rain.
    (b) Dense, tractless belukar being difficult to negotiate lowers his efficiency.
    (c) He is apt to become perplexed when large numbers of people are in a small area.

(d) He cannot differentiate between CT and SF. Full briefing to the patrol in the dispositions of our own troops is essential.
(e) He will point at monkeys, pigs etc.

7. **Uses.**—The patrol dog can be used:—
   (a) On reconnaissance patrols.
   (b) On fighting patrols.
   (c) As a sentry outpost.
   (d) In ambush positions.

8. **On Patrol.**—On patrol the handler and dog will normally lead. However, if the dog is being worked loose it may be possible for the dog to lead followed by the leading scout, provided the handler constantly has the dog in sight. This makes the handler's job a trifle less hazardous. In any case close contact must be maintained between handler and patrol leader. The normal procedure is:—
   (a) The patrol commander indicates to the handler the mission, disposition of own troops, the general direction of advance and any special local instructions.
   (b) The patrol is ordered to move out.
   (c) The patrol dog and handler with one escort armed with an automatic weapon, precedes the patrol at a distance which will permit immediate communication with the patrol commander. At night this would be about an arm's length; in daylight the distance will be greater but within easy visual signalling distance.
   (d) The patrol dog and handler move off, keeping generally in the indicated direction. He must be allowed to take advantage of wind and other conditions favouring the dog's scenting powers without endangering the patrol.
   (e) When the dog points the handler indicates by silent hand signal 'CT in sight.'
   (f) The patrol halts and takes cover.
   (g) Patrol commander proceeds quietly, utilising available cover, to the handler and dog and makes his plans.

9. **Sentry Outposts.**—The main value of the dog is to give timely warning of approach of, or attempts at infiltration by CT. The handler and dog are placed a short distance from the sentries: this distance will be within easy visual signal in daylight but much closer at night. A simple means of communication between handler

and patrol commander at night is a piece of cord or string, which is jerked to alert everyone. When alerted the patrol commander proceeds immediately to the handler to receive any information concerning the distance and direction of CT.

10. **Ambush Positions.**— In ambush positions, especially at night, the dog will give valuable warning of anyone's approach. His handler must always be beside him.

11. In all cases the local commander should take the advice of the handler as to the best employment of the dog or dogs. Only knowledge and experience will give familiarity with the powers and limitations of the unit's own particular dogs.

Section 4.—DOG HANDLERS

1. **General.**—The performance of a war dog is directly dependent upon the skill of the handler and the mutual understanding existing between him and his dog. The dog must be handled only by a trained handler. In Malaya all dogs and handlers are trained initially at the War Dog Training Wing RAVC, attached to the FARELF Training Centre.

2. **Operational Dog Section.**— Included in all operational dog sections is an RAVC element. Dependent upon the size of the section this element may be made up to three NCOs—Sgt., Cpl. and L/Cpl.

3. The RAVC NCOs are responsible for the continuation training, management etc. of the dogs. Where necessary they will also undertake the training of replacement handlers.

4. The RAVC NCO will be the commanders adviser on dogs. He will be responsible for:—

  (a) Advising the commander on all matters affecting dogs in his section.

  (b) Further training of dogs in their locations and keeping them at the height of operational efficiency.

  (c) Arranging for the deployment of dogs in accordance with the operational requirements of the commander.

  (d) Establishing and maintaining a veterinary pharmacy and as many first aid posts as necessary for the treatment of all sick and injured dogs.

  (e) Dissemination of information on the uses and limitation of dogs amongst the fighting personnel, especially the newly joined. It is useless to expect much from war dogs if there is a general antipathy to their use or if they are considered a nuisance.

5. After his return to his unit the handler must be given sufficient time for the proper care, management and continued training of his dog.

6. The notice at Appendix A to this Chapter should appear on all notice boards in kennels.

7. **Selection of Personnel.**— Potential dog handlers should be chosen from volunteers who have already received a sound basic military training and who are friendly and sympathetic towards dogs. This is a primary requisite. A dog will quickly sense an unsympathetic handler and its standard of performance will deteriorate. Other qualities for potential handlers may be listed as follows:—

(a) Intelligence.
(b) Patience and perseverance.
(c) Dependability. The dog's whole life depends upon its handler. Unless the handler is conscientious and reliable, capable of performing without strict supervision what he has been taught during his training, the dog will suffer.
(d) Resourcefulness. It is inevitable that situations will arise which do not appear in the text book. Improvisation by a resourceful man may save the situation.

Section 5.—KENNEL MANAGEMENT IN THE TROPICS

1. **General.**— Kennel management includes:—
(a) Kennel hygiene.
(b) Grooming.
(c) Foods and feeding.
(d) Exercise.

2. A high standard of care and management is required if the health and well-being of the dog is to be maintained. Fit and well cared for dogs are contented dogs: contented dogs are trained more quickly and will, of course, prove more effective on operations than ill cared for and unhappy dogs. In addition sickness is reduced to a minimum or, if present, is detected at its first onset.

3. **Grooming.**— The dog must be thoroughly groomed once a day. The procedure is as follows:—

(a) Vigorous massage of the coat with the tips of the fingers.

(b) Brush: first against and then with the direction of the hair.
(c) Comb: to remove dead and tangled hair.
(d) Brush with the growth of the hair.
(e) Remove discharges from eyes, nose and anus.
(f) Examine and clean ears: NEVER probe into ear.

4. **Foods and Feeding.**— The normal daily ration for a war dog is:—

Meat	$1\frac{1}{2}$ lbs.
Biscuits	$\frac{1}{2}$ lb.
Vegetables ...	$\frac{1}{4}$ lb.

5. The dog should normally be fed in the late afternoon or evening but the actual time will vary depending on circumstances. Sufficient time should be allowed after feeding for the dog to empty its bowels.

6. The dog should be allowed to consume its food undisturbed. After feeding all feed bowls must be removed and thoroughly scoured. Only in cases of known shy feeders should food be left in the kennel. The diet should never be changed suddenly but gradually, otherwise diarrhoea will result.

7. For feeding on patrol: see Section 6.

8. **Water.**— Water should be allowed without any restriction.

9. Insufficient exercise is the cause of constipation, stomach troubles and skin disorder. Free exercise must be given at first kennel parade, after feeding and before kennelling up at night. The amount of exercise will vary with the work done but must always be sufficient to keep the dog in a hard, fit condition.

10. **Kennel Hygiene.**— Kennels must be thoroughly cleaned and brushed daily. No bedding should be normally allowed in kennels. Food and water bowls must always be cleaned and when not in use properly stacked or turned upside down. Shelter must be provided for the dog from rain and sun. Regular disinfection and spraying of kennels in order to control ticks, etc., is often necessary. Kennels should be moved to fresh ground regularly unless they are on hard standings.

Section 6.—FEEDING ON PATROL

1. All dog meat is issued in tins of 1 lb. weight. The meat should be mixed with biscuit before feeding. Dogs should normally be fed in the late afternoon or evening but this will depend entirely on

operational requirements. Two principles of feeding must, however, be borne in mind:—
  (a) Never feed immediately after arduous work.
  (b) Never feed immediately before work.

2. If fresh meat is issued it should be fed raw to the dog. If bully beef is issued and the dog will not eat it, it is usually the salt which puts him off. Therefore the bully should be soaked for a few minutes, and the scum poured away. The dog should then feed satisfactorily.

3. If no special dog rations are available the dog should be fed with the same rations as the patrol. Some dogs love curry and rice.

Section 7.—VETERINARY NOTES FOR DOG HANDLERS

1. **Signs of Health.**— Signs of health in a dog:—
   (a) Alertness. The dog is bright, wags his tail and is pleased to see his master.
   (b) Passes urine and faeces normally.
   (c) Eats and drinks normally.
   (d) Eyes are bright and clean. Conjunctiva (mucous membrane of the eye) is salmon pink in colour.
   (e) Nose is usually cold and wet.
   (f) Skin is loose and the coat is glossy.
   (g) The breath is not offensive, the tongue and gum (if not pigmented) are salmon pink in colour.
   (h) The temperature is 101-102 degrees when quiet at rest.
   (j) The pulse is about 80 per minute.

2. If the dog does not look well it must be reported at once to the NCO or officer-in-charge.

3. Health is maintained by:—
   (a) Kennel hygiene.
   (b) Grooming.
   (c) Feeding.
   (d) Exercise.

4. **First Aid Treatment of Wounds.**—Types of wounds:—
   (a) Clean cut (incised), e.g. razor or broken glass.
   (b) Torn (lacerated).

(c) Punctured, i.e. dog bite.
(d) Bruised (contused).

5. Principles of treatment:—
    (a) Stop bleeding if severe (pressure or tourniquet).
    (b) Clip hair away.
    (c) Wash with warm water and soap.
    (d) Apply mild antiseptic solution, e.g. 1/1,000 acriflavine solution or weak Dettol.
    (e) Dust with sulphanilamide powder or boric acid powder.
    (f) Bandage if necessary.
    (g) Maggots. When a wound is neglected it quickly becomes fly blown with resulting maggot infestation. Treat with Lorexane.

6. If there is an injury to the eye or near the eye, it should be bathed gently with warm water. Soap or antiseptics must not be used on or near the eye.

7. **Elementary Nursing.**— A sick dog should be kept warm and given a light diet, e.g. bread and milk, rice pudding, steamed fish, egg and milk, a little offal twice or three times a day. Food should be removed if the dog does not eat it. Plenty of fresh clean water should always be allowed. He should be groomed gently and only given a little gentle walking exercise.

8. **Some Common Conditions:**—
    (a) 'Eczema.' This is caused usually by inadequate grooming, fleas or lice, errors in feeding and exercise. Treat the cause: change the diet: report to VO to ascertain exact cause and particularly to differentiate from mange.
    (b) Fleas or lice may be found when grooming. The dog should be dusted with Pulvex to kill them. If fleas are present, the bedding must be burned and Pulvex dusted round the kennel.

9. Ticks should not be pulled off. They must be anaesthetised with chloroform or dusted with Pulvex or burned off by touching their bodies with a lighted cigarette and they will then fall off on their own accord.

10. If a dog loses hair in patches it may be due to mange or ringworm. It must be reported at once as the dog must be treated by a Veterinary Officer. Mange and ringworm are infectious and

the dog must be isolated. Cases of so-called 'eczema' are often due to mange.

11. The dog may pass roundworms or tapeworms. If he does it must be reported to the Veterinary Officer.

12. **Constipation.**—Food should be made more 'sloppy' and a desertspoonful of medicinal liquid paraffin given.

13. **Vomitting.**—A dog can vomit very easily but if he keeps on doing it, it must be reported as he may have swallowed something or have kidney trouble.

14. **Diarrhoea.**—Diarrhoea may be due to a change in food or some disease. It should be reported.

15. **Heat Exhaustion.**— This condition occurs not uncommonly in unfit dogs. The dog becomes lethargic, refuses to work and attempts to get in the cool. His temperature rises rapidly up to 110°F or more and he appears extremely distressed. The dog should immediately be placed in the shade and cooled with cold water douches. Ice, if available, should be placed on and around him, until recovered.

16. If the dog looks off colour report it.

Appendix A

ADVICE TO DOG HANDLERS

1. As a trained dog handler you are responsible for the continued health and working efficiency of your dog. You must show zeal, enthusiasm and devotion to duty.

2. DON'Ts
    (a) Don't allow anyone to handle or become friendly with your dog. It is NOT a pet and has a job to do like yourself.
    (b) Don't throw sticks or other articles for your dog to retrieve.
    (c) Don't allow your dog to go chasing poultry or game.
    (d) Don't allow your dog to sleep in your own bivouac.
    (e) Don't overdo your obedience work or your dog will lose its initiative.

3. DO's
    (a) Do praise your dog for a command successfully obeyed or for a job well done.
    (b) Do insist on commands given being carried out.
    (c) Do allow your dog to relax and play when off duty.
    (d) Do ensure that kennel management is the best.
    (e) Do give your dog regular training.

XXI

CHAPTER XXI

TRACKING

Section 1.—INTRODUCTION

1. With the smaller numbers of CT operating in the jungle and a consequent reduction in the opportunities to secure kills, it is essential that full use is made of the specialised tracking resources available to the SF. These consist of:—
   (a) Sarawak Rangers (Iban trackers).
   (b) Tracker dogs.
   (c) Visual trackers drawn from suitable members of individual units.

2. This Chapter sets out the characteristics of the human tracker and the tracker dog, tracking techniques and the composition and employment of tracker teams.

Section 2.—THE SARAWAK RANGER (IBAN)

1. Recruited in Sarawak for service in Malaya against the CT, the Sarawak Ranger is carefully selected for his known ability to follow a track in the jungle. On arrival in Malaya he initially passes through the Sarawak Rangers Depot where certain administrative requirements are met and then undergoes a four weeks' tracking course at the Far East Training Centre at Kota Tinggi. The object of this training is to familiarise the Iban in working with military patrols, and to acquaint him with varying types of terrain with which he was not previously familiar.

2. Whilst at the Far East Training Centre he receives sufficient instruction in weapon handling to enable him to defend himself when engaged in anti-CT operations.

3. After completion of this training he is available for posting to an infantry battalion. Normally he serves only with British and certain Commonwealth battalions; both Gurkha and Federation Army units providing trackers from within their own resources.

4. The normal allotment of Iban trackers to an infantry battalion is 30. The sub-allotment within the battalion is a matter for the Commanding Officer to decide, but it is normal for the Ibans to be allotted on a permanent basis to companies, where they may be retained centrally, or more usually, further sub-allotted to platoons. In this way they become, to all intents and purposes, a member of

the platoon and identify themselves in every way with the platoon. Under day to day operational conditions the Iban normally accompanies his platoon, particularly when it is engaged on patrolling tasks.

Section 3.—THE VISUAL TRACKER

1. Although reference is made in this Chapter to the Iban tracker, a visual tracker may, in fact, be of any nationality, and references to visual trackers need not necessarily refer only to the Iban.

2. **Capabilities and Limitations of the Visual Tracker.**—A skilled tracker is able to follow a track by recognising the following signs which are inconsistent with normal pattern:—

   (a) Change in the colour of the vegetation.

   (b) Unnatural formations in the vegetation.

   (c) Bruises, breaks and cuts in the vegetation.

   (d) Water on certain areas whereas the remainder is dry.

   (e) Lack of water or dew on vegetation.

   (f) Mud or soil on grass or bushes.

   (g) Scars (or footprints) in bare or muddy ground.

   (h) Latex exuded from a bruised rubber root.

   (j) Disturbances in insect life.

3. Due to the fact that the visual tracker relies on sight, he is unable to track at night. He is not always able to recognise the end of a track, and because of the necessity to examine minutely the trail he is following, he tends to be unduly slow when engaged on a follow up.

Section 4.—TRACKER

1. **General.**— Tracker dogs, as issued, are trained to follow human ground scent. Trained, as they are, on the Reward System they must be allowed to earn their reward as often as possible. Failures on difficult tracks are to be expected, but these failures must not occur too frequently otherwise they will become disheartened. Following a failure the dog must, where circumstances permit, be given a simple track to enable him to earn his reward—usually a piece of meat.

2. **Operational Employment.**— The most important single factor in the successful employment of a tracking dog is TIME. The dog must be brought to the scene of the incident with all possible speed and NOT USED AS A LAST RESORT. It is

suggested that tracking dogs are held at base until a call for their services is made. When this happens they should be taken as near as possible to the scene of the incident by transport or helicopter in order that they may arrive fresh, not tired out by a long forced march. The degree of fatigue a tracker has reached will determine its usefulness.

3. Once it has been decided to use a tracking dog, the less 'fouling' of the area with extraneous scent the better. Objects liable to have been in contact with the person to be tracked should not be touched and movement over the area restricted to a minimum.

4. **Scent.**— Man, in common with animals, gives off a body odour which is specific for each person. This odour is constantly being exuded and traces of it remain in the path of a moving individual. Added to this body odour, there is the scent given off by the wearer's clothes, footwear, and those released by the bruising and breaking of vegetation and the crushing of small insects. The dog tracks a combination of scents known as a 'Track Picture.' The analogy is the connoisseur of music following the 'Theme' of a complicated major work. The dog becomes conscious of the scent through the air near the ground over which the individual has passed coming into contact with the delicate membranes lining the nose. It follows that the degree of discernment is directly related to the concentration of 'scent' in the air which the dog breathes.

5. **Tracking Conditions in Malaya.**— The ideal tracking conditions may be listed as follows:—
   (a) Air and ground temperatures approximately equal.
   (b) A mild day with a certain amount of moisture in the air with slow evaporation.
   (c) Damp ground and vegetation.
   (d) Ground overshadowed by trees.
   (e) Blood spilled on trail. It has been noted however that certain dogs become disturbed by the presence of blood or a body and their performance deteriorates.
   (f) A running CT who gives off more body odour than one who has walked away calmly.
   (g) An unclean CT.

6. Factors which adversely affect the 'Track Picture' include:
   (a) Hot sun.
   (b) Strong wind.
   (c) Heavy rain.
   (d) Roads (tarmac) on which cars travel.
   (e) Running water.

7. In Malaya the heavy growth of vegetation helps to combat the heat and retains more scent than one would expect in a temperate climate. Furthermore, a greater amount of vegetation is damaged by a running CT, thus producing an increased aroma.

8. Despite the knowledge that certain factors have a direct effect on the 'Track Picture' the degree of effect is frequently so variable that it is impossible to say with certainty when it should be sufficiently apparent to follow successfully. Nevertheless, it is known that tracks made late in the day can normally be identified the following morning and that tracks protected from direct sun's rays and tropical rain have been recognised after 36 hours or more.

9. **Night Tracking.**— As scent tends to remain more concentrated during the hours of darkness it may be assumed that dogs will track better at night than during the day. This assumption has been proved correct. However, to accustom them to the altered conditions they must be given regular night training. This is also necessary for the handler as a greater degree of skill is required in reading his dog. As frequent halts will be made during an operational night track these must be included when training.

Section 5.—TRACKING TEAMS

1. As seen in Sections 3 and 4 above, both the visual tracker and the tracker dog are subject to certain limitations. In order to exploit fully their special characteristics it is desirable that they be made complementary to one another. This can best be achieved by the formation of tracker teams consisting of both the visual tracker and the dog.

2. The formation of tracking teams may be done in several ways, but from the viewpoint of team spirit and familiarity with one another, it is desirable that permanent affiliations be built up and the teams kept intact.

3. The most important role that the team will be called on to perform will be an immediate follow up after a contact or an incident. It is necessary that a sufficient degree of centralisation be retained to enable a team or teams to be moved into position with the minimum delay. A balance must be struck between a desire to allot teams permanently to rifle companies, and centralised control at Battalion Headquarters level. It is also important that due allowance is made for wastage due to leave, sickness, etc. when teams are formed.

4. In order to achieve sufficient flexibility it should normally be possible to allow the Iban to live and operate with his platoon, as

shown in Section 2, and a tracker dog and handler to be married up with the team commander and Iban as and when required. It is suggested that at least one, and possibly two, complete teams be retained at Battalion Headquarters as a Battalion reserve. If it is to be a success the Tracker Team must be allowed to work as a set Team and changes in its personnel should be as infrequent as possible. Thus a team of trackers and cover-men working constantly together build up complete confidence in one another.

5. The following is a suggested composition of a tracking team:—

Team Commander (Sgt. or Senior Cpl.)	1
Iban trackers	3
Dog Handler	1
Tracker dog ...	1
Cover men ...	3

6. **Positioning of Tracker Teams after an Incident or Contact.** Circumstances will arise when an incident or contact will occur with either a visual tracker or a tracker dog present at the time. Although the ideal situation would be for the team complete to take part in the follow up, the commander on the spot will be in the best position to decide whether to wait for the marrying up of the whole team or to follow up immediately with whatever resources he has available.

7. Where such a situation occurs, and the sub-unit commander desires to complete his team before following up, the quickest method of moving the remaining elements of the team to the contact point must be adopted. The use of helicopters for this purpose must always be borne in mind.

8. The employment of the Battalion reserve team(s) under these circumstances should not be overlooked.

Section 6.—TRACKING TECHNIQUES

1. The following are factors which influence tracking and which must always be borne in mind:—
    (a) Type of vegetation.
    (b) Weather conditions.
    (c) Age of tracks.
    (d) Time of day.
    (e) Type of track.
    (f) Deception measures taken by the CT.

2. **Deception.**—CT will use any of the following methods to throw off trackers:—
 (a) Walking backwards.
 (b) Walking in a stream.
 (c) Jumping off to one side.
 (d) Splitting up into ones or twos.
 (e) Walking along logs or on stones.
 (f) Moving on ground over which it is difficult to track.
 (g) Covering their footprints with leaves etc. or brushing over their tracks.

3. **Counter-deception.**—The methods described above will DELAY a tracking team but the team commander must bear in mind that CT are not possessed with wings. A careful search of the immediate vicinity will show what method of deception has been used. The commander can then take steps to renew the follow-up.

4. Some suggested methods are:—
 (a) Direction of grass, twigs, ferns etc. These will always point in the direction of movement whether or not the footprints appear to be going the other way.
 (b) Search BOTH banks of the stream for about a mile up and down from the point of entry.
 (c) Use a "box" or "cross grain" search. (See paragraphs 5-7 below).
 (d) Trackers MUST be trained to report immediately to the team commander any attempt by the CT to split up. The team commander will then decide which party will be followed. The splitting up point should be marked so that the team can return to it and start again if necessary.
 (e) Examine any logs, stones, etc. in the immediate vicinity.
 (f) The team commander can "lift" the team and try a search along the edges of more favourable ground.
 (g) Examine the area on either side of the track for signs of disturbance in the leaves.
 Note:—Unless carried out by an expert, forms of deception will often only serve to give a clearer indication of where the track is!

5. **The Box Search.**—The Box Search is used when the leading tracker indicates that he has reached the last visible sign of the track he is following. Trackers must be trained never to pass beyond this

point without first informing the team commander of its exact location.

6. A simple drill for the Box Search is:—
   (a) Leading tracker halts the team and indicates the position of the last visible sign to the team commander.
   (b) This sign is marked for future reference.
   (c) The leading tracker casts ahead and to the flanks about 5-6 yards. This "Private" box search must be rigidly controlled by the team commander.
   (d) Tracker finds track—team continues.
   OR
   (e) Tracker fails to find the track.
   (f) Team commander orders the leading tracker (plus his "cover-man") to search to the limit of visibility or to 50 yards (whichever is less) to the FRONT and then circling to the LEFT REAR.
   (g) At the same time, the team commander orders another tracker (plus his "cover-man") to search within the same bounds of distance to the RIGHT REAR circling to the FRONT.

7. **The Cross-grain Search.**— Cross-graining is a technique carried out by a tracking team:—
   (a) When the team is searching for track information in a given area.
   OR
   (b) Should a Box Search fail.
   (Sketch at Appendix A refers).

8. **Information obtainable from a Visual Tracker.**— A visual tracker should be able to give some, or all, of the following information to his team commander:—
   (a) Direction of tracks.
   (b) Age of tracks.
   (c) Number in party.
   (d) Whether party is carrying loads.
   (e) Sex.
   (f) Weapons.

9. The information in sub-paragraphs (d) (e) and (f) above will not always be given but under certain favourable conditions they may be ascertained.

Section 7.—OPERATIONAL EMPLOYMENT OF TRACKER TEAMS

1. Based on the strength of the team as set out in Section 5, paragraph 5, the team allows for a relief system to be followed when a long follow-up is in progress.

2. The visual tracker when in the lead, must have a cover-man who acts as a second pair of eyes. This cover-man must never be more than two yards from his tracker when the latter is actually tracking.

3. The team commander must make an appreciation of each track or section of track and use the element of his Team which will produce the faster result.

4. Except when carrying out a "Box Search" the team will remain in SINGLE FILE. A suggested formation is shown at Appendix B.

5. **Rate of Movement of Tracker Team.**— Team commanders must always bear in mind the principles of movement and patrolling already laid down in this book. Speed must be related to the type of country being traversed. Silent movement must be achieved and halts every 10-15 minutes must be made to enable the team to LISTEN for CT.

6. It is most disheartening to follow a track for several hours, to find a CT camp and then discover that the process has to be repeated purely because the CT heard the team approaching.

7. Thus it will be appreciated that any reference to speed already made in this Chapter is purely relative.

8. **Use of Teams at Night.**— Commanders must remember that tracker teams can be used in the rubber at night. By using the dog element the team should be able to follow CT tracks to the rubber/jungle edge. There the team should base-up and continue the track at first light. Silence must be maintained in the base-up position as it will be more than likely that the CT are only a matter of two or three hundred yards from the rubber/jungle edge and are also in a base-up position. Teams must not attempt to follow up through any type of country in which it is not possible to move silently, i.e. jungle, belukar, etc.

9. **Employment.**—Tracker teams can be used, for any of the following tasks:—

    (a) To follow-up and achieve contact after a CT incident or initial contact.

(b) As a source of intelligence for commanding officers and company commanders.

10. Although in theory every follow-up by a tracker team should result in a contact, due to the various factors already mentioned, this will not be so in practice.

11. However, each follow-up should provide information either positive or negative which may at a later stage enable commanders to ascertain the location of either:—
   (a) CT camps or
   (b) CT spheres of activity.

12. Information, positive or negative, should result also from teams when used in their subsidiary role in paragraph 9 (b) above. It should be noted that when used in this role the dog should not be included in the patrol but a signaller with wireless set should be added thus enabling the team commander to call in the dog should the need arise.

13. To assist commanders to identify possible CT camp sites or spheres of activity each unit and sub-unit should have a track map. On this map every track discovered in the unit or sub-unit area should be charted. This should be done irrespective of age or length of the track. Each track charted should be labelled to show the following points:—
   (a) Direction.
   (b) Age.
   (c) Number in party.
   (d) Length of track.
   (e) Any special features.

14. **Follow-up Platoon.**— Tracker team commanders should always bear in mind that they are not "Killer-Groups" but an aid to their commanders to destroy the CT. Thus each tracker-team when used to follow-up tracks must be partnered by a follow-up group of a size detailed by commanders. The team commander must ensure that as soon as he locates a CT camp he must halt his team and inform the commander of the follow-up group, so that effective action may be taken to ensure complete elimination of the CT.

15. **Training.**— It must be remembered that visual trackers— as well as tracker dogs—lose their skill at tracking if continuation training is not carried out. This training can be achieved by laying a quite simple track over about a mile of country twice or three times a week. In addition, training of this nature will build up a team spirit and thus help ensure successful results.

XXI
Appx A

Appendix A

CROSS GRAIN SEARCH

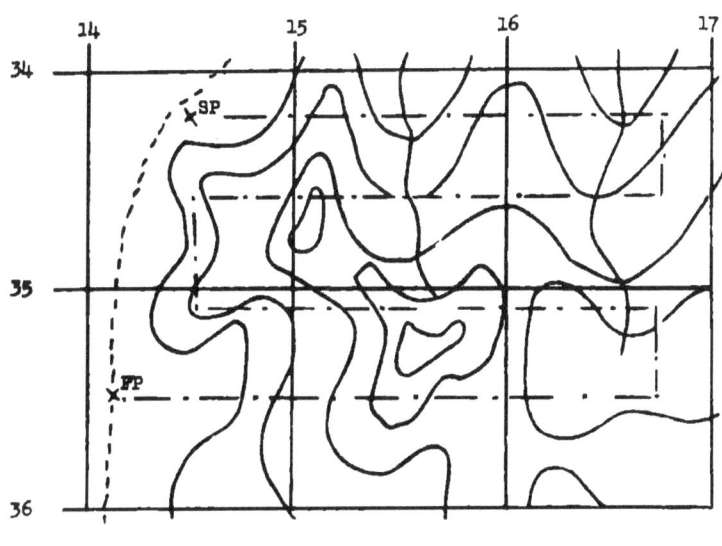

LEGEND. SP — Start Point.
         FP — Finish Point.
         —.— — Path taken by team.

Appx B

Appendix B

TRACKER TEAM FORMATION

The following are suggested formations but can be varied to suit the task in hand.

1. Using Visual Tracker:—

(a)	Tracker	— Follows actual track.
(b)	Team commander	— Covers serial (a).
(c)	Tracker	— Watches flanks for any attempt at deception.

TACTICAL BOUND

(d)	Cover-man	— Cover-man for serial (a)
(e)	Cover-man	— Cover-man for serial (c)
(f)	Cover-man	— Cover-man for serial (h)
(g)	Dog and Handler	—
(h)	Tracker	— Resting but available for Box. Search.

2. Using Dog:—

(a)	Dog and Handler	—
(b)	Tracker	— Covers serial (a)
(c)	Team Commander	—

TACTICAL BOUND

(d) Cover-man
(e) Cover-man
(f) Cover-man
(g) Tracker
(h) Tracker

PART THREE
ADMINISTRATION

CHAPTER XXII
OPERATIONAL RATIONS

Section 1.—INTRODUCTION

1. The basic principle adopted in feeding the soldier in Malaya is to provide him, as far as possible, with fresh food of the type to which he is accustomed. If for any reason this is not possible (e.g. turnover of reserve supplies, transport difficulties or operational reasons), resort must be made to preserved food such as canned meats, vegetables, biscuits or pack rations.

2. Under certain conditions, it is an advantage to pack in one container a complete day's requirement of tinned foods either for one man or for a group of men, e.g. an infantry section.

3. The problem as regards jungle operations in Malaya is to produce an easily carried and suitable ration for patrols which operate in the jungle over long periods, bearing in mind that it is essential in these conditions that the ration provides both variety and sufficient bulk.

Section 2.—TYPES OF PACKS AVAILABLE IN MALAYA

1. The following types of special ration packs in use in Malaya are described in Appendix A to this Chapter. Lists of contents and notes on their use are contained in the appendices shown below:—

Type of Pack	Detailed composition shown at Appendix
BT 10 Men	B
BT 24 Hour (UK)	C
BT 24 Hour (Local)	D
BT 24 Hour (SAS)	E
BT 14 Day Light Weight	F
GT 10 Men	G
GT 24 Hour	H
MT 2 Men	J

2. Contents and sizes vary according to the particular use for which packs are designed, e.g.:—

(a) 10 men composite ration pack (normally referred to as 'Compo Rations')—designed for bulk or party feeding where it is not possible to issue normal fresh rations.

(b) 24 hour rations.—Designed for individual feeding where bulk or party feeding is impossible for operational or supply reasons.

Section 3.—AIR SUPPLY

1. Fresh rations, as well as ration packs, can be demanded when troops are being supplied by air. As these must be consumed the day they arrive, the proportion normally should be one day's fresh rations to three or four days tinned.

2. In addition to normal items, the demanding unit can arrange for extra cigarettes or other articles to be obtained on payment through NAAFI.

3. Broadly speaking, the Air Despatch Coy RASC is prepared to drop any supplies or amenities urgently required operationally, which can be supply dropped, and if available.

4. For further details see Chapter XVII, Section 4.

Appendix A

GENERAL DATA ON SPECIAL RATION PACKS

Serial No.	Type of Pack	Detail of Packing	Average gross weight of one pack	Average gross weight of one ration	Detailed composition shown at Appendix
(a)	(b)	(c)	(d)	(e)	(f)
1	BT 10 men Compo (produced in UK)	Ten rations (less biscuits) in fibreboard case, 16¼" x 11" x 10". *N.B.* When bread is not available or cannot be accepted, biscuits service will be issued at the scale of 9 ozs. per ration.	37 lbs. to 38½ lbs. (7 types)	3 lbs. 7 ozs. without biscuits; 4 lbs. with biscuits	'B'
2.	BT 24 hour (produced in UK)	Ten rations (complete) in fibreboard case, 28" x 12" x 8".	47 lbs. to 48½ lbs. (4 types)	4 lbs. 3 ozs.	'C'
3.	BT 24 hour (produced in FARELF)	Ten rations (complete) in fibreboard case, 24" x 10" x 6½".	39¾ lbs.	3 lbs. 10 ozs.	'D'
4.	BT 24 hour (Special Air Service) (produced in FARELF)	Ten rations (complete) in fibreboard case, 22" x 11½" x 7".	41 lbs. to 43 lbs.	3 lbs. 14 ozs.	'E'
5.	BT 2 men x 7 days light weight (produced in FARELF)	14 rations in fibreboard case, 19" x 9½" x 9½".	36 lbs.	2 lbs. 7 ozs.	'F'
6.	GT 10 men compo (produced in FARELF)	Ten rations (complete) in fibreboard case, 16¼" x 12½" x 8½".	37 lbs. and 36 lbs. (2 types)	3 lbs. 6 ozs.	'G'
7.	GT 24 hour (produced in FARELF)	Ten rations (complete) each in a tin packed in fibreboard case, 24" x 10½" x 7".	39 lbs. and 38 lbs.	3 lbs. 9 ozs.	'H'
8.	MT 2 men (produced ex Police through local contract)	Twelve rations in wooden case, 18" x 14" x 10".	50 lbs.	3 lbs. 4 ozs.	'J'

Appendix B

DETAILED COMPOSITION OF BT 10 MEN COMPO RATION PACK

Note:—
- (1) In order to give variety these packs are produced in seven types (A, B, C, D, E, F, and G).
- (2) Where bread is not available or cannot be accepted, biscuits service will be issued at the scale of 9 ozs. per man per day.
- (3) These packs are designed to feed:—
    - (a) 10 men for 1 day.
    - (b) 5 men for 2 days.
    - (c) 3 men for 3 days.

Commodity and type of container	A	B	C	D	E	F	G
No. 1 Tall Cans—							
Oatmeal Blocks	10	10	10	—	—	10	—
Bacon	45	—	—	—	—	15	—
Sausage	—	45	—	—	—	30	—
Ham and Eggs	—	—	45	—	—	—	45
Bacon and Beans	—	—	—	48	—	—	—
Sausages and Beans	—	—	—	—	48	—	—
Tea	6	6	6	6	6	6	6
Sugar	14½	14½	14½	14½	14½	14½	14½
Stewed Steak	—	96	—	—	—	—	—
Steak and Kidney Pudding	—	—	96	—	—	—	—
Meat and Vegetables	—	—	—	160	—	—	—
Irish Stew	—	—	—	—	160	—	—
Casserole Steak and Onions	—	—	—	—	—	96	—
Mutton Scotch Style	—	—	—	—	—	—	160
Peas	—	10	10	—	—	—	—
Beans	—	—	—	—	—	16	—
Diced Mixed Vegetables	—	—	10	—	—	—	—
Carrots	—	10	—	—	—	10	—
Vegetable Salad in Mayonnaise	30	—	—	—	—	—	—
Potato Mash Powder	12	12	12	—	—	12	—
Treacle Pudding	—	42	—	—	—	—	—
Rice Pudding	—	—	48	—	—	—	—
Jam Roll Pudding	—	—	—	45	—	—	—
Ginger Pudding	—	—	—	—	42	—	—
Apple Pudding	—	—	—	—	—	—	45
Luncheon Meat	—	32	—	—	—	32	—
Hamburgers	—	—	32	—	—	—	—
Rice Cake	—	—	—	20	—	—	—
Ham and Beef	—	—	—	—	32	—	32
Chocolate and Sweets—							
Chocolate	20	20	20	20	—	20	—
Sweets	4	4	4	4	4	4	4
Raisin Chocolate	—	—	—	—	20	—	20
Clear Gum	5	5	5	5	5	5	5
Matches (Box)	1	1	1	1	1	1	1

Appendix B—Continued

Commodity and type of container	Amount in each type in ounces						
	A	B	C	D	E	F	G
Water Sterilizing Outfit (Tin)	1	1	1	1	1	1	1
Salt Dispenser	2	2	2	2	2	2	2
Paludrine (Tabs.)	10	10	10	10	10	10	10
A 1 Tall Cans—							
Fruit Canned	48	—	—	—	—	48	—
Salmon	32	—	—	—	—	—	—
½ A 1 Tall Cans—							
Sugar	7	7	7	7	7	7	7
Sweets	5	5	5	5	—	5	—
Clear Gums	—	—	—	—	5	—	5
Cheese, Processed	16	16	16	16	16	16	16
Margarine	15	15	15	15	15	15	15
Jam	18	9	18	9	18	9	18
Marmalade	—	9	—	9	—	9	—
300 x 111 Cans—							
Tea	$1\frac{1}{4}$	$1\frac{1}{4}$	$1\frac{1}{4}$	$1\frac{1}{4}$	$1\frac{1}{4}$	$1\frac{1}{4}$	$1\frac{1}{4}$
Sugar	$1\frac{1}{4}$	$1\frac{1}{4}$	$1\frac{1}{4}$	$1\frac{1}{4}$	$1\frac{1}{4}$	$1\frac{1}{4}$	$1\frac{1}{4}$
Various—							
Preserved Meat	72	—	—	—	—	—	—
Milk Condensed Unsweetened	32	32	32	32	32	32	32
Latrine Paper (Sheets)	100	100	100	100	100	100	100
Can Opener (Nos.)	1	1	1	1	1	1	1
Contents List	1	1	1	1	1	1	1
Soap G.P. (Tablets)	1	1	1	1	1	1	1
Reclosure Lids (Nos.)	2	2	2	2	2	2	2

Appendix C

BRITISH 24-HOUR RATION (GS)—TYPES A, B, C & D ONE MAN FOR 24 HOURS

1. This ration is packed individually in a cardboard container, with tin-liner containing 10 x 24 hour rations.

2. Each individual ration is sub-divided into 4 packets consisting of:—

(i) Breakfast Packet.
(ii) Snack Packet.
(iii) Main Meal Packet.
(iv) Sundries Packet.

Schedule of Contents

	Type 'A'	Type 'B'	Type 'C'	Type 'D'
(a) *Breakfast Packet*—				
Biscuits Service -	3 ozs.	3 ozs.	3 ozs.	3 ozs.
Oatmeal Block -	1 oz.	1 oz.	1 oz.	1 oz.
Sausage and Beans	5¼ ozs.	—	—	—
Bacon and Beans -	—	5¼ ozs.	—	—
Chopped Bacon -	—	—	5 ozs.	—
Ham and Eggs -	—	—	—	5 ozs.
Jam - -	2 ozs.	—	2 ozs.	2 ozs.
Marmalade -	—	2 ozs.	—	—
Tea - -	¼ oz.	¼ oz.	¼ oz.	¼ oz.
Sugar - -	1 oz.	1 oz.	1 oz.	1 oz.
(b) *Snack Packet*—				
Biscuits Sweet -	2 ozs.	2 ozs.	2 ozs.	2 ozs.
Chocolate Milk (Blended) -	2 ozs.	2 ozs.	2 ozs.	2 ozs.
Clear Gums -	1⅛ ozs.	2¼ ozs.	1⅛ ozs.	1⅛ ozs.
Boiled Sweets -	2 ozs.	—	2 ozs.	—
Butter Scotch -	—	1¾ ozs.	—	—
Mars Bars - -	1⅛ ozs.	—	—	1⅛ ozs.
Spangles - -	—	—	—	1½ ozs.
Nuts and Raisins -	—	—	1⅛ ozs.	—
Tea - -	¼ oz.	¼ oz.	¼ oz.	¼ oz.
Sugar - -	1 oz.	1 oz.	1 oz.	1 oz.
(c) *Main Meal Packet*—				
Biscuits Service Plain - -	3 ozs.	3 ozs.	3 ozs.	3 ozs.
Preserved Meat -	5 ozs.	—	—	—
Ham and Beef -	—	5 ozs.	—	—
Liver and Bacon -	—	—	5¼ ozs.	—
Steak and Kidney Pie - -	—	—	—	5 ozs.
Vegetable Salad in Mayonnaise -	4 ozs.	—	—	—
Beans in Tomatoes	—	—	5 ozs.	—
Spaghetti in Tomatoes -	—	5¼ ozs.	—	—
Diced Mixed Vegetables -	—	—	—	4 ozs.
Mixed Fruit Pudding -	4 ozs.	—	—	—

Appendix C—*Continued*

Schedule of Contents

	Type 'A'	Type 'B'	Type 'C'	Type 'D'
(c) *Main Meal Packet*—				
Treacle Pudding	—	3½ ozs.	—	—
Rice Pudding with Sultanas	—	—	5 ozs.	—
Ginger Pudding	—	—	—	5 ozs.
Cheese	1½ ozs.	1½ ozs.	1½ ozs.	1½ ozs.
Tea	¼ oz.	¼ oz.	¼ oz.	¼ oz.
Sugar	1 oz.	1 oz.	1 oz.	1 oz.

(d) *Sundries Packet—same for all types—*

Milk (in Tube)	2 ozs.
Salt (in Dispenser)	5½ grms.
Chewing Gum (in Pkt.)	4 tabs.
Flare Matches (in Tube)	4 Nos.
Paludrine	1 No.
Can Opener	1 No.
Toilet Paper	10 Sheets
Contents List	1 No.

Appendix D

BRITISH TROOPS 24-HOUR PACK RATION MK III (LOCAL)

Commodity:	Type 'A'	Type 'B'	Type 'C'	Type 'D'
Breakfast Meal—				
Rolled Oats	1 oz.	1 oz.	1 oz.	1 oz.
Sausages and Beans	8 ozs.	—	—	—
Bacon and Beans	—	8 ozs.	—	—
Frankfurters	—	—	6 ozs.	—
Kipper Snack	—	—	—	3¼ ozs.
Tea	¼ oz.	¼ oz.	¼ oz.	¼ oz.
Sugar	2 ozs.	2 ozs.	2 ozs.	2 ozs.
Milk in Tin	2¾ ozs.	2¾ ozs.	2¾ ozs.	2¾ ozs.
Snack—				
Chocolate	2 ozs.	2 ozs.	2 ozs.	2 ozs.
Barley Sugar	2 ozs.	2 ozs.	2 ozs.	2 ozs.
Mars Bars Nos.	1	1	1	1
Oxo Cubes Nos.	1	1	1	1
Tea (2 Pkts.)	¼ x 2	¼ x 2	¼ x 2	¼ x 2
Sugar	1 oz.	1 oz.	1 oz.	1 oz.
Main Meal—				
Biscuits Service	4 ozs.	4 ozs.	4 ozs.	4 ozs.
Steak, Onions and Peas	12 ozs.	—	—	—
Beef and Vegetables	—	12 ozs.	—	—
Irish Stew	—	—	12 ozs.	—
Steak and Beans	—	—	—	12 ozs.
Curry Powder	⅛ oz.	⅛ oz.	⅛ oz.	⅛ oz.
Rice	4 ozs.	4 ozs.	4 ozs.	4 ozs.
Tea	¼ oz.	¼ oz.	¼ oz.	¼ oz.
Sugar	1 oz.	1 oz.	1 oz.	1 oz.
Processed Cheese	—	—	2 ozs.	2 ozs.
Jam	2 ozs.	2 ozs.	—	—
Raisins	1½ ozs.	1½ ozs.	1½ ozs.	1½ ozs.
Sundries—				
Milk in Tubes (2 ozs.) Nos.	1	1	1	1
Chewing Gum (Packets)	1	1	1	1
Salt	1 oz.	1 oz.	1 oz.	1 oz.
Paludrine Tablets Nos.	1	1	1	1
Toilet Paper Sheets	10	10	10	10
Contents Lists	1	1	1	1

XXII
Appx E

Appendix E

BRITISH TROOPS 24-HOUR PACK RATION MK III (LOCAL) SAS ONLY

Commodity:	Type 'A'	Type 'B'	Type 'C'	Type 'D'
	Amount in each type in ounces			
Breakfast Meal—				
Rolled Oats	1	1	1	1
Sausages and Beans	8	—	—	—
Bacon and Beans	—	8	—	—
Frankfurters	—	—	6	—
Kipper Snack	—	—	—	3¼
Tea	¼	¼	¼	¼
Sugar	2	2	2	2
Milk in Tin	2¾	2¾	2¾	2¾
Snack—				
Barley Sugar	1	1	1	1
Oxo Cubes Nos.	1	1	1	1
Tea	½	½	½	½
Sugar	1	1	1	1
Main Meal—				
Biscuits Service	4	4	4	4
Steak, Onions and Peas	12	—	—	—
Sausage and Vegetables	—	12	—	—
Irish Stew	—	—	12	—
Beef and Vegetables	—	—	—	12
Curry Powder	¼	¼	¼	¼
Rice	6	6	6	6
Tea	¼	¼	¼	¼
Sugar	1	1	1	1
Processed Cheese	2	2	2	2
Ghi Butter	2	2	2	2
Raisins	1½	1½	1½	1½
Sundries—				
Milk in Tubes (2 ozs.) Nos.	1	1	1	1
Chewing Gum (Pkts.)	1	1	1	1
Salt	1	1	1	1
Paludrine Tablets Nos.	1	1	1	1
Toilet Paper Sheets	10	10	10	10
Contents Lists	1	1	1	1

Note:—The total quantities of tea and sugar are each packed in one packet.

Appendix F

2 MEN x 7 DAY LIGHT WEIGHT PATROL RATION

Item	Amount
P. Meat	84 ozs.
Soup Dehydrated Onion	12¼ ozs.
Vegetable	10½ ozs.
Cabbage Dehydrated	7 ozs.
Rice (Enriched)	63 ozs.
Curry Powder	3½ ozs.
Nestum	14 ozs.
Biscuits Service	28 ozs.
Processed Cheese	28 ozs.
GHI Butter	10¼ ozs.
Oxo Cubes	14 Nos.
Raisins	16 ozs.
Tea	7 ozs.
Sugar	49 ozs.
Powdered Milk	21 ozs.
Boiled Sweets	14 ozs.
Orangeade Powder	14 ozs.
Salt	7 ozs.
Paludrine Tablets	14 Nos.
Matches Boxes	7
Cigarettes	100 pieces
Hexamine Cookers	2 Nos.
Hexamine Refills	5 Nos.
Toilet Paper	100 sheets
Contents List	1 No.

Appendix G

GURKHA 10 MEN COMPO RATIONS
(10 Rations contained in one wooden box)

Item	Amount Fish Pack	Amount Meat Pack
Rice	210 ozs.	210 ozs.
Dhall Moong	36 ozs.	36 ozs.
Chillies Dried	½ oz.	½ oz.
Sugar	27½ ozs.	27½ ozs.
Fruit Dried (Vine)	5 ozs.	5 ozs.
C.V. Tablets	10 Nos.	10 Nos.
Tea	7½ ozs.	7½ ozs.
Potato Mash Powder	10 ozs.	10 ozs.
Curry Powder	1 3/7 ozs.	1 3/7 ozs.
Salt Refined	10 ozs.	10 ozs.
Milk Tinned	32 ozs.	32 ozs.
Vegetables Tinned	40 ozs.	40 ozs.
Herrings Tinned	28 ozs.	—
Sardines Tinned	4½ ozs.	—
Mutton Curry in Ghi	—	35
Ghi	17½	—
Leaflet	1 No.	1 No.

Appendix H

GURKHA 24 HOUR PACK RATIONS

(Twelve tins to a wooden case)

Item	Fish Pack	Meat Pack
Rice	18 ozs.	18 ozs
Dhall	4 ozs.	4 ozs.
Biscuits Service	3 ozs.	3 ozs.
Potato Mash Powder	1 oz.	1 oz.
Sugar	3 ozs.	3 ozs.
Salt Refined	$\frac{1}{2}$ oz.	$\frac{1}{2}$ oz.
Salt Tablets	5 Nos.	5 Nos.
Tea	1 oz.	1 oz.
Fruit Dried	2 ozs.	2 ozs.
Curry Powder	$\frac{1}{8}$ oz.	$\frac{1}{8}$ oz.
C.V. Tablets	1 No.	1 No.
Milk Condensed	4 ozs.	4 ozs.
Sardines	$4\frac{1}{2}$ ozs.	—
Mutton Curry	—	$3\frac{1}{2}$ ozs.
Ghi	2 ozs.	2 ozs.
Chillies Dried	$\frac{1}{8}$ oz.	$\frac{1}{8}$ oz.

Appendix J

MT 2 MEN PACK RATIONS

Serial No.	Commodity	Quantity per pack (of two rations)
1.	Rice	34 ozs.
2.	Sugar	6 ozs.
3.	Salt	2 ozs.
4.	Tea	2 ozs.
5.	Groundnuts or Dried Fruit	4 ozs.
6.	Biscuits	8 ozs.
7.	Sweets	4 ozs.
8.	Milk Condensed (2 x 2 ozs. tube)	4 ozs.
9.	Meat	8 ozs.
10.	Fish Curry Tinned (1 x 5 ozs.)	5 ozs.
11.	Curry Gravy	4 ozs.
12.	C.V Tablets	2 Nos.
13.	Matches	1 packet
14.	Tin Opener	1 No.
15.	Contents List	1

CHAPTER XXIII

FIRST AID AND PREVENTATIVE MEDICINE

Section 1.—FIRST AID

1. It is essential that every man on operations should understand not only the basic methods of First Aid to the injured, but also general health, in other words the principles of Preventative Medicine. This in particular applies to senior and junior leaders who are responsible for the health of their men.

2. Many a soldier has been saved from death or permanent disability because immediate First Aid was rendered, and many have died as a result of their comrades lacking the knowledge or the confidence to apply First Aid.

3. **First Aid.**— saves lives and stops pain. It is but common sense plus a little specialised knowledge.
   - (a) A lightly wounded man, if given first aid, can go on fighting. It is therefore essential to act quickly.
   - (b) A badly wounded man looks pale and sweaty. Be prepared for this. Calm him and also the men under your command.
   - (c) Do not disturb a wounded man too much unless you have to. Nature will tell him how to lie in the safest and most comfortable position.
   - (d) Look, think and then act—there may be three men wounded at once. Treat the most urgent first. Keep under cover. Any fool can be brave and get killed; be brave and don't get killed, and save your friend instead. Look, think and then act.
   - (e) Equipment:—
     - (i) First field dressing is carried by every man.
     - (ii) Each section carries a first aid pack.
     - (iii) Extra medical equipment and dressings are carried by medical orderlies.

4. When a man gets hit beside you:—
   - (a) CALM YOURSELF.
   - (b) STOP HIS BLEEDING.
   - (c) KEEP HIM WARM.
   - (d) REASSURE HIM (words of comfort are an important first aid measure).

5. **Wounds.**— At the time of injury pain is seldom felt. The sensation is very like a blow that you may get when boxing.

6. **When to give a man a drink.**— Give a wounded man a drink of anything you have—but do NOT give a drink to a man with a wound in his belly, or to a man who cannot swallow. You will kill him if you do. Remember—no drink to these two men. But you can moisten their lips.

7. **Stop Bleeding.**— Bleeding of a slight or severe degree accompanies all wounds. A man can bleed to death very quickly. SO ACT PROMPTLY. Remember bleeding can be stopped by the firm pressure of a dressing accurately applied on or into a wound. The dressing acts as a splint and helps to immobilize the injured part. After the dressing has been applied have faith and do not remove it to see if the bleeding has stopped.

8. **Shock.**— Shock lowers vitality; it kills more men than do bullets. It is increased by fear, cold and pain. Restore, by encouragement, the peace of mind of the wounded man. Reassure him by the quiet and methodical way you go about giving first aid. All movement of the wounded man must be gentle and reduced to a minimum. Pain is allayed by immobilization. If pain is severe morphia should be given. Avoid an overdose. Do NOT repeat until the end of four hours. If morphia is given to a man to be evacuated inform somebody of the fact. If possible give hot sweet drinks—tea or soups.

9. **Abdominal Wounds.**— All cases should be treated as of first urgency. The object is to get the wounded man quickly and comfortably to surgical aid. Do not give this man anything to drink.

10. **Chest Wounds.**— The small perforating wound requires little direct attention save the application of a dressing. If the wounded man coughs up blood explain to him that it must be expected. Reassurance and calmness are essential for his peace of mind. Some of the larger wounds are of the valve type and suck in air, they require immediate first aid. The man finds it difficult to breathe. Seal the wounds off with elastoplast or the firm application of a dressing into the wound itself. Bind the dressing firmly to the chest. Transport the patient in the position most comfortable to himself.

11. **The Jaws and Face.**— The impact of the blow may cause a temporary loss of vision. The first sign is usually a trickle of blood on the face or in the mouth. The patient may faint. A patient

with a severe jaw wound should be laid stomach down on the stretcher with his head projecting beyond the canvas and the forehead supported by a bandage sling between the handle bars. This prevents the man swallowing blood and saliva and his tongue falling back. Keep the foot of the stretcher higher than the head to ensure drainage.

12. **Broken Bones.**—To allay pain and shock and to prevent the splintered bones damaging blood vessels, nerves and muscles, the bones together with their surrounding tissues and muscles must be immobilized by splinting. Support the broken limb with a well padded splint. Place the limb in its most natural position and you cannot go wrong. Do not let the limb flap around or the sharp ends of the splintered bones will cut the vessels, nerves and muscles to pieces. A broken arm should be bound firmly but not too tightly to the chest. After splinting the broken lower limb bind it to the other, foot to foot, knee to knee and thigh to thigh.

13. **Injury to Spine.**—In all cases of fracture of the spine, the patient must be transported on his back. Pads should be placed to support the neck and the small of the back. It is vital that the injured man is not bent or twisted when moving him as it may kill him. If the man is unconscious make sure his tongue or false teeth do not fall back and choke him.

14. **Burns and Scalds.**—If a limb has been burnt, elevate and immobilize it. If proper medical attention is not available apply a dressing to the burn. Pain may be allayed by giving morphia and shock by frequent hot drinks to which a little salt has been added.

15. **Phosphorus Burns.**—Hold under water—pick out the pieces of phosphorus. Keep the wound wet.

16. **Artificial Respiration.**—For the apparently electrocuted or drowned. In the former case first free the victim from the current without electrocuting yourself and then ensure that after this he is earthed. In the case of the apparently drowned, after removing the man from the water he should be laid down with the head lower than the feet.

THE IMMEDIATE APPLICATION OF ARTIFICIAL RESPIRATION IS VITAL. THERE IS NOT A SPLIT SECOND TO WASTE:—

(a) Turn the man onto his belly.

(b) Head turned to one side resting on his folded wrists.

(c) See that there is no obstruction in the mouth—false teeth or weeds.

- (d) Kneel astride the man's head.
- (e) Place your hands on the back of the man's chest, fingers splayed out.
- (f) Keep your arms rigid and let your weight fall on the man's chest and at the same time squeeze—count one, two, three.
- (g) Recover and grasp the man's arms just above his elbows, pull both his arms back (i.e. towards you) until his body is just off the ground. Count four, five, six.
- (h) Complete the procedure as described at the rate of 10-12 times a minute.
- (j) CONTINUE THIS IF NECESSARY FOR AN HOUR. The operation is tedious. A team of two or three operators will be needed.

17. **Snake Bite.**— This rarely causes death in Malaya.
    - (a) Look at the bite:—
        - (i) Multiple small punctures are non-poisonous.
        - (ii) Two fang marks are due to a poisonous snake.
    - (b) Treatment:—
        - (i) Apply a tourniquet to stop the flow of the blood in the vein. (The tourniquet is the most dangerous of surgical appliances. It MUST be released every 30 minutes for a few minutes either until the injured part begins to bleed or until you can feel the pulse).
        - (ii) Incise the punctures and the swollen areas to a depth of one-quarter inch to get free bleeding.
        - (iii) Suck out the venom.
        - (iv) Apply a dressing.

18. **Poisonous Trees.**— Poisonous trees secrete an irritating oil which produces a severe rash. The affected areas should be washed with a strong soap solution and a coating of soap left over the area.

Section 2.—FIRST AID TO HEALTH

1. **Malaria.**—Malaria is prevalent everywhere in Malaya outside the large towns. In operational camps you should carry out the following precautions:—
    - (a) Take one tablet of Paludrine each day at a fixed time.
    - (b) Avoid unnecessary exposure of the body between 1800 hours and 0600 hours by wearing slacks, long sleeved shirts, etc.

(c) Use mosquito repellent on exposed skin, hands, face after 1800 hours.

(d) Use head and hand nets impregnated with mosquito repellent; they are particularly useful on night patrols. These are contained in your Anti-Malaria Wallets.

Paludrine must be taken for 28 days after leaving a malarial zone, and also while on leave in Singapore, Penang, etc. This is most important. Stopping for even one day may lead to an acute attack.

Dysentry and other Intestinal Diseases.

2. **Food.**— If you eat only clean food and drink clean water, you will avoid these diseases. Make every effort to ensure that food is kept clean during carriage and during its preparation. Food or drink should not be purchased from villages or unlicensed vendors. The most dangerous items are cold drinks and ice cream. The local custom is to use human excreta as manure for growing vegetables and fruit. These foods must not be eaten.

3. **Clean Water.**— In the jungle, water is generally obtained from streams. Village wells are polluted and should be avoided. All drinking water must be purified before use. This is done by Water Sterilizing Tablets contained in small individual outfits.

(a) The water bottle is filled with water, as clean as is obtainable.

(b) A white tablet from the individual outfit is added and the bottle shaken.

(c) After half an hour the water is fit to drink.

(d) A blue tablet added at this time (not before) will remove the taste of chlorine.

(e) Cloudy water cannot be sterilized. So strain it through cloth or a bag-water filter ('Millbank Bag'). Purification should then be carried out as detailed above.

(f) Boiling (and if desired, making tea) will purify any water.

Men who drink water straight from streams may escape disease —but not for long.

4. **Jaundice** (Leptospirosis).—The germ which causes this disease is found in streams infested by rats and rodents. The slimy banks of streams are particularly dangerous, especially with bare feet. The centre of a swift running stream is less likely to be infected.

5. **Scrub Typhus.**— This is caused by the bite of a very small mite insect. It is prevented by smearing mite repellent on clothing. Mite repellent is available in all units. Use it. When applying it, pay particular attention to socks, lower ends of slacks, fly openings, waist, cuff and neck openings. Mite repellent remains in clothing after washing but should be reapplied each fortnight.

6. **Skin Diseases.**— The hot sweaty climate leads to many skin diseases, for example, ringworm of the foot and body and jungle sores. These diseases are more common in persons recently arrived in this country because they have not learned the importance of frequent washing of the body. Two showers (at least) daily are recommended. Even if showers are not available the person who wants to keep clean can always do so. Powder for foot and body should always be used after washing. Clean clothing is also most important. Socks should be changed twice daily. Rubber soled footwear, e.g. jungle boots, should not be worn any longer than necessary. Feet should, whenever possible, be exposed to the air.

7. **Leeches.**— Leeches are common in the jungle. They may be quite small and snail like. They gain access to the body through the lower ends of slacks, lace holes in boots or any opening in the clothing and then attach themselves firmly to the skin where they engorge themselves with blood. They are painless and cause little harm but their bites may later result in ulceration.

   (a) Do NOT pull leeches off. Touch them with a lighted cigarette, or put a drop of insect repellent on them.

   (b) Mosquito repellent (mentioned in connection with malaria, i.e. DMP) if freshly smeared on clothing, socks, slacks, fly area and boots is effective in keeping them away.

8. **Veneral Disease.**— Remember that all local women concerned may be infected. Sheaths and prophylactic packets are available in units, etc. and should be used as necessary.

Section 3.—SUMMARY

Visible First Aid Equipment.

1. **For Wounds.**— FIRST FIELD DRESSING carried by all ranks on operations.

2. **For Malaria.**— PALUDRINE suppresses malaria. A tablet a day taken at a fixed hour. This routine is continued for 28 days after leaving a malarial area whether on posting or on leave.

Invisible First Aid Equipment.

1. To assure your good health the following immunisations are provided:—
    (a) Small-pox.—Vaccination every two years.
    (b) Enteric Fever.—Annual TAB inoculations.
    (c) Tetanus.—Inoculation every year.
2. **Don't.**—
    (a) Eat locally grown salads. They are polluted.
    (b) Drink minerals or fruit drinks prepared in villages. Ice used for these is usually made from polluted water.

www.ingramcontent.com/pod-product-compliance
Lightning Source LLC
Chambersburg PA
CBHW070958160426
43193CB00012B/1831